I0813428

(w)Ego by The Why Factory (TU Delft)

Authors: Winy Maas, Javier Arpa Fernández, Adrien Ravon, Felix Madrazo

How can we turn every dwelling into a desirable home? *(w)Ego: Dream Homes in Density* investigates participatory processes and applies them to housing design. These processes establish a negotiation between the desires of each of the residenWts of a housing block and help determine the design of their units. (w)Ego explores these negotiations through the development of gaming processes that leverage the specific dreams of each resident and transform them into spatial requirements. This way, novel housing typologies emerge within a truly human-driven, dreamy architecture.

This book brings together research undertaken by students from The Why Factory at TU Delft and students from IIT Chicago, RMIT Melbourne and Bezalel Academy Jerusalem who collaborated with The Why Factory. This research explores the co-creation and negotiation of architecture through computational models, progressing from an experiment with social media users to reveal their dream homes, to the development of a video game through which a group of future residents negotiate their housing desires in real time, to the subsequent implementation of software to manage conflicts. Each pedagogical experiment asks: How can gaming facilitate and visualize the beauty of the individual dream within a collective context? How can we build a dream living space that can adapt with us as individuals and as a collective as time goes by?

Why? We believe that this intensity of desires, diversity and density, when applied to housing, can optimize land use, help combat social inequalities and counteract the centrifugal forces condemning urban development to urban sprawl. This book is an invitation to keep on exploring housing futures and, together, build collective processes that recognize individual needs while imagining ways in which those needs are met in new, responsive and responsible models for the production of collective spaces.

Table of Contents

Table of Contents

From Me to We

Winy Maas

Freedom

We love liberty and the freedom to live where we want to, make a home where, when and how we want to, adapt ourselves and our homes to changing circumstances throughout our lives.

The Limits

But the world limits us. We cannot all live in fields, forests and nature. We need to keep space open for that. And we want to live together in communities, cities. To be inspired, collaborate, share facilities, have fun.... That leads to a need for cities. A need that will get even bigger in the coming years, as the population of the planet grows by another 4 billion people.

Cages

But then, in these cities, we find ourselves stuck with the current housing stock and approach. The result is often a horrendous landscape of uniform prefab elements stacked on top of each other in an endless repetitive vista of towers and slabs. Why have we lowered ourselves to being creatures condemned to live in a mass of multiplied 'cages'? Why should we want to live in a profit-driven product that reduces our options in life to fit within limited variations of the same basic floor plans? Where is our freedom?

From Ego To (w)Ego

How can we improve on this? Can architecture reflect the liberty and variety of the individual and shape a future with more and more responsible options? How can we expand this individual freedom and fantasy while positioning it in a dense world? How can we negotiate with our neighbours and environments to find an optimal balance? Here, freedom and imagination meet responsibility and collaboration. Here, ego becomes (w)Ego.

(w)Egoism

Welcome to our (w)Egoistic society; welcome to those who want to live together in density.

This vision advocates architecture as a device, inviting us to move from fear to curiosity, from individualism to togetherness. (w)Ego investigates the freedom of designing and making your own dream house within dense circumstances. How do we negotiate our dreams with our neighbours? How can individual desires fit into a collective model that works optimally for everyone? And then, can we scale up this model and apply it to cities and the planet? When do egos become (w)Egos?

This research is an invitation to explore ways of thinking and designing that reveal this myriad of possibilities. It imagines and tests future housing models that facilitate citizens' creativity, trigger curiosity, embrace diversity and don't shy from conflict as part of the design process. (w)Egoism happens at the moment when we can cooperate without losing a sense of ourselves, and, by doing so, create something greater than any of our individual dreams.

Fear

Our epoch is witnessing global anxiety. In a world subject to the effects of dramatic climate change, declining resources, loss of biodiversity, societal inequity, political unrest, rapid population growth, rampant urbanization, capitalist exploitation of the earth, and a related and exponential consumption of space, design disciplines must work towards radical solutions. The present urges us to tackle these urgencies, and to engage with the responsible design of our planet, our cities, buildings and products. We must build an environment that is healthier, more inclusive, more responsible, more human, more sustainable and more resilient.

How to address these urgencies? How to defeat fear and egoism? From XS to XL, we need to act. Everybody has a role to play, and everybody should have a voice to speak out loud. Participation, bottom-up initiatives, direct democracy, and the invention of new forms of engagement and solidarity are ways for everyone to take action and responsibility in the building of the future.

Collaboration

Simultaneously, a global agenda supported by worldwide collaboration, regulations, collective knowledge and technological innovations is taking shape, urgently inviting humanity to think with a longer-term perspective.
The sustainable development goals defined by the United Nations is one of these invitations. Opening borders, universal basic income, affordability, the ongoing growth of the global middle class, inclusiveness, the lessening of inequalities, the reduction of global warming, and transnational solidarity movements show us that we can shape change, and require us to keep on acting collectively towards those common goals.

Housing

(w)Ego addresses these challenges through the prism of collective housing. How can a multitude of individual dwellings respond to the planetary housing crisis? The making of the city is a political act where housing needs to be defended as a right and not as a product. We believe that housing is a tool that can be used to build a better society, to overcome fear and egoism, consumerism and inequalities, promote diversity and celebrate the plurality of our planet.

What are the tools and architectural devices capable of inspiring curiosity, cooperation, innovation and empowering everyone to design their own life and live together in density? The future of cities is a collaborative work, through which we shape what we are to one another. There is therefore a need to work with others to do something we couldn't do on our own.

Cities are in constant evolution. They are never finished. They comprise the foundation and promise for a better society.

What Came Before This

During the past 25 years at the architecture and urban design practice MVRDV and the past 13 years at the global think tank and research institute The Why Factory, the issue of how to design good and innovative forms of collective and affordable housing has been intensely tackled. From the Double House in Utrecht, via the Silodam in Amsterdam, Ypenburg in The Hague, to Oosterwold, Almere's Freeland, the Vertical Village, PoroCity, Anarcity and Barba, we have been exploring new models of collective housing.

In the Double House in Utrecht, we found two couples who wanted to live in their dream homes on one plot. Through a series of therapeutic sessions, a new puzzle of co-living emerged, where the negotiations between the couples solidified into an optimized design. Both dreams now coexist in a limited spatial envelope.

In the Silodam in Amsterdam, we shuffled neighbourhoods of different signatures to find the most efficient and affordable juxtaposition.

In Oosterwold, a new garden city next to Almere, we proposed that 20,000 inhabitants could design whatever they want as long as they didn't harm their neighbours. And as long as they took a share of the total autarchic 'pie' by adding their bit to the collective infrastructure: water, food, greenery, energy, facilities, roads. This is gradually creating a city made by and through the negotiation between its new dwellers. Where roads curve around stubborn owners, leading to a surprising townscape.

In the Vertical Village, we explored the world of stacking one's highly individual house onto others, in a cloud of houses. The Housemaker, a design program, helps you to design your dream home. The Villagemaker, a value-based distribution tool, then positions it in a juxtaposition that you want and can afford. Infrastructure follows.

In PoroCity, we explored how to escape the typical monstrous monolithic towers by opening them up, allowing for cavities of all scales, for collectivity, energy, cooling, plant and animal life. In a series of tests, we explored the balance between the homes and the 'unhomes'.

In Barba, we explored the ultimate potential of ultra-elastic materials that can shape co-living on the go and respond spatially to our smallest needs.

(w)Ego is the latest step in that long and collective journey.

The Dialectics of Our Time

(w)Ego starts with a critical investigation of the dialectics of the current world, by exploring the forces that shape the suburban dream. We seek to analyse these forces, as the drivers behind a selfish operation that consumes so much space on our planet. The average suburban dream sets itself in opposition to the alternative of a doomed world of endless cages, stacked in towers and slabs, multiplied to enormous proportions.

Endless Dreams

(w)Ego then builds dreams, by investigating what different kinds of houses can be imagined, based on potential residents from everywhere, from any country or any culture, just as our contemporary cities are completely mixed. How extravagant can their ideas be? How limited are they? This leads to a catalogue of potential clients and their houses.

The Envelope

(w)Ego continues with an investigation of how these differences can be incorporated within a given envelope like a slab, a tower or a block. Suddenly egos become (w)Egos. How to negotiate and make space for others? How can we get the best outcome for everyone without homogenizing their dreams? This chapter develops a series of tools, games, and software that can facilitate and visualize the beauty of the puzzle that comes alive. In (w)Ego, you can design what you want. But you cannot harm your neighbours. When you live in dense conditions, you have to relate to your neighbours. Suddenly, your dream home becomes a shared project; and the relation you create with your neighbours becomes a catalyser for curiosity, openness and creativity. These negotiations then 'solidify' into optimal designs for cohabitation in which dwellings fit together like pieces of a puzzle. Ego becomes (w)Ego.

Neighbours

(w)Ego shows that this kind of cohabitation is an intriguing world. In every distinct house you feel the presence of your neighbours. You don't hear them, but the unusual shapes of the walls and floors make you wonder: How do they live? What might their house be like? This makes you want to visit your neighbours. Ego becomes (w)Ego.

Infrastructure

(w)Ego moves on to the forming of infrastructure. Stairs, corridors and lifts follow the negotiations, and nestle in between private constraints. This leads to interior streets that go around neighbours who have special demands, echoing and characterizing these demands. Ego becomes (w)Ego.

Satisfaction

(w)Ego checks the level of satisfaction by means of a separate tool. For each game, satisfaction levels are calculated at different stages of iteration and negotiation. Which approach to negotiation achieves maximum satisfaction? Unexpectedly, but in retrospect perhaps it was obvious, the Blind Game leads to the highest level of satisfaction. Ego becomes (w)Ego.

Tests

(w)Ego has been tested on site. In Eindhoven and Shenzhen, test houses were built to scale to investigate fire codes, routings, sizes, relations. Thousands of visitors have explored them and given their views. In Chicago, a test house was built with developers. How far can this go? How might brokers and the market react to this new model?

OntheGo

(w)Ego then questions how to adapt over time. Can we make an ever-changing 'puzzle' of dreams? This stage takes the concept of a hotel where a different set of guests stay each night. The guests state their requirements and dreams before arrival; the hotel re-forms itself during the day to meet their wishes.

The Rack

OntheGo imagines a rack of rails that facilitates moveable boxes, contains bedsheets, food, and etcetera, to form new walls, floors and ceilings. The racks are used as lifts to move users up to their destinations, temporarily pushing the neighbours a little away during the journey. Sensors allow for ultimate adaptation in multiple coinciding situations. While you are partying, OntheGo makes sure your neighbours can sleep undisturbed.

The Dream

(w)Ego can be a step towards a future where new materials would allow us to be even freer, denser, more flexible and more innovative. Adapting your space as you wish, expanding when desired and shrinking when needed, (w) Ego explores the first makeability of these dreams and society, and the first steps towards life in a fully adaptable environment.

(w)Ego is about the future of our planet and the way we inhabit it. About cities and density, about freedom and desires, about users and technology, about design and automation. About curious individuals who want to live together, and to be ever more responsible. (w)Ego is an invitation to dream about our future. It's an invitation to optimism. It celebrates and facilitates the first articles of many of our constitutions, where we offer a world of freedom but don't harm our neighbours.

Welcome to (y)our (w)Ego world.

Berlin Voids, Berlin, Germany – MVRDV, 1991

Double House, Utrecht, Netherlands – MVRDV, 1997

Silodam, Amsterdam, Netherlands – MVRDV, 2003

Ypenburg, The Hague, Netherlands – MVRDV, 2005

Oosterwold, Almere, Netherlands – MVRDV, 2011

Vertical Village, Individual, Informal, Intense – The Why Factory (TU Delft) and MVRDV, 2011

PoroCity, Opening up Solidity – The Why Factory (TU Delft), 2018

Barba, Life in the Fully Adaptable Environment – The Why Factory (TU Delft), 2015

Part 1

What's the impact of most of us wanting to live in cookie-cutter versions of an ideal home? Imagine what our world would look like if its nearly eight billion inhabitants all lived in a detached house…

The population of the planet is projected to reach 11.2 billion by the year 2100. By that time, according to the World Economic Forum, we will need to build 2 billion new homes. This is an opportunity to reshape how the architecture of housing impacts the way we live (and vice versa) – and how it shapes the world we live in. How can we best live together in the coming 10, 50, 80 or 100 years?

This chapter investigates the impact of egoism at a planetary scale. The paradox of our current urban challenge is that although living in the city remains the best solution to diminish our impact on the environment, we all want to live a life that is not standardized. How can we solve the seemingly unsolvable conflict between freedom and density? Can architecture, via new design processes, come up with solutions that satisfy our individualistic desires while mitigating our footprint?

Ego

Landscapes of Egoism

The Why Factory (TU Delft)

Winy Maas, Javier Arpa Fernández, Adrien Ravon, Lex te Loo with Léandre Sassi

Text by The Why Factory

Egoistic, selfish, private, personal... the built environment often expresses our nature in a very coercive way. All over the planet, detached houses, private driveways, gated communities, malls, SUVs, golf courses, parking lots and other everyday trappings are the physical manifestations of an egoism that has become generic. We live in a shared state of excess and saturation that verges on the absurd.

This visual essay looks at 18 cases of extreme glut and how that impacts our cities, the way we live, consume, share or privatize spaces and resources on a planetary scale. Each case sets out the statistical evidence of the environmental, social and ethical cost of egoism.

Egoism doesn't make our cities better places to live in. On the contrary, it makes cities less innovative, less accessible, more congested, more polluting – and increases fear and inequality. This collection of facts and images depict the ugly face of an impossibly egoistic world.

My, My, My

The following series of satellite images is a compilation of absurd examples of egoism and its consequences for our planet. From oversized individual desires to unsustainable collective landscapes, this collection of images, facts and data shows the results of egoism in design. It starts with some of the most egoistic and exuberant dwellings on Earth and develops into the most repetitive, monotonous, and segregated pieces of city fabric. What would urbanism look like if we all lived in dwellings with panoramic views, access to our personal rooftops, individual swimming pools, private driveways, and personal waterfronts? What would our Planet look like if 8 billion inhabitants could park their own jumbo jet in front of their home, live in a McMansion, or own a second house? Each of these examples is a manifesto against egoism and a life void of responsibilities.

My Skyscraper

My Rooftop

My Jumbo Jet

My Backyard

My Personal Suburbia

My Pad in the Sky

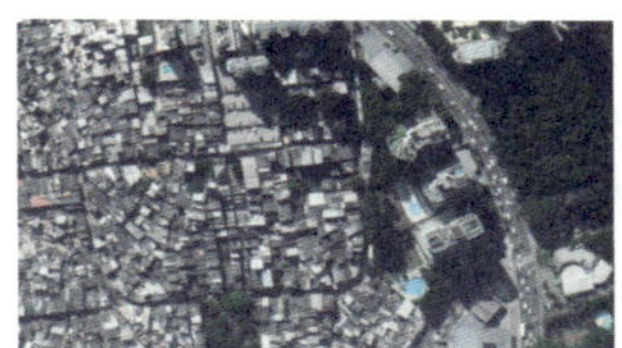
My Condo

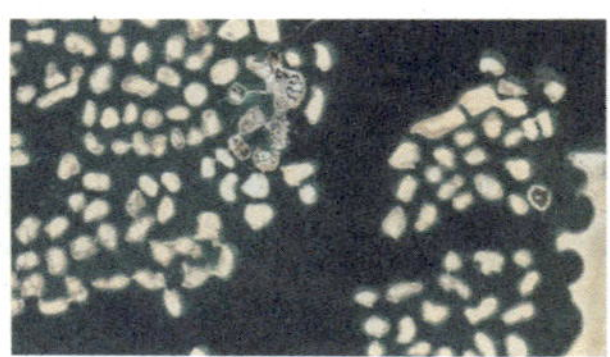
My Island

My Retreat

My McMansion

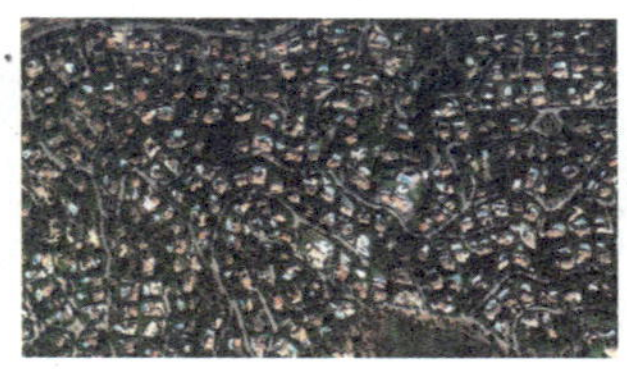
My Swimming Pool

My Finca

My Castle

My Dead End

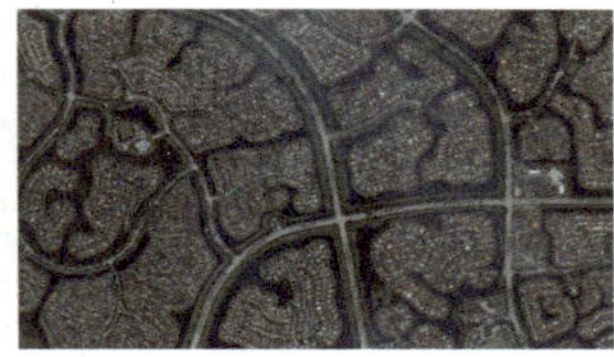
My Waterfront

My Oasis

My Block

My Space Trip

My Skyscraper

Antilia.
Mumbai, India

Antilia is the residence of the Indian billionaire Mukesh Ambani.

It is one of largest private homes in the world, and one of the tallest buildings in Mumbai.

- 173 m tall
- 27 floors
- 4,532 m2 (plot area)
- 37,000 m2 (floor area)
- 2 billion USD (1.65 billion EUR) construction costs
- 168 car garage
- 3 helipads
- 9 high-speed elevators
- 1 snow room

My Penthouse

Kingfisher Tower Penthouse.
Bangalore, India

In 2016, the shell of a replica of the White House was built atop Kingfisher Tower in the heart of Bangalore City. Located on the 33rd and 34th floors of this ultra-high-end millionaires' apartment tower, the penthouse was intended to be the private residence of Indian businessman Vijay Mallya. The house remains unfinished, after Mallya moved to the UK, fleeing charges of financial crime in India. The completed home was supposed to have a wine cellar, a heated indoor pool, outdoor infinity pool, gym, salon, spa, helipad, and many more luxuries.

- 20 million USD (16.52 million EUR) construction costs
- 3,716 m2 built-up area
- 33rd and 34th floors
- 1 private entrance with a private garden, personal lobby and lift
- 100 car capacity private car park

My Jumbo Jet

Jumbolair.
Ocala, USA

Jumbolair is a private airport for an exclusive gated community, Jumbolair Aviation Estates. With a runway capable of accommodating a Boeing 737, Jumbolair has the longest private runway in the United States. John Travolta's estate is one of 17 ultra-luxurious properties with runway access. The house has been designed around jets, with two taxiways leading directly to its front door. It can accommodate five airplanes. John Travolta's own, a Boeing 707, is parked in his yard.

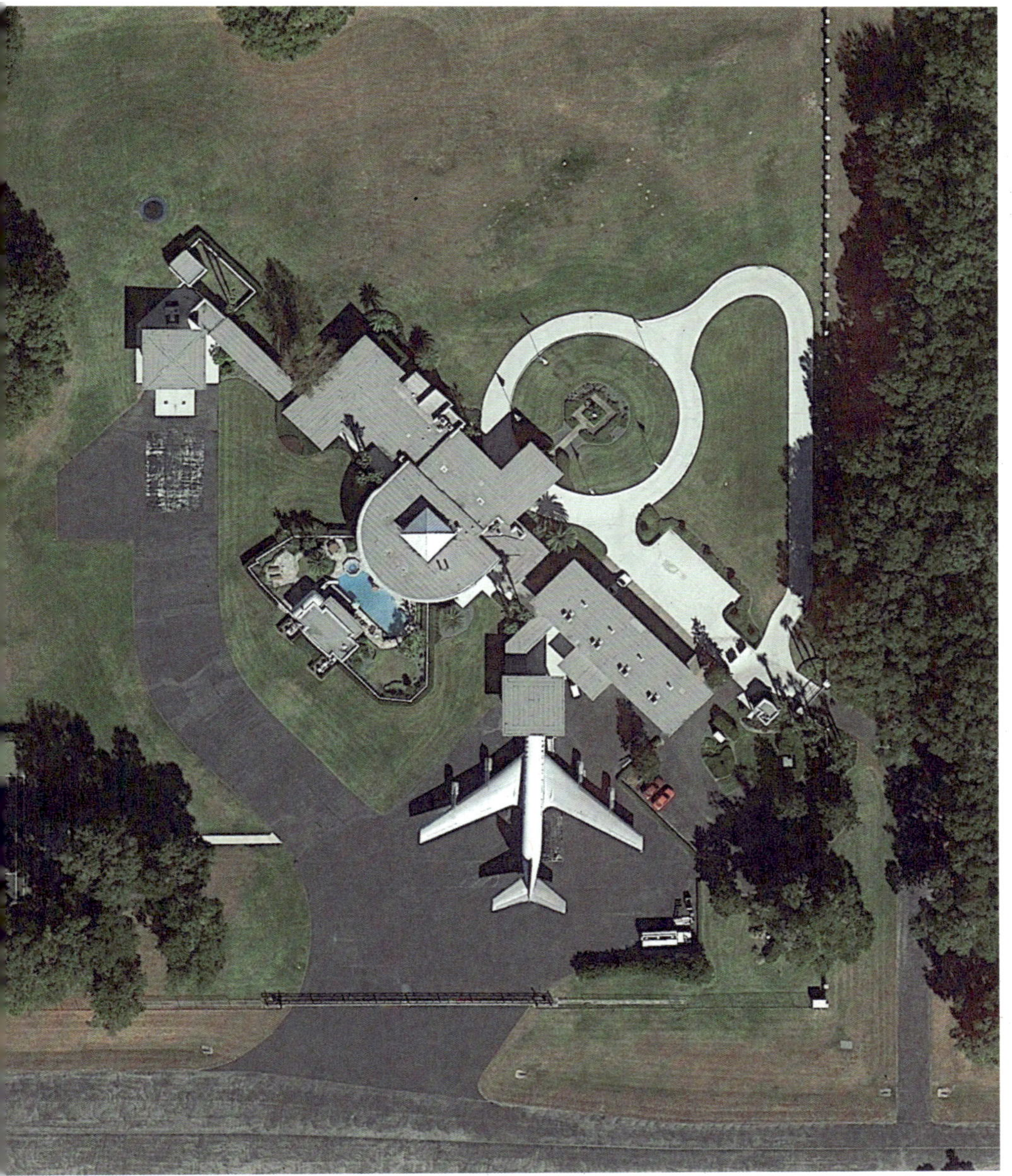

- 222 ha community
- 17 developed estate lots with runway access
- 2 taxiways
- 2,300 × 64 m of asphalt runway
- 1,110 × 30 m grass runway
- 10.5 million USD (8.67 million EUR) selling price of John Travolta's house

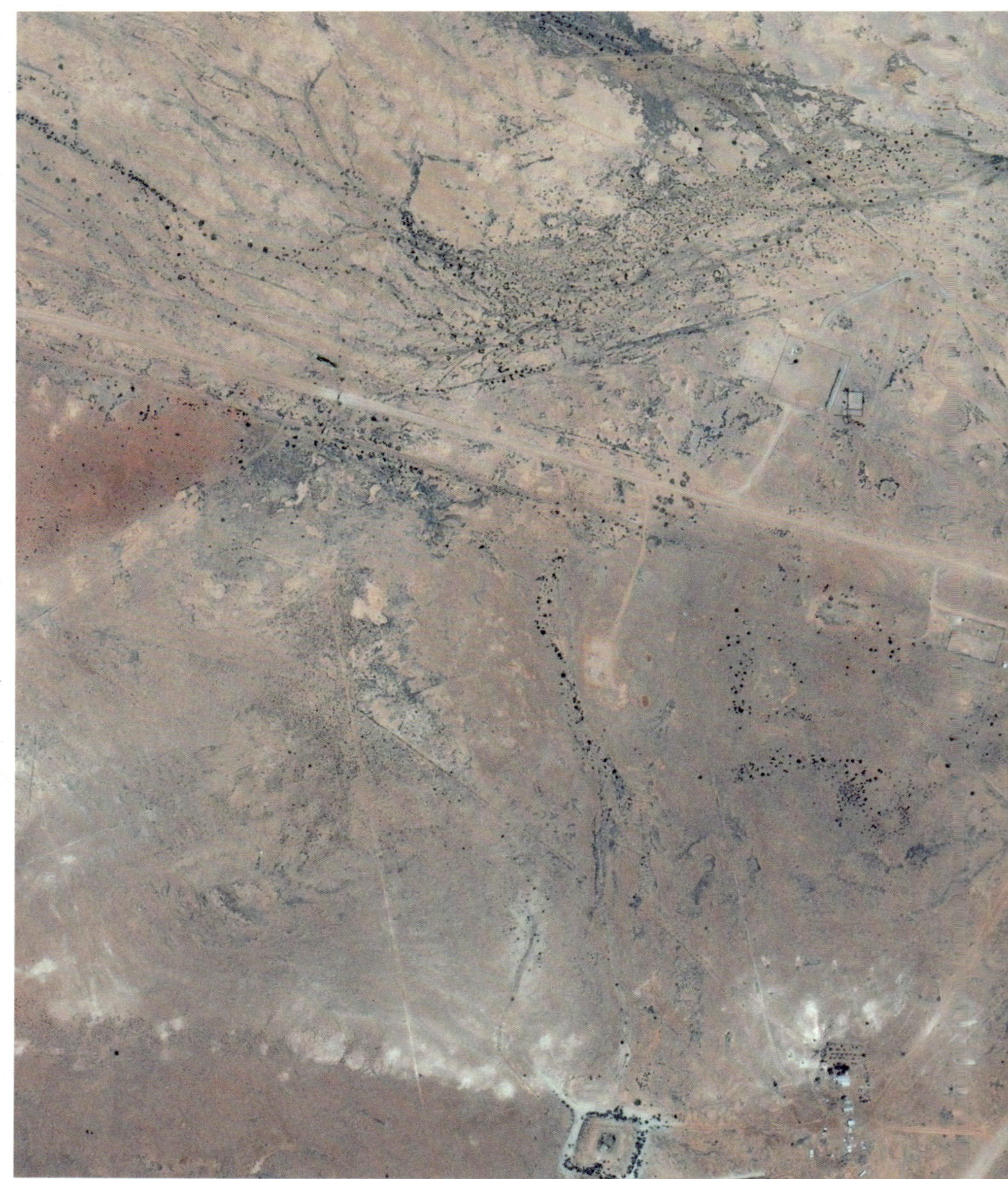

My Backyard

Anna Creek Station.
Australia

Anna Creek Station is the largest individual private land holding on the planet. This cattle station is almost the size of Sicily and is privately owned by the Australian mining magnate Gina Rinehart. Its huge size allows the herds to migrate within the property to response to seasonal changes in the weather. About 100 of Australia's largest cattle stations are bigger than the largest American ranch.

- 23,677 km2 area
- 1.3% of Australian land
- 9,500 head of cattle, with capacity for up to 16,500
- 10-20 staff

My Personal Suburbia

Palazzo Steyn, Steyn City.
Johannesburg, South Africa

Steyn City is a private residential development initiated by a South African billionaire, Douw Steyn.

The estate is two and a half times the size of Central Park in NYC, or four times the size of Monaco. It is an exclusive residential development, with a private water reservoir, private schools, and sport facilities such as a golf course, rugby field and riding stables.

Palazzo Steyn is the billionaire's personal home within his own city. The sprawling mansion is the most expensive residence in South Africa.

- 810 ha of land
- 6 billion ZAR (0.36 billion EUR) initial investment in 2015
- 5.5 billion ZAR (0.33 billion EUR) second investment in 2019
- 3,000 m2 floor area Palazzo Steyn mansion
- 2.5 ha Palazzo Steyn property
- 250 million ZAR (15.11 million EUR) value of Palazzo Steyn property
- 1 personalized city

My Pad in the Sky

432 Park Avenue.
New York, USA

Known as a 'pencil tower', this is a supertall, slender skyscraper overlooking Central Park. It is located amid similar ultra-luxury residential skyscrapers – the so-called Billionaire's Row – in midtown Manhattan. 432 Park Avenue has some of the most expensive residential units in NYC and is one of the tallest residential buildings in the world. Amenities include golf-training facilities, private dining and screening rooms, a fitness centre, a 23-metre-long swimming pool and a library. Lately, residents have complained about malfunctions, leaks, and disturbances due to heavy wind sway. The project has

been described as 'an architectural emblem for rising inequalities' in a city that has long been unaffordable.

- 425 m tall
- 85 floors
- 125 condominiums
- 38,500 m2 floor area
- 770 m2 surface area of the largest unit
- 370 m2 surface area of medium-sized units
- 3.7 to 4.72 m high ceilings
- 1.25 billion USD (1.03 billion EUR) construction costs
- 18 million USD (14.86 million EUR) median unit selling price
- 80 million USD (66.06 million EUR) penthouse selling price

My Condo

Paraisópolis favela and Morumbi condominiums. Sao Paulo, Brazil

Paraisópolis is the second largest favela in Sao Paulo. It is surrounded by the wealthy district of Morumbi. In 2004, photographer Tuca Vieira took a photograph of the Paraisópolis favela, separated by just a wall from the picture-perfect wealthy towers of Murumbi. The juxtaposition was striking and upsetting. On one side, sun shaded, cascading swimming pools on balconies, private tennis courts and well-maintained lawns. On the other, steel sheet rooftops, poorly built housing and inadequate infrastructure, including visible drainage overflows. The image remains a worldwide symbol

of social inequalities between rich and poor and their built environments.

- 11.4 million Brazilians live in informal settlements
- 15% of Sao Paulo's population lives in informal settlements
- 100,000+ inhabitants in Paraisópolis's 0.75 square kilometres
- 32,281 inhabitants in Murumbi's 11.4 square kilometres

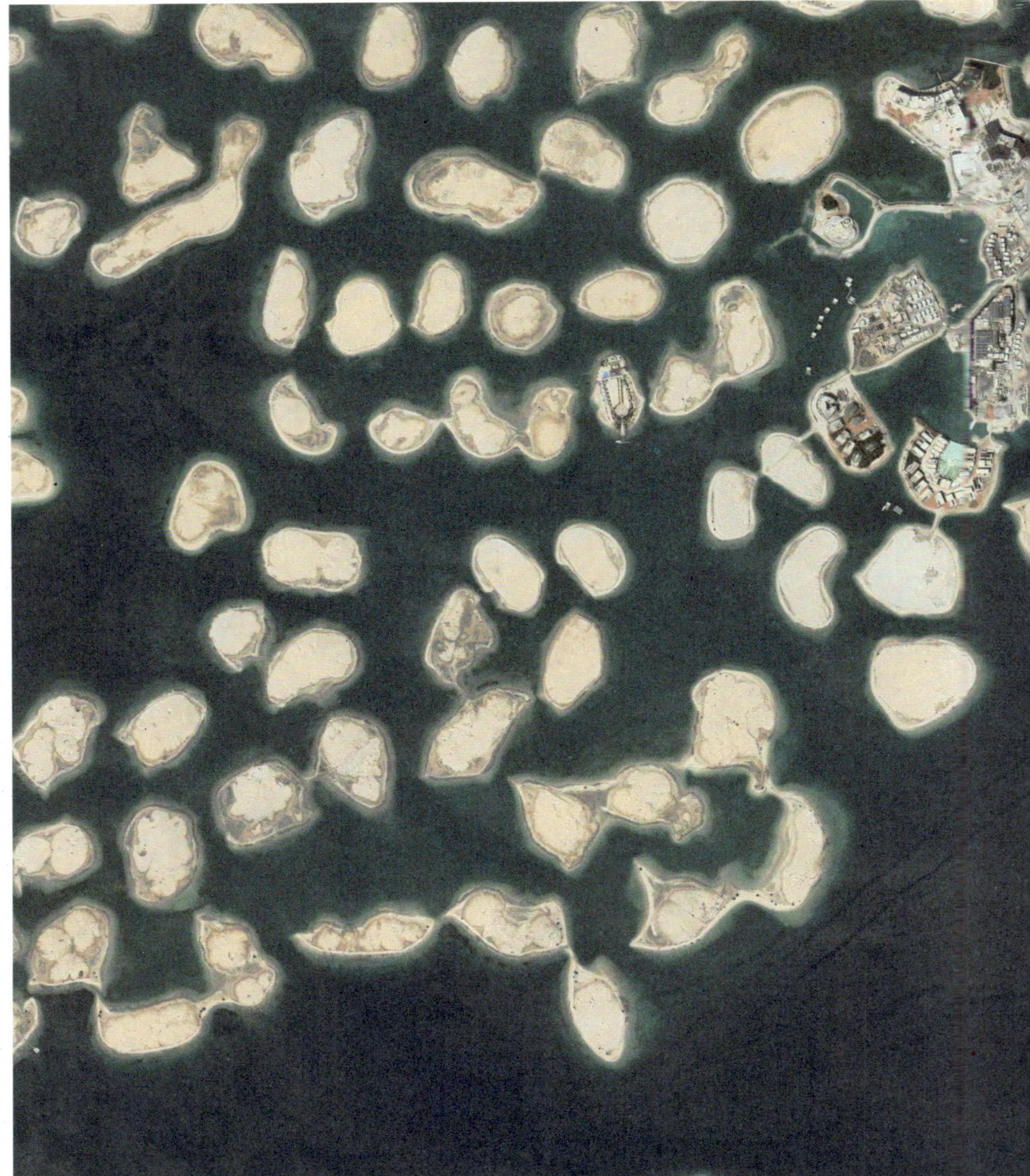

My Island

The World Islands.
Dubai, United Arab Emirates

The World Islands are a collection of man-made islands designed in the shape of the world map.

Located 4 km from Dubai's coast, the development can only be reached by boat, seaplane, or helicopter. Sales of the individual islands are by invitation only. Initiated in 2008, the project as of today is mainly undeveloped: only two of the 300 islands have been built on.

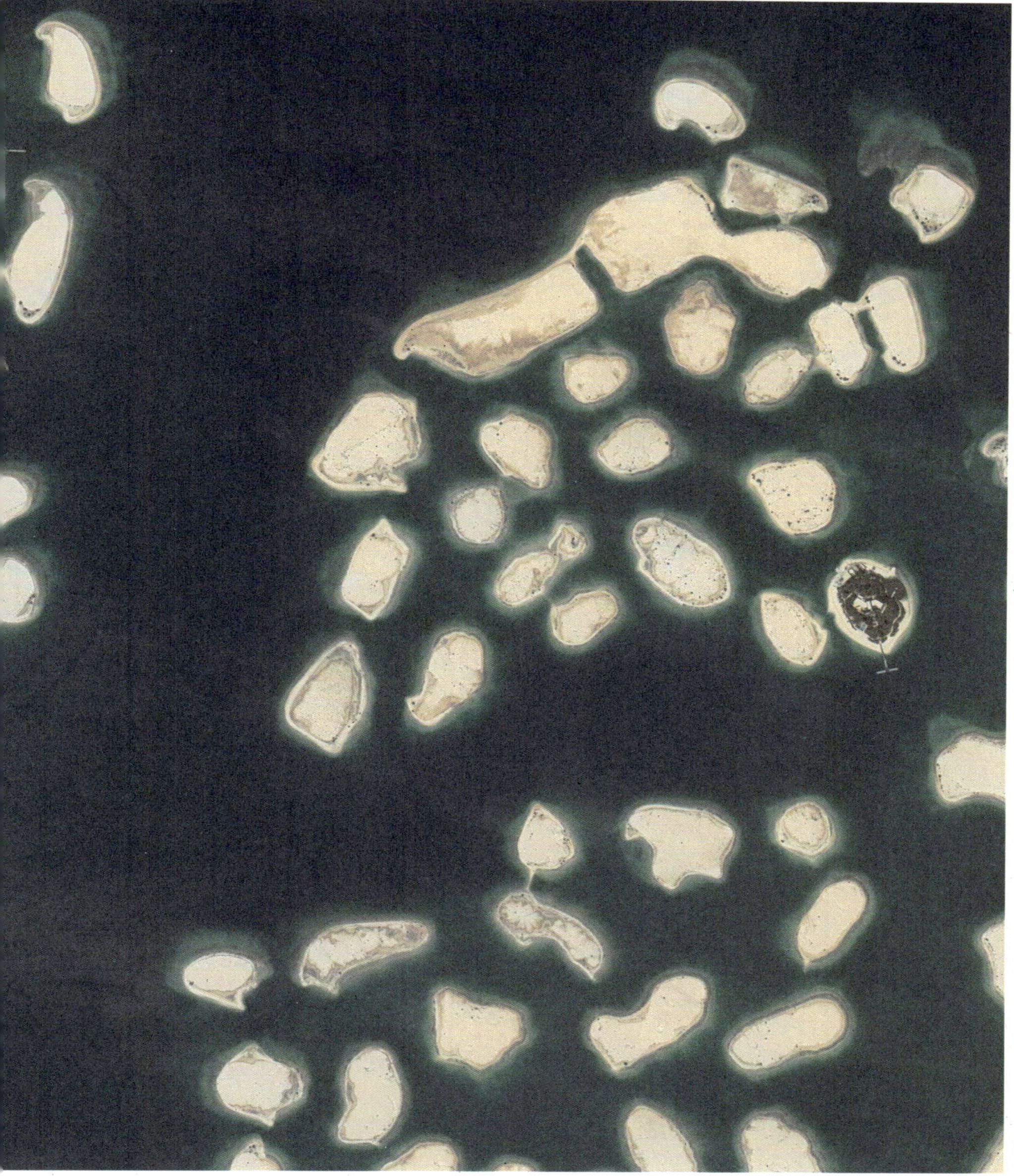

- 300 artificial islands
- 5 years of dredging
- 320 million m3 of sand
- 25 million tons of rock
- 386 million tons of rock
- 14,000 to 42,000 m2 islands
- 100 m average distance between islands
- 6 × 9 km area of development
- 232 km of exclusive beachfront
- 13 million USD (10.74 million EUR) estimated development costs
- 15 to 45 million USD (12,.39 to 37.16 million EUR) cost range of an island
- 60 billion USD (49.55 billion EUR) of debt

My Retreat

The Hamptons.
New York, USA

The Hamptons are a seaside resort located in the East end of long island, two and a half hours distance by car from Manhattan. Characterized by oceanside, rural atmosphere, historic charm, and exclusivity, they are one of the wealthiest a summer colony, providing escape from the city and where residential real estate prices rank among the highest in the U.S.

It is a popular celebrity-spotting. Hundreds of celebrities have a home in the Hamptons, including J-Lo, Calvin Klein, Paul McCartney, Steven Spielberg, Robert De Niro and Beyoncé.

- 1.6 million USD (1.32 million EUR) median property value
- 5,900 m2 – the floor area of the biggest home in the Hamptons
- 90,000 USD (74,297 EUR) median household income
- 90% of residents are white

My McMansion

Suburbian fabric.
Dallas, USA

Commonly known as McMansions, mass produced and supersized houses have been proliferating in north American suburbs since the 50s. And they're getting bigger. For several years, architecture critic Kate Wagner has been reviewing those designs of excess and opulence head over to mcmansionhell.com

- 90 m2 average house size in 1950 in the U.S.
- 140 m2 average house size in 1970 in the U.S.
- 220 m2 average house size in 2004 in the U.S.
- 280 m2 average floor area of a McMansion
- 30% larger than the average new house
- larger than 80% of houses
- 3 m average ceiling height of a McMansion
- 3 car garage or more
- 1 two-storey portico

My Swimming Pool

Suburban fabric
Saint Tropez, France

U.S. is the number one consumer of private swimming pools, followed by France. Those markets are supported by the growing demand for individual houses in both countries. Residential swimming pools are becoming increasingly popular around the world and in many different climates. With their democratization, they are now a must-have residential recreation component.

- 10.6 million residential swimming pools in the U.S.
- 3 million residential swimming pools in the state of California
- 309,000 public swimming pools in the U.S.
- 2.5+ million private swimming pools in France
- 20,000 EUR estimated average cost to build an in-ground swimming pool

My Finca

La Finca.
Madrid, Spain

Located in the municipality of Pozuelo de Alarcón, whose population enjoy the highest income per capita in Spain, La Finca is a low-density development. Each villa claims to be a unique palace, although they are all designed by the same firm (A-cero). Amenities include private swimming pools, gyms, home cinemas, shooting rooms, and even bunkers. Following its residents' obsession with safety and privacy, the villas and the whole area have a double perimeter fence, movement detection, sensors and private patrols for surveillance. The isolated luxury residential area is often quoted as being the most exclusive ghetto in Spain.

- 12 million EUR selling price of a mansion
- 3,000 to 10,000 m2 surface area of land plots
- 5 to 7 million EUR average selling price of mansions

My Castle

Burj Al Babas.
Mudurnu, Turkey

Burj Al Babas is a failed residential development of identical miniature Disney-like castles. Developers originally envisioned the complex as a luxury vacation destination for a community of wealthy tourists. Construction started in 2014. The company went bankrupt in 2018 after nearly 80% of the villas were built. The housing development is currently abandoned.

- 100 ha
- 732 houses planned in 2014
- 587 houses completed to date
- 2,500 construction workers involved
- 370,000 to 500,000 USD (305,440 to 412,760 EUR) house price range
- 324 m2 average plot area
- 200 million USD (165.1 million EUR) estimated value
- 27 million USD (22.29 million EUR) company debt

My Dead End

Section Seven.
Las Vegas, USA

Cul-de-sacs are non-through roads with only one inlet and outlet, and usually a circular shape at the end to facilitate the turning of cars. Since the 1950s, there has been extensive use of cul-de-sac in suburban land subdivisions, worldwide. Cul-de-sacs were supposed to increase traffic safety, but they actually rely on and encourage car transportation. These days their selling point is a sense of privacy that adds value to a property; developers love them for their low cost compared to a grid, and how flexibly they can cram more properties onto any topography. They have dramatically negative

consequences for environmental, health and social issues.

- 10,845,867 dead-ends in the world (as mapped on OpenStreetMap)
- 5% of American commuters use public transit, 3% walk, 1% ride a bicycle; the rest drive
- Residents on gridded streets drive 26% less than residents on cul-de-sacs

My Waterfront

Suburban fabric
Weston, USA

Florida is characterized by extensive water resources. With the urbanizatior of the State during the second half of the 20st century, many low dense communities were built around the creation and incorporation of water bodies. Developers created canals and lakes to maximize the amount of waterfront properties. Weston, ranked as the best place to live in Florida, is a perfect example. It is built right up against the Everglades, a swampy ladnscape vital to Florida's fresh water supply. This watery suburbia is causing significant damage to the natural landscape and the environment.

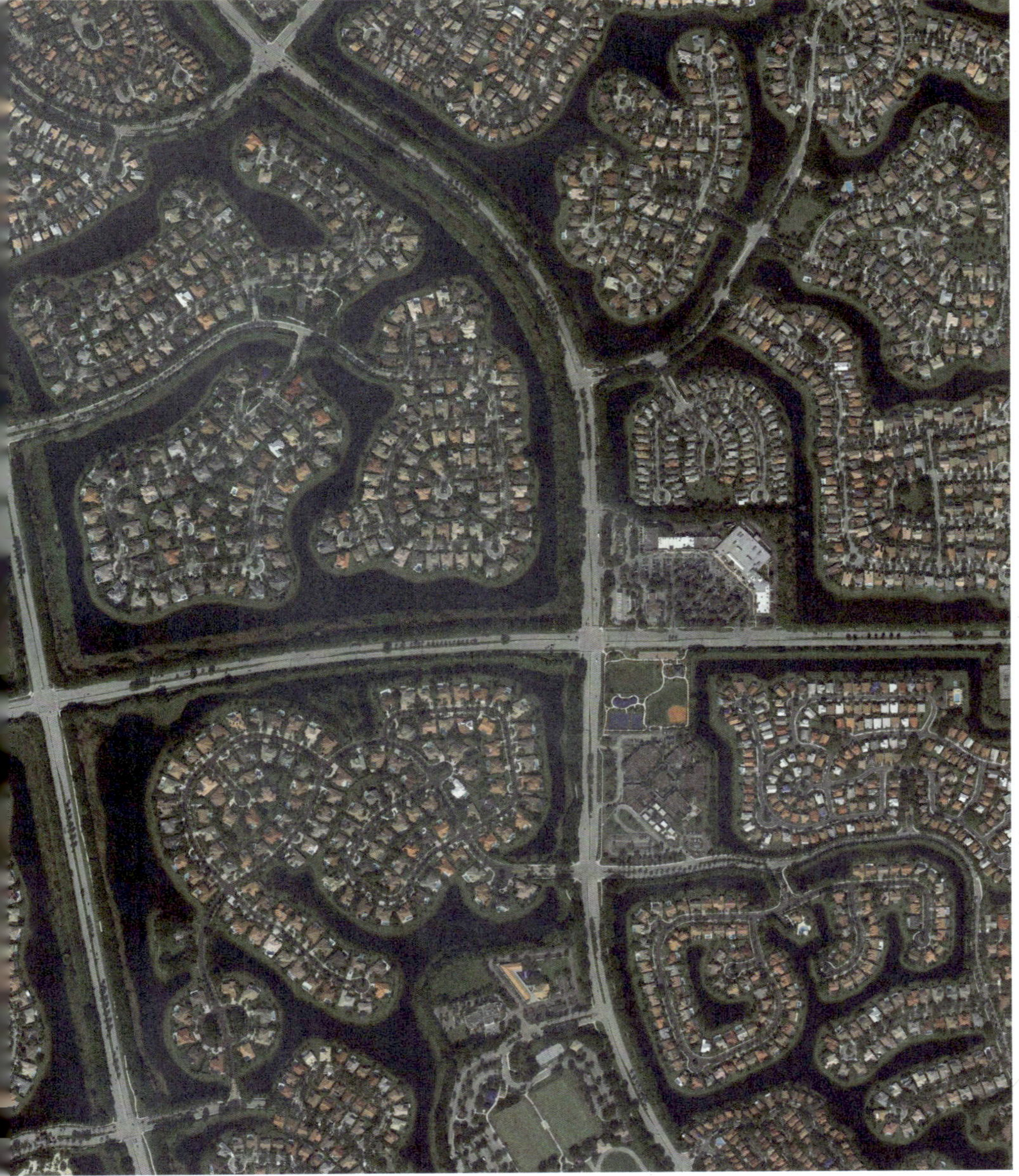

- ¾ of Florida's population lives in coastal counties
- The sea level is rising along the Florida coast six times faster than at any time in recorded history
- Florida is one of the most vulnerable places on Earth to climate change
- Over 50% of Florida's 825 miles of beaches is eroding
- 77.6% of workers in Weston drive to work alone; 3.55% have 'super commutes' in excess of 90 minutes

My Oasis

Madinaty.
New Cairo, Egypt

Madinaty is an exclusive gated community made up of villas and luxury apartment blocks, being built in the desert outside Cairo. It is a new town extension to New Cairo, itself a satelite new town of Cairo built in the 1990s. Madinaty will include vast green areas, golf courses, hospitals, business centers, hotels, educational institutions, sports and social clubs, household services, and entertainment facilities, as well as "innovative and unique services on its fringes which will cater to the needs of nearby towns", including a 40-acre water park.

- 33.6 million square metres land coverage
- 600.000 future inhabitants
- 120.000 apartments
- 80.000 villas
- 42.1 billion EUR total budget
- 42% of Egypt's population lives below the poverty line
- 0% taxes paid during construction, by government exemption

My Block

Hefei.
China

Hefei is the capital city of China's Anhui provicence, a major producer of rice, soybean and tea, and a regional hub for coal and steel production. The Evergrande Hefei Center T1, under construction in the regional capital's new Central Business District but currently paused, will be 518 m tall when completed, and include a financial centre and hotel. Evergrande, a Chinese developer, is reported to be at risk of financial collapse due to huge short-term debt in 2021.

- 518 m, tallest tower in the Anhui province
- 112 floors above ground
- 9 years predicted construction time

My Space Trip

Earth Orbit

Since the summer 2021, it's possible to travel outside of our Planet for recreational purposes. Each space 10 min ride costs about 450,000 Eur per person and emits 100 times more CO2 than a regular flight. The impact of such orbital travels appears as the ultimate ego-trip.

- 450,000 EUR per person for a 10-minute ride
- 100 times more CO_2 than a regular flight
- 400 tonnes of fuel to reach suborbital space
- Average 120 km^2 launch site

Dream Homes?

The Why Factory (TU Delft)

Tutors: Winy Maas, Ulf Hackauf, Adrien Ravon

Student: Jayson Johnstone

Text by Adrien Ravon

What's your dream home? You've probably been building one in your mind since you were a child. How different is your dream home now? And how different is it from mine?

Dream homes are often depicted as single-family villas with a private garden. This image projects the innocence of a child's sketch, but its ubiquity is alarming. It suggests that the range of options from which we patch together our dreams of a home is limited, perhaps constrained by our lack of references, but more likely by trends, speculation and advertising. How free are our desires of what is already commonplace, or of what our neighbours dream of?

Through this experiment, we explore the potential of social media to be a liberating environment for creativity and the realization of individual desires. It focuses on Pinterest, a popular social network launched in 2010 that quickly evolved into a search engine and participatory image database. This chapter explores ways of translating generic images and data analysis into architecture. Starting with a survey of Pinterest users compiling images as reference for their dream home in their 'home feed', the research proposes a methodology for quantifying the importance of constituent parts of the dream of each 'Pinner'. Individual items are compared, assigned a weighting in the definition of the dream home, and collaged into personalized architectural visions. How different are these composite visions from the norm, and from each other?

This exercise challenges the generative power of AI and the use of personal data for targeted advertising through the medium of user-generated collages. Can we take back control of dreams aggregated by machines?

The Perfect Home Collection

Imagine nine children's drawings of their dream home. They are all likely be detached houses, with luxurious facilities such as pools and slides, perhaps a car, but probably no bins, and no shed. They might have gardens or trees near them, and they're probably bathed in sun. The houses they sketch are rather similar. They are not the houses that these children actually live in, or houses that exist in a precise location, but rather a normative representation of 'home' that seems to be anchored in our collective psyche.

This set of mental images of drawings of houses is in some ways similar to the set of pictures that Google Images would produce for the search item 'dream home': the houses all seem oversized and are positioned in the centre of the page; most have pitched roofs and a chimney or turret; a private driveway leads to the welcoming front door located in the centre of the facade, and a garden delimited by a fence surrounds the house (in the image, we may have already stepped past the fence, but we know it is there); there will be hints of outdoor leisure activities as well as indoor warmth. In short, we've all pictured the idealized suburban single-family home.

Visual-content-oriented social media helps to build collective imaginaries. It constantly feeds us new information based on our tastes and our community, broadening and building on our interests. But how free are we to dream of new things? On Pinterest or Instagram, the range of routes (or scrolls and clicks) for us to explore new things creatively is limited by what is offered by others. How free can our desires be if we glean them from what already exists, what our friends say they like, or from prompts for the new thing that is already in a warehouse near us – waiting for us to desire it? Are there tools for safeguarding and enhancing individual expression and creativity in an era driven by the standardization of dreams?

Pinterest: An Individual Archive of Collective Tastes

Dreams are often described in oversimplified terms, flattened or reduced to impossible images. To learn more about the way dream homes are composed, we followed eight real users on Pinterest. The users remain anonymous in this chapter, but their visions of home tell us a lot about the collective imaginaries, perhaps as much as about theirs.

Turning to Pinterest for answers may not be as odd as it sounds – it is finely tuned to our individual tastes, and has a crowd-sourced archive of the little things that make a space special: isolated huts in the forest, practical kitchens, a detail of a rug you think is from Morocco, a stylish, stripped-back Modernist living room, humble floors made perfect by adding yoga or cats, or that penthouse with a panoramic view that you know would give you the head space you need to dream.

Pinterest, a contraction of the verb to pin and the noun interest, is described by its founders as a '*visual discovery engine… where you can find useful and relevant things that inspire you to do stuff*'[1]. The San Francisco-based company has evolved into a collection of more than 240 billion 'relevant things'[2] since its foundation in 2010. Users turn to Pinterest for answers to everyday questions in life: 'What should I cook?'; 'What should

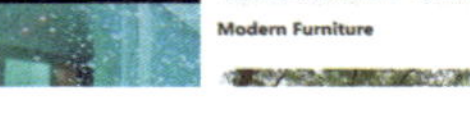

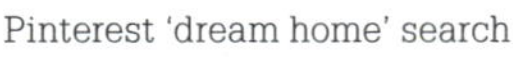

Pinterest 'dream home' search

I wear?'; 'What should I like?' In short: 'How should I live, and what does that look like?'

Recently estimated to be worth 21 billion USD[3], this dream bank is fed by the clicks of 450+ million monthly active users – potential consumers. From a consumerist point of view, the platform is very close to becoming a catalogue of products, but if we look at it from a collaborative point of view, it's also a tool for creation. With it, users can become designers and describe their dream home with images sourced from others. What if the real transformative potential of Pinterest is its use as a *participatory design engine*? And what can we learn from this collective mosaic of desires?

The previous figure shows 1000 images selected by the eight Pinterest users as a way of enriching their personal dream home collection. We used this set of images as a collective database to analyse the desires of these users by sorting, counting and categorizing these images, then transforming the sets into spatial propositions.

Decoding Dreams

Even though our brains grasp things visually, we often use words to describe these images to others, or search for them online with a written approximation. But words are rarely enough to describe your dream home.

This experiment set out a methodology for reconstructing dream homes based on Pinterest data. To transform each dataset into an input for the design of a house, we set out to decode and sort the meaningful elements of each image according to criteria which we could then use to inform an architectural and programmatic arrangement.

We began by tagging the 1000 images collected from Pinterest according to 56 categories, which include type of room, architectural elements that define spaces (such as a pitched roof, vault, mezzanine, columns, etc.), types of window, materials, objects and surrounding environment. This series of tags were used to create a resident profile card, compiling all the design information to generate a person's dream home.

Recent developments in machine learning and artificial intelligence mean that software is increasingly able to take on a role similar to that of the architect, translating words or other datasets, such as numbers, incomplete sets of images or metadata, into 'complete' images. What if this experiment were coded into a data-harvesting design program? For example, in the picture of a bathroom shown on page 79, a computer program developed out of this exercise would be able to automatically recognize and identify a series of elements, and extract them from the visual composition. Image recognition in computer sciences is based on a series of algorithms able to identify objects, places, and other discrete visual data, and match that with an existing database. By doing so, the script will recognize that this is a picture of a bathroom, because of other references present in the database as well as the identification of towels and a bathtub in the image. Further, a program – much like our researcher – would recognize the bathtub at the bottom left of the image and calculate its presence and the space it takes up in the composition.

What else matters in this image? In this typical Pinterest image, what is architecture, and what just décor or clutter? And how would a program

Collective mosaic of dream home of eight Pinterest users

identify and categorize items? An artificial intelligence could identify objects, materials and architectural elements. It could identify the laminate on the floor. It would estimate that the room has a high ceiling, recognize its vaulted shape, count two twin sinks and one large window offering a view towards a lush green exterior; the window, the view and the exterior qualities might be logged as three distinct but interrelated items. And so, it would analyse what the space is composed of, and sort it into a series of tags per type: bathroom as the type of room; high ceiling, vaults and a view of the forest as the dominant spatial features; large windows, twin sinks and bathtub as the significant elements; wood, mirror and ceramic as the materials; and brown, green and white as the predominant colours.

Dream Home Dataset

A quick look at the collection of images provides an overview of the differences and similarities between the eight dream homes of our eight sample Pinterest users. At a glance, the relative importance of the different types of room, signature architectural elements, view, materials, size and surroundings is clear. How many times a type of image is pinned gives an indication of each user's priorities.

After decoding each image, counting the number of times its elements occur and defining a profile card, an algorithm would link this dataset to Photoshop and assign a degree of opacity to the image, depending on its place in the hierarchy of importance of a user's Pinboard. The transparency assigned to each image is therefore a direct reference to how, and how often, the constituent elements of an image appear in each dataset.

For instance, if a user obsessively compiles images of helicoidal staircases, this might signal a strong desire for a duplex. If another user pins only folding ladders and step stools, we could assume they are keen on DIY, while a collector of both rope-ladders and split staircases might – despite the grandeur implied by the latter – be obsessed with escape strategies. According to our methodology, the choice of stairs (or no stairs), as anecdotal as it may seem, is a major marker of our understanding of what makes our ideal home.

Dreaming in Style

User A's collection of pins of wooden attics with exposed beams recalls the idealized image of a chic-cool loft. As important as the structure, a series of free-standing bathtubs seem to be the essence of this dream home: an antique roman tub teleported into the interior of a heavily pastel-coloured chalet. User D would probably also like this house.

User G loves views down onto, through and out of things, and is into round windows, curvy stairs and arches on a big scale and with a splash of colour. Geometry and scale are important elements of what makes their dream home. So is colour.

There are no people in these dream homes, but there's plenty of furniture and soft furnishings. There's an oversized sofa, all those free-standing bathtubs, cushions, perfectly full bookshelves, rocking chairs *en rotin*, fashionably designed lighting, curtains, Eames chairs, and a ladder with no clear use leaning against the wall. Sometimes, furniture seems more important than the space itself – it's easy to project yourself onto an XXL sofa.

Analysis of image components

There is a clear trend for plants, inside and outside. Greenery signals a sense of well-being. For some users, extensive lawns are a strong desire. For others, a carefully-placed easy-to-care-for succulent is preferable.

Kitchens are mainly enclosed, with no need for outdoor views. They are mostly conditioned by the archetype of the island kitchen. Sinks matter. As do swimming pools; almost every collection has one.

The maximization of height seems to be important too, interchangeable with skylights. Both give a sense of luxury through space. Choice of material matters to most users. Wood is perhaps the most popular – every user has pinned some, and one user is particularly dedicated to it – followed by marble, exposed stone and brick.

Having analysed, categorized and weighted each collection of images, visions of the eight users' dream homes could now be fabricated.

Looking at the grid of desires of each user, it is hard to imagine a coherent architectural or spatial vision emerging from such a mash-up of desires. But the Pinterest dream homes on the following pages have a depth of spatial suggestion, atmosphere and sense of interiority that is greater than the set of found images that generated them. There's a strong sense of transition between spaces, foregrounding experience rather than function and spatial organization. They are strongly dream-like and yet feel much more real and personal than the cookie-cutter images from which they are composed.

Dream Homes Review

The collages are blurry, like most of our dreams. They are full of nuances and possibilities. They produce immersive spaces where the delimitation between desires fades away, revealing a productive gradient from one dream to another. When a user has a very clear image of what their living room should look like, the resulting image is in focus and in it we can recognize composite desires – hybrids of existing styles, scales and spaces that appear new when mixed. Sometimes, where the desires are a bit more uncertain, the relationship between elements of the dream home remains blurry. But it is in this blur that there may be most space for transformation. The blur makes space for potential new dreams and negotiation – an ambiguity within which we can compromise, invent, innovate and create.

What is blurry in the data, or in one person's reading of a space, may not be in others'. The unknowns can make space for new visions and space to keep dreaming, to adapt and build on what we like most. It allows us to move on from our initial set of desires. Almost like the first render impression an architect could produce for a client, these collages give us a spatial feeling of what this space could be, while highlighting what type of definition the dream might still be missing.

The collages are not static. They are an instance of a visual composition in evolution – an architecture that *is becoming*. These visions and desires are not frozen or static, but in constant flux. What kind of architecture could absorb this idea of evolution and adaptability?

The Next Dream Home

Pinterest, in the context of our experiment, is more than an archive of images. This research takes a set of users with mainstream, replicated

Space		Kitchen	Dining	Living	Bed	Bath	Office	Media	Circulation	Storage	Exterior	Sum
	Pins	11	7	9	8	5	2	1	3		12	58
	Exterior Doors	2		5	2		1		2		4	16
	High Ceiling	1	2	3	1	1						8
	View	1	1	3		1					1	7
	Open rooms			4			1		2			7
	Gable										5	5
	Stairs	1	1	1					1			4
	Courtyard			1	1						1	3
	Garret			1	2							3
	Cantilever										2	2
	Mezanine			1								1
	Outside			1								1
	Vault											0
Objects	Windows	1	4	5	6	1	1		1		7	26
	Ornament	1	1		2		2		1		1	8
	Column	1	1	1			1				3	7
	Fireplace		3	1	1							5
	Pool								1		4	5
	Bath tubs					3						3
	Corners	2										2
	Balcony										2	2
	Vegetation										2	2
	Storage				2							2
	Shower					2						2
	Skylight				1							1
	Arch			1								1
	Wine Cellar			1								1
	Hot Tub										1	1
	Lawn										1	1
	Pool Table			1								1
	Swing										1	1
	Screen											0
	Furniture											0
	Water Garden											0
	Garden											0
	Aquarium											0
	Bowling											0
	Tennis											0
	Bar											0
	Library											0
	Zen Garden											0
	Shutters											0
Environment	Ocean		1	1							2	4
	City	1		1								2
	Forest					1						1
	Moutains			1								1
	Lake											0
	Plaines											0
Material	Paint	9	4	5	7	2	1	1	1			30
	Wood	6	4	3	3	1	2		2		5	26
	Glass		2	3	1		1				4	11
	Stone	2	1	2					1		4	10
	Tile	2				3					2	7
	Steel	1		1							3	5
	Plaster					1			2		1	4
	Wallpaper		1	1	1	1						4
	Mirror	2				1						3
	Concrete			1	1							2
	Shingles										2	2
	Stainless Steel		1									1
	Carpet							1				1
	Gold											0
	Brick											0

A dream home dataset example

sets of desires and develops a methodology for spatializing these into non-standard, three-dimensional dreams. Through this exercise, users take control of dreams generated by machines. They become makers of their own dreams, turning marketing-generated content into the shared building blocks of their dream homes.

These collages were manually put together, but could easily be automated. The experiment could also be taken one step further: back to the original users for input. Picture a user pinning another ideal bathroom to a board, and seeing a summary collage of their dream home updating itself – a suggestive spatial mash-up of desires. In a scenario in which software could generate our dream homes in real-time based on a categorization and weighting of a series of desirable images, users would be able to intervene in the production of the space and critically edit their own desires, engaging in the cumulative process of design.

Imagine a software that would allow this level of analysis of our desires – those we know and those we don't know – and that includes the user as an active negotiator in how the desire evolves.

Taking as a starting point the idea that data harvesting, targeted advertising and artificial intelligence learns from our desires in order to sell us new ones or shape our actions without us knowing, this experiment set out to program a negotiation tool that transforms our desires into the production of space. The next chapter explores how much a dream can be distorted and condensed through this process, or evolve as it negotiates space with others, while demonstrating that potential overlaps and differences can lead to new forms of compatibility.

The (w)Ego Game is a computer-aided investigation into how dream homes can coexist collectively, in density. We will look at how these can evolve, by adjusting their parameters to make space for the collective, into unique spaces with latent, unimagined potential.

Dreams evolve over time.
The image of a dream home is not something precisely defined. It is a kind of atmospheric, blurry vision that leaves freedom and space for negotiation and discovery – a discovery that comes from interaction with the dreams of other people, and is at its core evolutive and social.

User A – The Loft – Dream Home Images Collection

User B – The Modern – Dream Home Images Collection

User A – The Loft – Dream Home Blend

User B – The Modern – Dream Home Blend

User C – The Attic – Dream Home Images Collection

User D – The Chalet – Dream Home Images Collection

User C – The Attic – Dream Home Blend

User D – The Chalet – Dream Home Blend

User E – The Palace – Dream Home Images Collection

User F – The Villa – Dream Home Images Collection

User E – The Palace – Dream Home Blend

User F – The Villa – Dream Home Blend

User G – The Duplex – Dream Home Images Collection

User H – The Penthouse – Dream Home Images Collection

User G – The Duplex – Dream Home Blend

User H – The Penthouse – Dream Home Blend

I-City

The Why Factory (TU Delft),
MVRDV

Winy Maas, Bas Kalmeyer,
Tiham Salij, Leo Stuckardt,
Sander Mulders, Jeroen Zuidgeest

Tutors: Winy Maas, Felix Madrazo,
Sander Mulders, Ania Molenda

Student: Dalia Zakaite

Text by The Why Factory / MVRDV

What sort of city results when everyone chooses to live by themselves? This visual essay builds on the individual desire of owning a detached house and expands it to a city of one million inhabitants.

The study begins by showing one million capsules for individuals that never interact with each other: in other words, this is the most egoistic approach to urbanism and housing. By taking users' egoism as a starting point for our research, then challenging it, this chapter speculates on what happens to the egoistic ideal when two users get close to each other. What happens next when they are connected? And when more join? How does a system of users emerge? The essay speculates on how interactions between individuals, groups and collectivities can shape the future city. When do individuals become part of a collective? When, and where, do they fight? When, and where, do they share? When does collective intelligence happen?

This chapter ends with an impossible vision of an endless three-dimensional suburb, exploring the potential of a more porous density based on both our boundaries and the bonds that bring us together.

The Unit

Sometimes I wonder how I would behave if our current society fell apart. What would happen if I had to start from scratch? Would it be completely from scratch? Like with Adam and Eve? Or could I rely on some of the teachings of our civilization? Of thousands of years of development? Would my equipment still work? Could I rely on help?

If so, what would my contemporary survival package then

be? What is the minimal architecture that I need? What is the 'Existenz' Building?

I-City starts with a survival unit containing all the basic elements which are needed to survive individually. It provides a small semi-artificial ecosystem as a safe haven in which to live, grow food and produce energy, allowing everybody to organize all their needs individually and be fully autonomous, independent from others.

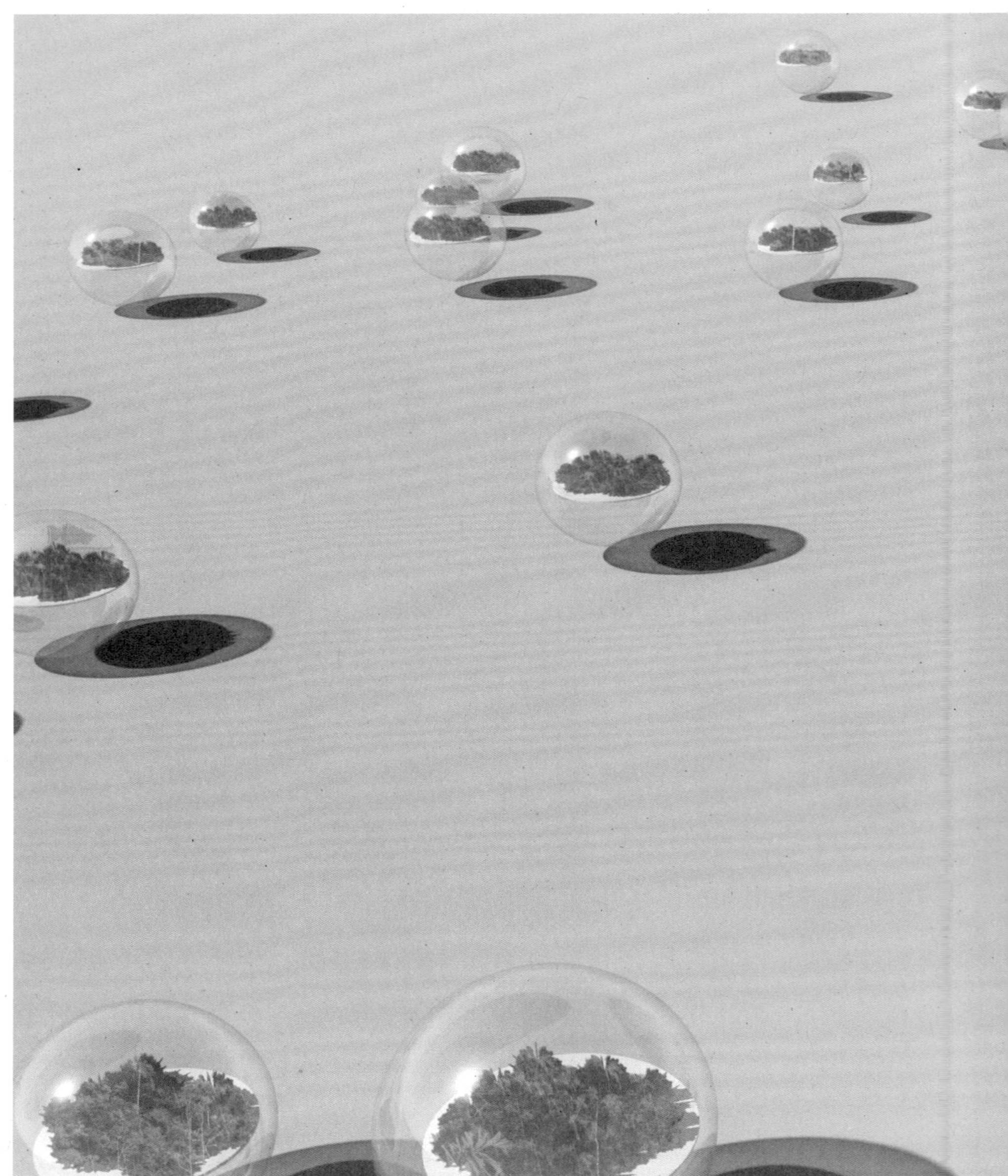

Floating Units

I-City starts out as individual units, but social relations and stability, efficiency and safety concerns are drivers for the development of communities and clusters.

Connecting Units

An individual unit can open up in order to connect to a neighbouring unit by controlling the adhesive aspects of the fabric of its Skin.

Sharing Units

The Bubbles' Transportation Amenities make it possible to connect or move to another neighbourhood.

It allows you to connect with other units and share your space and amenities, whenever and wherever you want.

Clusters

And it came alive. I-City became a We-City, where people started living together like clans, according to a model of specialization and exchange, with one cluster being focused on generating energy, another one focused on producing food, and so on. As such, clusters optimize production and raise living standards.

The Base Plate

The Base Plate is made out of light biodegradable and re-printable material. It forms the base of your compound, upon which all other elements are positioned. By adding surface with the Printer (explained later), self-customization provides the possibility to tune your environment to your needs.

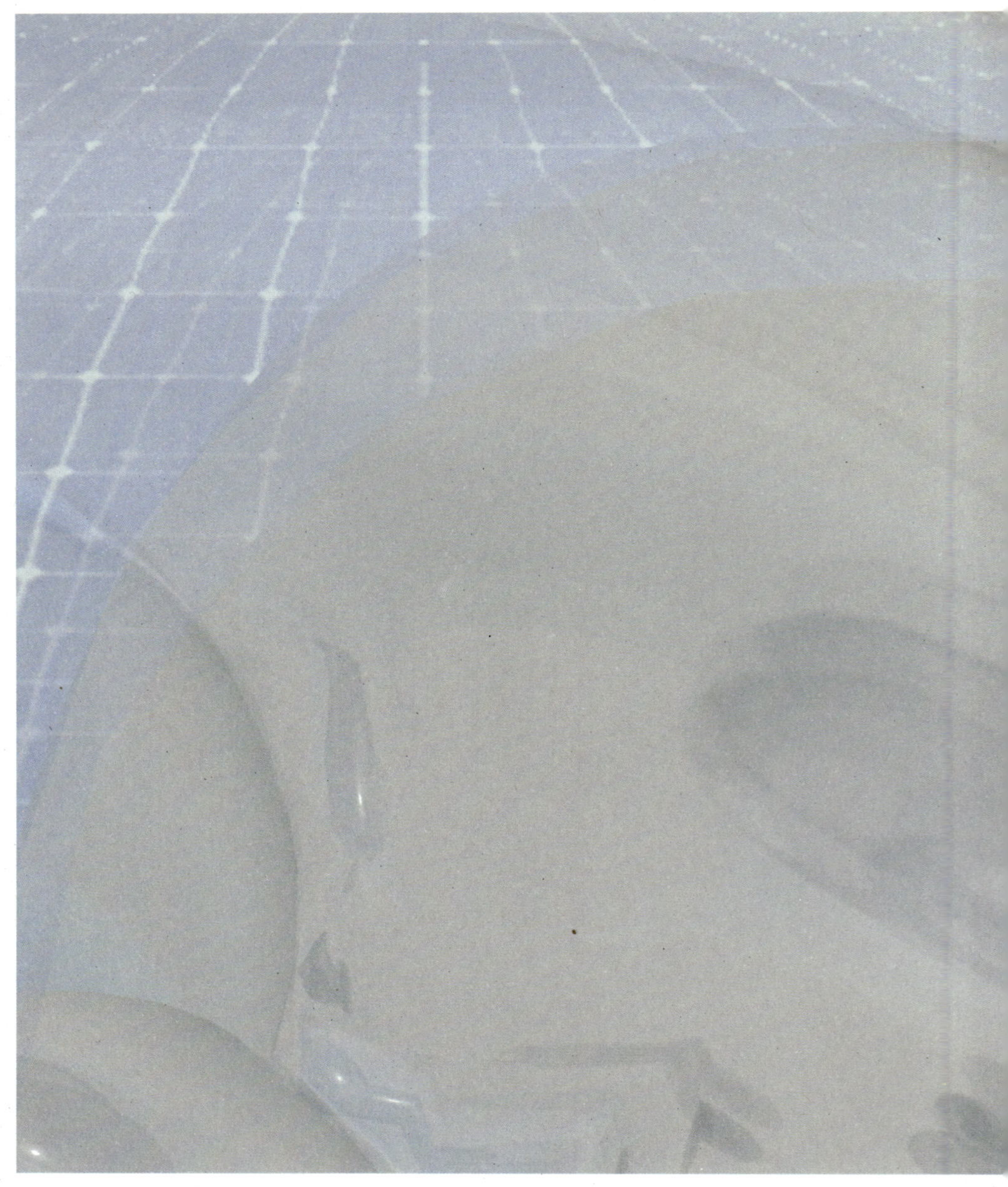

The Skin

The Skin is the basis of the independent safe bubble. It creates a protected interior for living, literally defining your living environment. The Skin of the sphere consists of a nanotechnology surface. The Sunlight Filter takes out harmful radiation from the sun, the Air Purification Membrane filters out the little amount of usable oxygen still left on our planet.

The Food Production Rack

A meticulously composed Rack takes care of the collection of water and highly efficient food production, able to provide a healthy, vegetarian diet for a family of four people.

The Water Condenser

The Water Condenser continuously distils water from the air within the bubble for the provision of clean water for consumption, personal hygiene and the production of food.

The Energy Production Unit

The Solar Power Membrane, integrated into the Skin, takes care of the production of energy gained from the increased strength of the sun. The Waste Processer is a mini-energy plant that generates energy from residual products from the Food Production Rack and the Printer. The collection of water, food production, waste disposal and energy production are integrated into one Rack, working together in order

to create an optimum output and guarantee the stable production of all needed elements.

The 3D Printer

With the Printer, additional elements are produced. Based on 3D Printer Software, running on solar power and using natural materials such as sand, metal or biodegradable plastic, a wide variety of products for bubble inhabitation can be printed on demand.

The Transportation Amenities

The Skin is built up as a double layer, acting as the Non-Direct-Usable Emissions Storage. It uses helium-type gasses to levitate, which enables the Spheres to connect with others at any location. The Levitation System uses these gasses for transportation. Every object that is airtight can be filled with the gas, making it possible to move around. The Ground Anchor makes it possible to connect to any location or element.

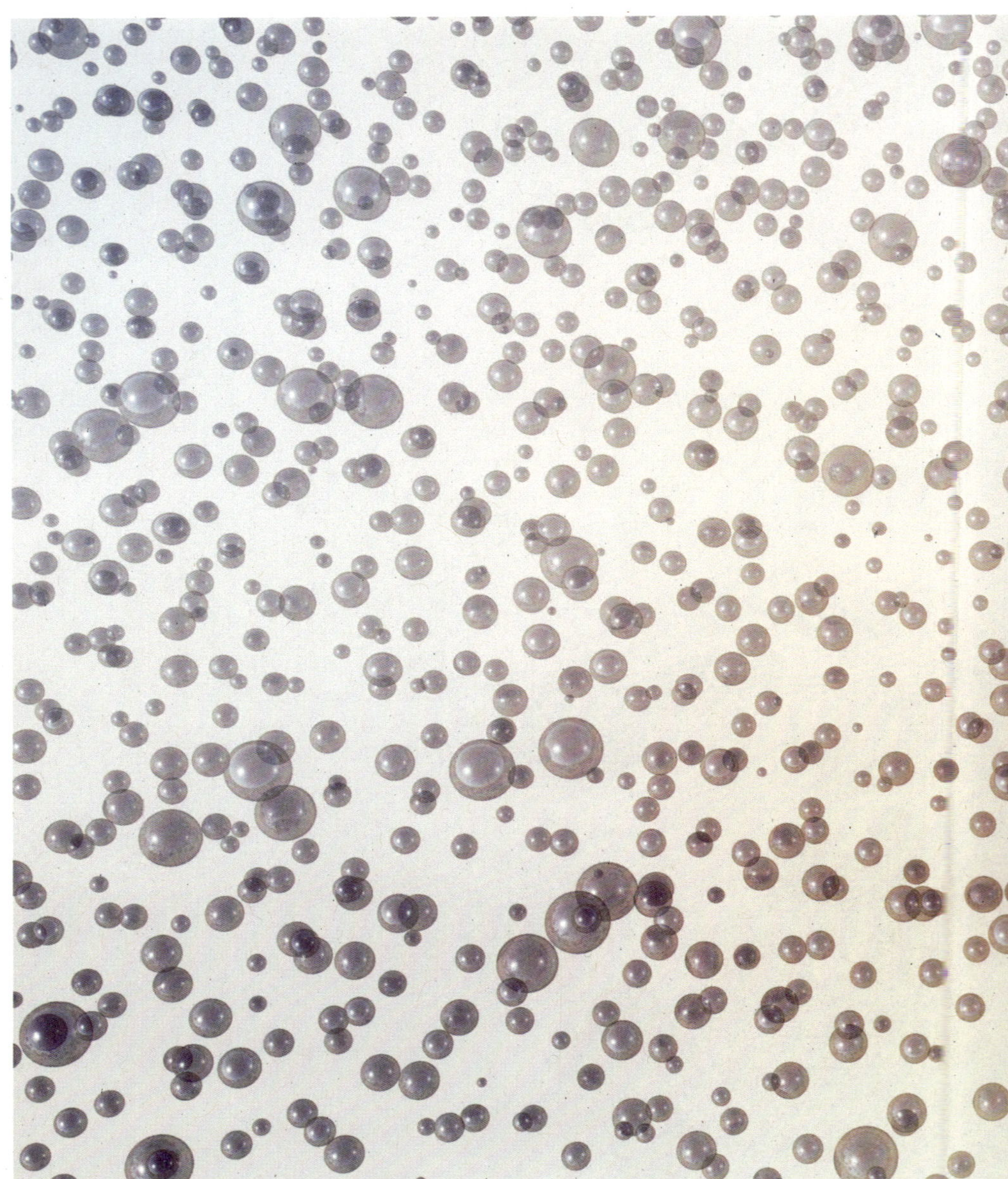

Impossible Egos

This impossible vision reminds us a kind of three-dimensional suburb, in motion. How would the governance of this city evolve? How long would individual bubbles last, in motion and taking part in multiple transactions? Even in the most egoistic scenario, a sense of collectiveness appears as the number of inhabitants grows.

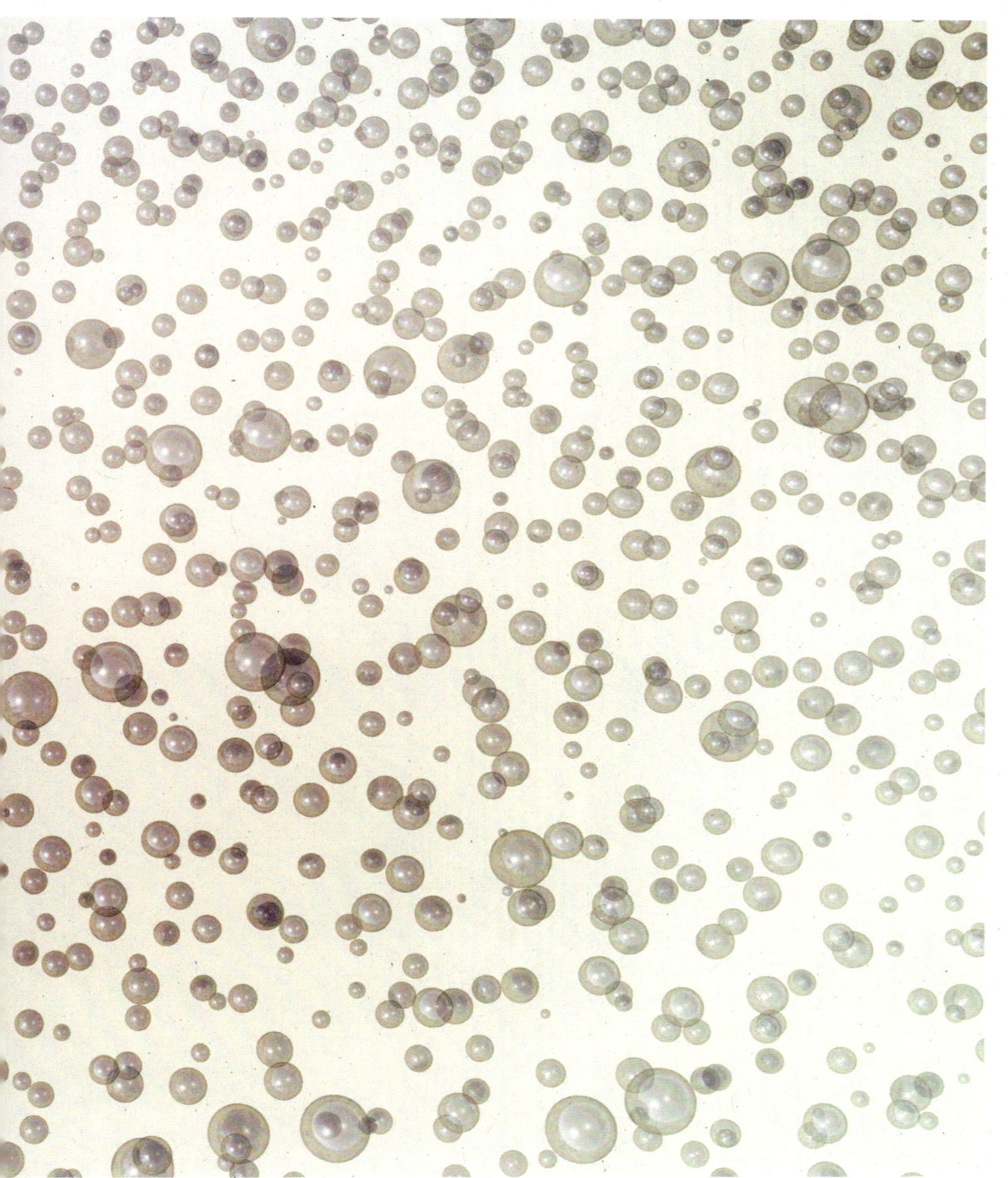

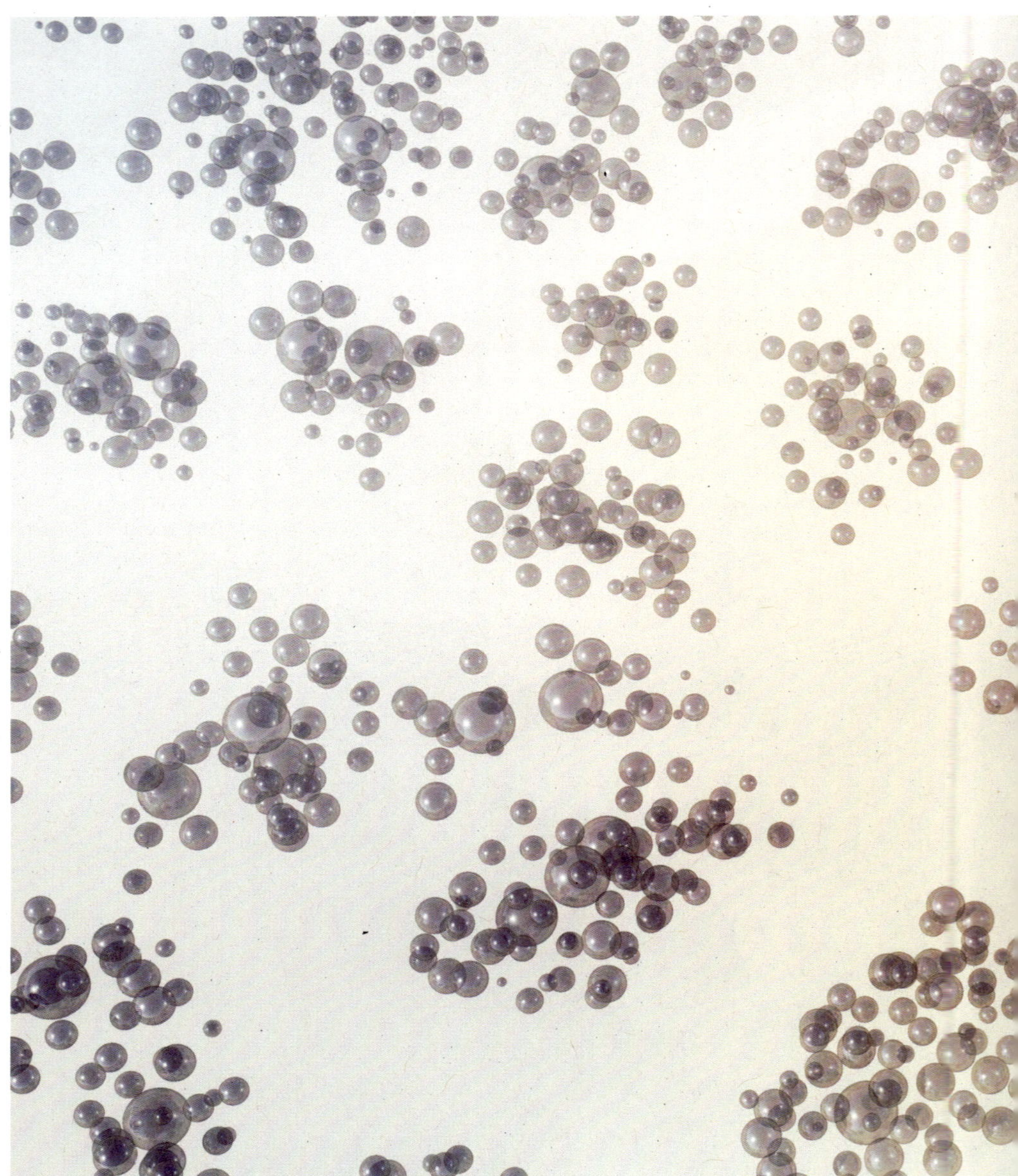

A Cloud-like Urbanism

The city becomes increasingly interconnected. Here you may live wherever you prefer, however you want, taking your bubble with you. I-City makes housing units flexible and independent enough to incorporate others and to adapt to their structures, without compromising independence.

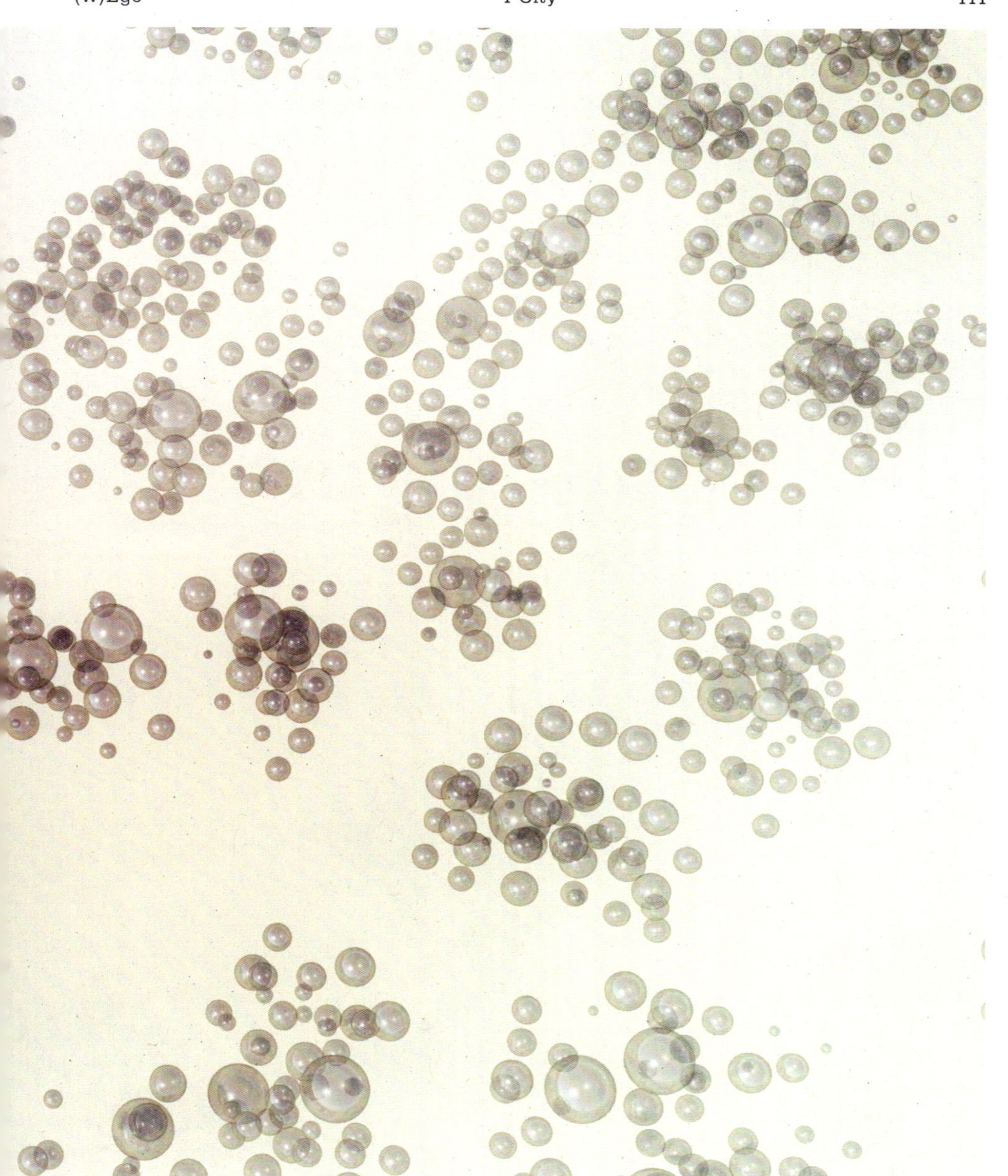

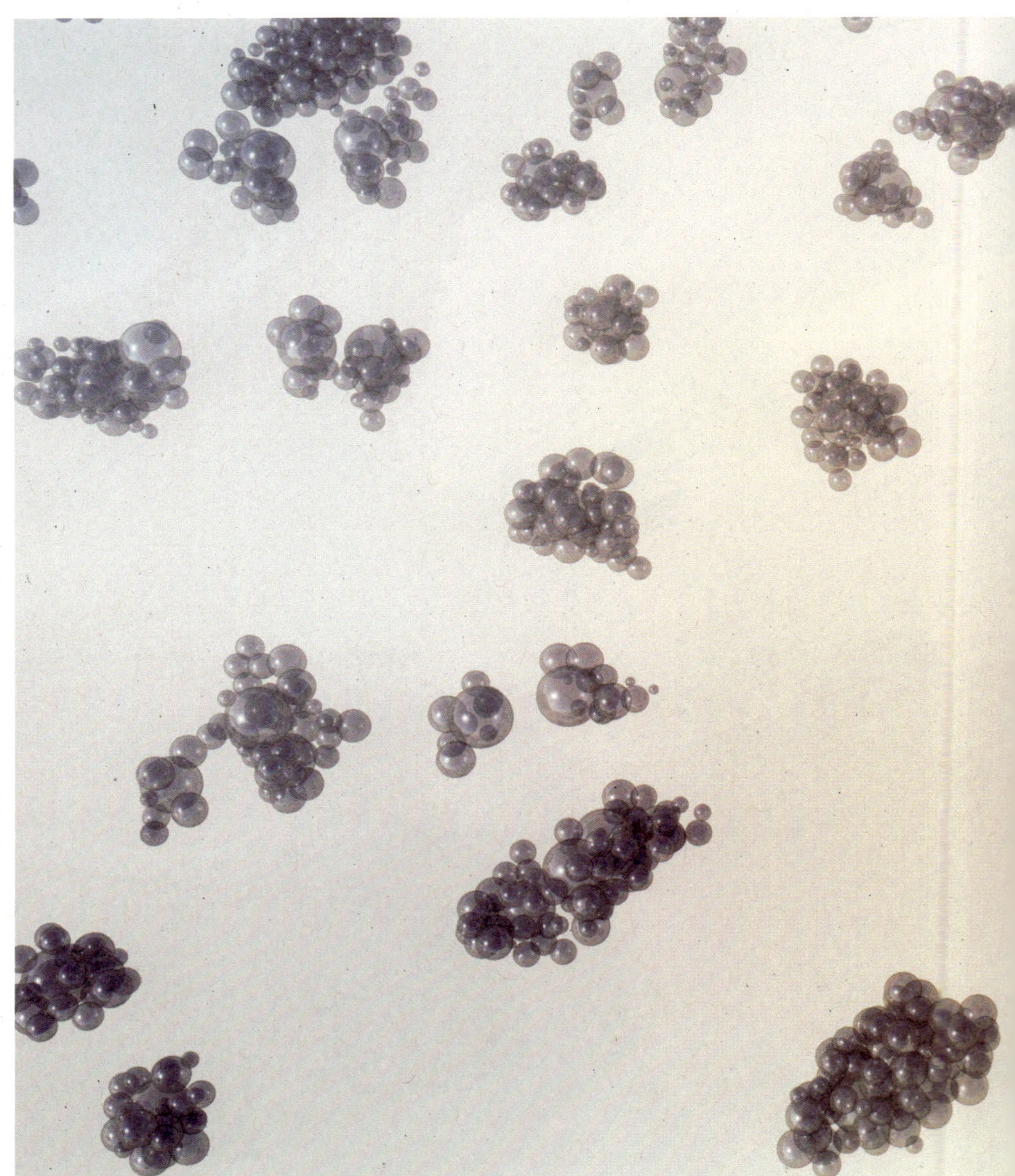

We-City

A We-City is emerging. A city, based on personal settings, but with a collective drive. After all, we all need our neighbours!

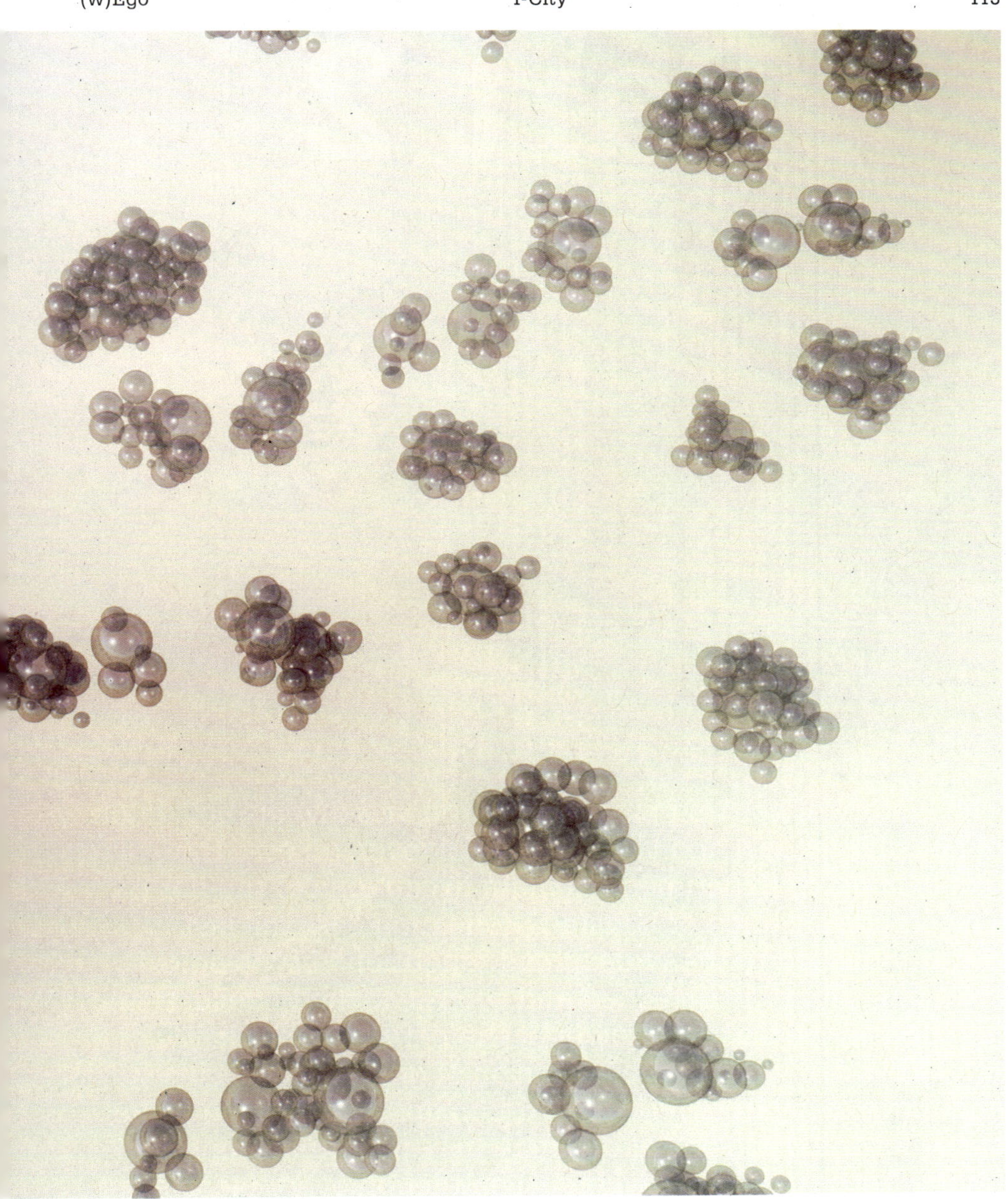

Part 2

The history of housing presents a large and diverse collection of housing models and typologies. However, all over the globe, housing experiments remain exceptions to the norm. The standardization of housing production over the last century has led to the widespread repetition of typological solutions: from the detached and semi-detached house, to the row house, the slab, the tower or the perimeter block.

How can we halt the extrusion of generic floorplans and move away from relentless urban sprawl? Can we make space for true typological diversity in dense urban contexts? Might 'Tetris' – a game where, even though every piece must fit together seamlessly, possibilities are endless – have something to teach the design professions? Could a video game help us design more innovative housing, spatially, typologically and sociologically?

(w)Ego

Housing Dialogues

The Why Factory (TU Delft)

Interview with Marja Elsinga, Dick van Gameren, Birgit Hausleiner, Paul Kuitenbrouwer, Nelson Mota and Mo Sedighi

Text by Javier Arpa Fernández and Adrien Ravon

(w)Ego is a pledge for density. It suggests that the spatial organization of housing has to be three-dimensional and that neighbours are the key for such development. But what are these shared spaces – flexible, public, social, bottom-up, top-down, incremental, reused and experimental – like in real life? What built examples of housing reveal the potential of living together in density?

In these conversations on housing, we engage with six housing experts from the Faculty of Architecture and the Built Environment at Delft University of Technology. From the Netherlands to the Global South (and back), this chapter looks at the precedents, trends, hopes, designs, developments and policies that have shaped innovative housing models across the world. Considering housing as a right and not a product, how can we make housing more affordable globally? How can architecture express diversity? What are the social and environmental impacts of 'good' and 'bad' housing on our cities? What approaches can we learn from the Global South? This discussion reflects on current and future housing urgencies, affirming a necessary optimism for the planet.

Flexibility is a very old idea

Interview with Dick van Gameren
by Javier Arpa Fernández

Javier Arpa Fernández: How far do you think The Why Factory's (w)Ego research is from reality?

Dick van Gameren: The ideas of flexibility, adaptability and customization are not new ones. How can we create dwellings adaptable to users' needs? How can everybody have a house as an expression of their own wishes and desires? How to start combining that in an urban situation? I think that, in the end, the idea of adaptability is the main issue. Can a building still change over time? This has never been really solved. There have been many projects where the internal layout was completely flexible. But in the end, they became rigid solutions. The mechanical services or installations are always the issue, especially in the Dutch context. In the Netherlands, the use of concrete structures, which allow for very little change, is widespread. Housing construction in the UK is based on a structural frame plus drywall, which allows for some more flexibility. Housing flexibility thus depends on building cultures.

At the same time, there are many examples of people coming together with a precise idea of the house they want to build so as to suit their needs. This is the case with cooperatives. There are beautiful examples, like Thalmatt 1 in Bern (Switzerland) by the architecture collective Atelier 5, where 18 completely different units were built together as one project by a group of individuals working collaboratively.

There are many other examples, probably not as extreme as what The Why Factory proposes, but they are there. Especially during the last crisis, when the housing market ground to a halt ten years ago, the cooperative model was embraced not only by individuals, but also by municipalities. When housing corporations and commercial developers stop building, it's time for cooperatives to take over, and that leads to really interesting projects. In any case, the reality is that cooperative housing remains kind of 'niche'. Many users are still not interested in it at all, as they are more interested in pursuing the standard than reaching the exception.

Building collective housing where each unit is entirely customized is an old ideal that has never been fully solved. It keeps being addressed, just like (w)Ego is doing.

JAF The Faculty of Architecture and the Built Environment at Delft University of Technology is engaged with the 1M Homes Initiative[4], aimed at pushing the construction of affordable housing in the Netherlands. What is your opinion about this initiative?

DVG Programmes to build large numbers of new housing have happened in the past many times, and with success. What should be new is to better reflect on what we are actually building. That's why (w) Ego is very interesting, since there is a tendency to focus on the total numbers (one million homes in this case), but not on variation and customization.

Over the last one hundred years, people could afford more and more personal space, but nowadays units need to be smaller and smaller so as to remain affordable. At the same time, more and more people live a more individual life, resulting in the need for dwellings for households of only one or two persons.

In this sense, it's quite a pity that many post-war housing interventions were demolished in the 90s. This was because the technical quality was not so good anymore, but also because we all thought they were too small and nobody wanted to live there anymore. And now, the housing being built is actually smaller than the demolished post-war projects. Such mistakes should really teach us that we need to develop an approach where housing size is not fixed and where you have possibilities for change and adaptation over time.

In a certain period, often only a single type of housing is produced. In the late 2000s, for example, during the financial crisis, the production of student housing became dominant. It was built in large numbers, and is nowadays often occupied by young starters. The units are very small and can't accommodate growing families. This approach doesn't have a great future. If you build neighbourhoods lacking typological diversity, where everything is the same, they will be outdated after 20 years, as users' lives change. Residents' needs will change and they will be forced to move out.

This is now a problem in the typical Dutch suburban neighbourhoods built in the 70s. If you analyse Tanthof in Delft, the residents really like it. But there is only one typology of single-family terraced housing, which forces the elderly to move out, as they need smaller, more comfortable dwellings on one level.

This is just an example, but I think that what we should really look at now, with the 1M Homes Initiative, is not so much the quantity but where and what we want to build. If you leave housing in the hands of the market, developers will go for the average to minimize risk. They will keep building two-bedroom, 80 m2 homes, increasing the endless repetition of suburban terrace houses and extending the city throughout the countryside.

As soon as the ambition of building one million homes within 10 to 12 years was announced, a debate on how we are going to do it immediately emerged. Will we build them within the existing city limits or will we keep building new Vinex-like[5] areas on the polders? Of course, many developers are against building them within existing cities: they find this too expensive and are keen to produce new towns like Almere. Many people, especially in this faculty, are against that, and would rather build towers in the city. But only building towers is also a danger: in my opinion, building just towers with too many small units is again only proposing one kind of housing typology.

So that's why the (w)Ego experiment is interesting: can units be more customized, and especially, can they change over time? As I said before, flexibility is a very old idea, and there are many examples from the past. I don't mean it as a criticism, but let's not forget customization is an old architectural ideal. We designers keep thinking about it, but it may not necessarily be the prime goal of people looking for a place to live in the city.

JAF 600 million homes need to be built in the world to meet current demand. Do you think that Western Europe's affordable housing policies are exportable to other places, mainly to the Global South?

DVG I think the 'European approach' has a very limited role to play there. Africa, India, Bangladesh, etc., are places where I work with my team at the Global Housing research group at Delft University of Technology. There, we address the enormous need for affordable housing. We really don't talk about customization. In a way, you're just happy if you can achieve a certain quality in the unit itself, and especially within the urban setting, because that is often where things go wrong.

I am concerned about the failure of certain projections in those areas of the world. For example, a few years ago India planned the construction of 15 million new housing units in five years. It didn't happen. During the first year of the programme, they didn't achieve even 1 per cent of that ambition. And they will never manage to do it. Because 15 million units, even in a country as big as India, is enormous. It's not realistic; nevertheless, the need is there. If you look at Africa, you can come up with the same figures.

Another aspect of concern is how, in places like Mumbai or Dhaka, where half of the population live in informal settlements, slum replacement projects often create a kind of vertical slum condition. There, the question is once more how to create a decent living environment for people with minimal or no means at all.

JAF You just mentioned decent environments. Standards can vary enormously from the Netherlands or Austria to India or Bangladesh, although people are the same anyway. What, then, is adequate housing?

DVG Yes, that's true. Changes to standards go step by step, also here. For example, at the end of the nineteenth century, places like London or Amsterdam were slum cities. They changed gradually. But the number of inhabitants was much smaller, and there was more time to do it.

Now everything is going so much faster. That is the big problem: can we

Incremental housing Aranya, Indore, India. Designed by Balkrishna Doshi (Photo: Dick van Gameren)

ever eradicate slums in the growing cities of the Global South? Some say that it is impossible, that there will always be slums, because cities keep growing exponentially.

In Dhaka, a family can live in a room of 3 by 3 metres, without any daylight, or ventilation, inside a giant warehouse covered with corrugated iron, and somewhere in the building there is a tiny shared kitchen and a space to do the washing. In the Netherlands we would not find that acceptable.

JAF I have the impression that we try to bring our knowledge and expertise to the outside world but we never do the opposite exercise. What models from the Global South could we import in places like the Netherlands?

DVG That's an interesting question. There are some very interesting experiences in the Global South aimed at embracing the idea of customization and building your own house. They mostly remain experiments, starting with a very basic unit, which people can extend over time. There are some beautiful examples of low-rise, high-density projects that start in the most basic way and change over time, allowing for these changes. I think that's very interesting. Here, we hardly allow change because it could immediately affect others, our neighbours. Here, in our own context, everything tends to be fixed. There are a lot of quite successful examples there that have to do with the incremental idea. I think we could certainly learn from that.

JAF Are you optimistic about the future of our planet?

DVG I'm an optimistic person. I want to be optimistic. But to be honest, when we do these design studios and studies in the Global South, it's difficult to be optimistic as you realize the enormous challenges we need to tackle.

On the other hand, I think we have managed to address all the extremely bad living conditions we knew in Western Europe until recently. So why should we not be able to solve housing scarcity problems in other parts of the world? We have to be optimistic. I think rampant urbanization and the question of how to create cities where people can live in a decent environment are incredible challenges that we need to address, now.

We focus a lot on the energy issue, but how are we going to house the global population? The housing crisis is possibly as threatening as the climate crisis.

Thalmatt 1, Bern, Switzerland. Designed by Atelier 5 (Photo: Dick van Gameren)

Thalmatt 1, Bern, Switzerland. Designed by Atelier 5 (Photo: Dick van Gameren)

Incremental housing Belapur, Navy Mumbai, India. Designed by Charles Correa (Photo: Dick van Gameren)

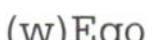

What is adequate for one person is not adequate for another

Interview with Marja Elsinga
by Javier Arpa Fernández

Javier Arpa Fernández: What are the pressing issues regarding housing?

Marja Elsinga: I'd say the pressure on cities. People want to live in cities but it's very hard for them to afford the housing there. Most people who live together do so because they can't afford other options. We are facing an enormous design challenge: how to make people like living together.

The flexible housing that (w)Ego presents can be a way for people to think about their desires and needs. What do we need in terms of privacy? What spaces can we share?

How can we include and combine our preferences in a physical structure?

JAF Many citizens still dream of a single-family home. Do you think it's possible to make citizens dream of collective housing?

ME The younger generations travelling the world are searching for communities to connect to. When you are mobile, you live for a while in a city where you do not have a social network. There is a whole mobile generation now that dreams of home as a place where you meet people, where you are not on your own in your single room.

JAF Would you say then that other groups, like families, would never dream of collective housing?

ME I do not dare to say so. I live in the inner city of Delft, where there are people living in very small houses with children, searching for some connectivity in the city and being happy in limited spaces.

Yet, there is still a vast amount of families that prefer to have their own villa with a garden and total privacy. Many users are quite conservative and tend to favour the single-family housing model, as do the building and the real estate industries.

JAF At the Faculty of Architecture and the Built Environment you are working on the 1M Homes Initiative , aimed at producing those many affordable housing units by 2030. What is your contribution?

ME The 1M Homes Initiative is an opportunity to rethink our position as a faculty. It is necessary to innovate in the field of housing, and such innovation must come from the University. Our ambition is to rethink housing systems together with the private sector.

Building so many new homes is nowadays quite a challenge for the Netherlands. In the past, there used to be a lot of public funding, but the subsidies are gone and we must rethink what adequate housing is. Once the public support is gone, we cannot afford certain standards anymore. Still, I believe it's the duty of the government to think of the future of spatial planning, the landscape impact and the needs of the citizens. The right to housing is in our Constitution[6], after all.

A revision of the essentials of housing is necessary to make this possible. It is fundamental to re-think what people need, but also the way we want to build in the city. We want to describe what the future of housing will be in terms of energy, circularity, digitization, institutionalization or participation. The 1M Homes Initiative embraces all dimensions of housing. It's about design and new technologies, but also about what adequate living is today.

Of course, what is adequate for one person is not adequate for another. Nevertheless, there is a bottom line. Adequacy is the balance between privacy and social life, it is health, and being able to live the life that you want to live.

JAF 600 million more homes are needed in the world as we speak, and there are a lot of good examples in Western Europe that we might want to export in order to solve this problem. But what do you think are the design, governance or organization examples that we could import from other places?

ME We should look at self-organization, participation, and people doing things by themselves.

In the Netherlands, we have a long history of the government regulating everything, which makes bottom-up initiatives very difficult. If you look elsewhere, there are neighbourhoods where residents plan their own infrastructure and dwellings. There is a lot of power and experience in building housing with the community in other places, which I find really inspiring.

I recently read a PHD dissertation about bottom-up initiatives in Brazil, a country full of dynamism. Citizens there are worried about climate change and public life, but have no trust in their government, so they organize themselves to tackle the challenges. The WikiHouse, for instance, offers the possibility of designing your own house from a shared digital archive. Homes are affordable and zero energy.

On the other hand, there is China, where the speed of construction is frightening to a certain extent. But there is a lot of innovation at the same time. Green and healthy buildings are really a top priority at universities. The capacity to change things in China is astonishing.

JAF What do you teach students?

ME My courses are about why housing is so relevant and how housing is organized, especially affordable housing; affordable defined as fitting within your income – in other words, not more than 30 per cent or 40 per cent of your income should be spent on housing.

Housing is a basic need and a very important part of the economy. I teach how to combine these differen dimensions of housing and how housing policies work in the Netherlands. In our country, 58 per cent of the population own their home, 30 per cent rent from the public sector and 12 per cent rent from the private sector. In this context, we look at what the government does, what the subsidies are, what the legislation is and how taxation works.

WikiHouse, De Stripmaker, Almere, The Netherlands (Source: WikiHouse.cc)

JAF Do you think that the housing market is going towards more regulation in the Netherlands?

ME I see how most of my students struggle to find an apartment when they complete their education. They do not qualify for a mortgage or the social rental sector; only the private rental sector is an option for them. This is partly due to deregulation.

Nowadays municipalities are considering the idea of regulation again. In particular municipalities that see that young people or essential workers such as police, teachers or nurses would like to live in the city, but they cannot afford it. That's why the private rental sector might be increasingly regulated.

I think the Netherlands has undergone excessive deregulation and that more regulation is necessary. That's a matter of principles. I think it is the role of the government to protect consumers as well as to protect lenders from themselves. It is about financial stability in society as a whole. I believe the government has the task of preventing societies from derailing.

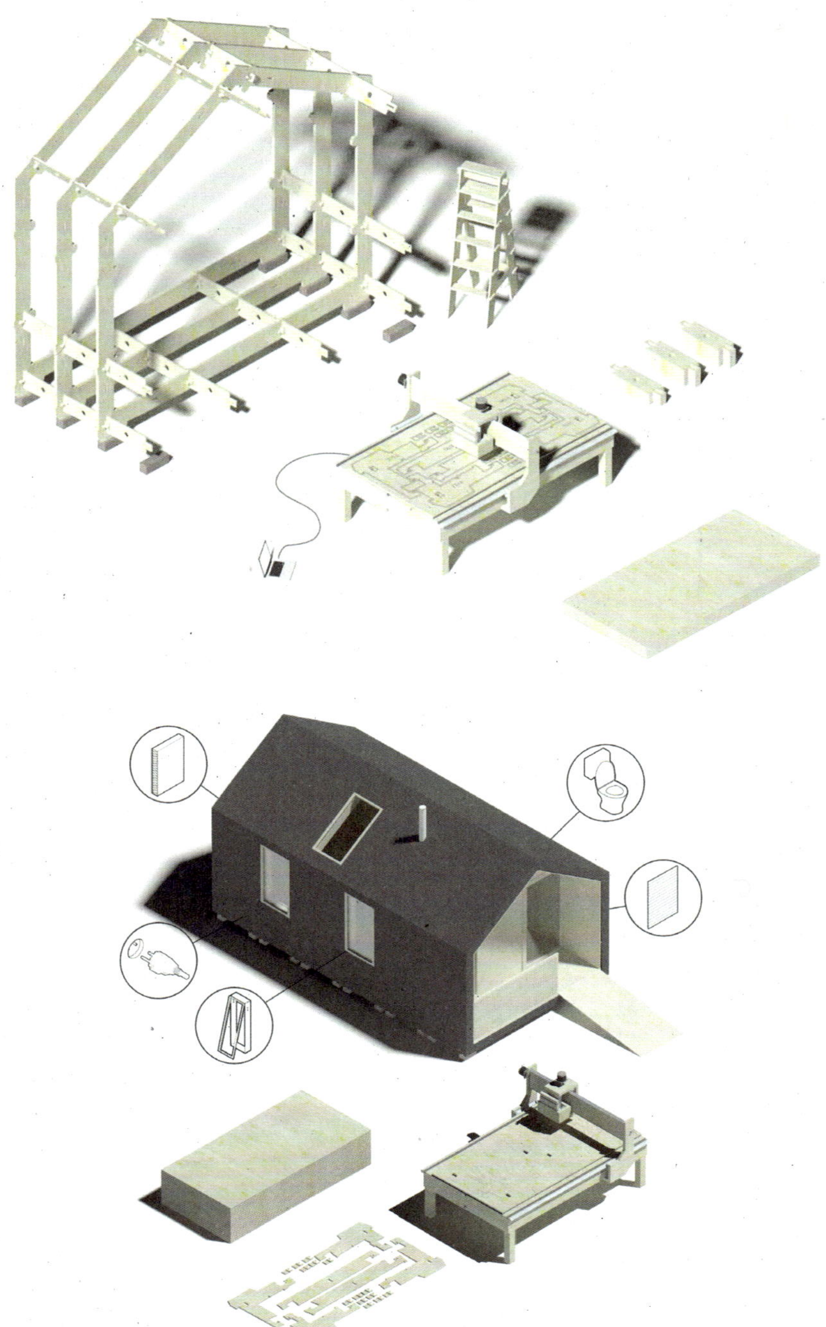

WikiHouse building parts (Source: WikiHouse.cc)

BouwEXPO Tiny Housing, Woningbouw Atelier, Almere, The Netherlands (Source: woningbouwatelier.nl)

Input from the citizens cannot be bypassed

Interview with Nelson Mota
by Javier Arpa Fernández

Javier Arpa Fernández: What do you think are the major global urgencies in terms of housing?

Nelson Mota: Access to affordable housing is an urgency, be it in Europe, the United States or the so-called Global South, where cities grow extremely fast. I understand that affordable housing applies not only to the urban poor but also to other income groups. In my opinion, affordable housing must cover not only low-cost emergency housing, often driven strictly by efficiency criteria, but also the needs of the middle-income groups whose access to decent housing is also threatened.

Another urgency is related to time and resilience. If we develop rigid housing solutions which do not accommodate the possibility of growth and change through time, the chances are that resources are allocated to something that may not perform properly shortly after construction.

We really need to consider these two factors and try to see what design can contribute in order to achieve a good trade-off between affordability and resilience.

JAF How do you define affordable housing?

NM According to UN-Habitat, households should not allocate more than 25 per cent or 30 per cent of their available income for housing, either to pay their rent or to pay monthly loan instalments, whatever the wage or household income is. Above such a percentage, you may suffer food deprivation, health challenges and so on, and housing is not 'affordable'.

JAF Would you say that this definition of affordable housing is applicable all over the world?

NM Absolutely. It's applicable to London, Amsterdam or Kinshasa, to formal or to informal housing. In slums, rents are higher than in formal public housing because residents must pay rent to the slum lords. This percentage is typically much higher than in the so-called formal markets. It's also a major challenge.

JAF As the 1M Homes Initiative is launched in the Netherlands, following a longer tradition of housing programmes in the country aimed at meeting the growing demand, what other places in Europe should we look at in terms of social housing?

Bouça Housing in Porto. Designed by Alvaro Siza (Photo: Nelson Mota)

NM Vienna is probably the best example, despite the recent neoliberal turn. They have been trying to engage with the local communities to produce housing. Projects are not only developed by state-owned corporations, but also by small-scale organizations that own the land and develop housing at a smaller scale. The system is still regulated and based on an efficient system that guarantees high-quality housing. As a result, the average size of a subsidized rental apartment in Vienna is far bigger than the average social housing in the rest of the European Union, and the costs are much lower than in London, Amsterdam or the Nordic cities.

In Vienna, living in social housing does not carry a stigma. On the contrary: it's a privilege. This is crucial in order to keep the liveability of our cities. In other places, like Portugal, social housing is unfortunately highly stigmatized. No-one aspires to live in social housing. Even renowned developments like Bouça in Porto, designed by Alvaro Siza in the mid-70s, had little success. Only half of it was actually built at first. Later, in the early 2000s, the cooperative that developed the project finally decided to complete the whole scheme, once Siza became a world-famous architect. When the new units were offered to the members of the cooperative, only a few of them actually occupied the homes, as almost everyone preferred to move to the outskirts where they could afford bigger dwellings. Finally, the houses Siza designed, in the heart of Porto, were sold at a very cheap price to young architects and designers. This is how far this stigma of social housing can go.

In Barcelona, city mayor Ada Colau's administration is trying to promote new approaches to housing that can cater to new ways of living, where residents engage in the whole process from the beginning, making a better trade-off between what the developer gets as a profit and what the user gets as a dweller. These co-housing experiences are alternatives to the traditional real-estate-driven policies, often aimed at increasing profit and not necessarily quality.

JAF Do you think then that the European tradition of top-down affordable housing is over?

NM I think that it has to be reconceptualized. The point is to see what top-down policies work and keep them. Then we need to try to complement those policies with bottom-up initiatives. This doesn't mean that the state is relinquishing its role entirely. The state plays an essential part in terms of regulation, funding and land policy. A complete withdrawal of the public sector from the provision of affordable housing would be tragic and should be avoided by all means. But input from the citizens cannot be bypassed: we need cooperation between top-down and bottom-up.

JAF Outside Europe, how do you think the huge amount of decent, affordable housing needed can be provided?

NM This is a challenge that requires a collective effort in terms of governance, management and design. Land ownership is absolutely crucial for affordable housing. Firstly, why don't we start by giving people living in informal settlements proprietorship of the land they occupy so that these settlements become formal? Residents would finally own the land where they build, feel they belong to the neighbourhood and participate in its maintenance. Secondly, when the land is privately owned, which is the case in many countries, you can hardly launch a governmental programme. A counter example of this is Ethiopia, where the state owns the land, being capable of delivering a great deal of affordable housing very quickly. However, both cases also have drawbacks. In the first case, these new millions of home owners became an easy prey for the financialization of housing. In the latter case, the state may employ totalitarian tactics to uproot citizens from their long-standing community bonds and rights to the city.

Regardless of the case, I believe design also plays a definitive role in overcoming the dramatic housing shortage. We know the consequences of developing extremely efficient, cheap, and quick projects. These projects provide people with running water and sewage in the short term, but what will be the consequences in 5, 10, or 15 years' time in terms of maintenance, patterns of inhabitation, public health or liveability?

How can we contribute to improving provision with better policies, housing models and strategies? In the 70s and 80s, the Sites and Services Project[7] sponsored by the World Bank became quite popular. That's in my opinion one of the best examples of a combination between top-down and bottom-up initiatives. From South America to Africa to South Asia, the World Bank programme permitted the construction of more than three million dwellings. This scheme sets the infrastructure (services) and establishes a division of plots (sites) from which people could develop units over time, based on their own initiatives. The whole investment would go to the infrastructural backbone at the urban scale, and the expansion of dwelling units would be developed with loans that residents received.

JAF This is a successful policy model. Was it successful in terms of design?

NM It has not always been successful. But I think that it's worthwhile revisiting the model and maybe upgrading it. Balkrishna Doshi, for instance, designed the Aranya

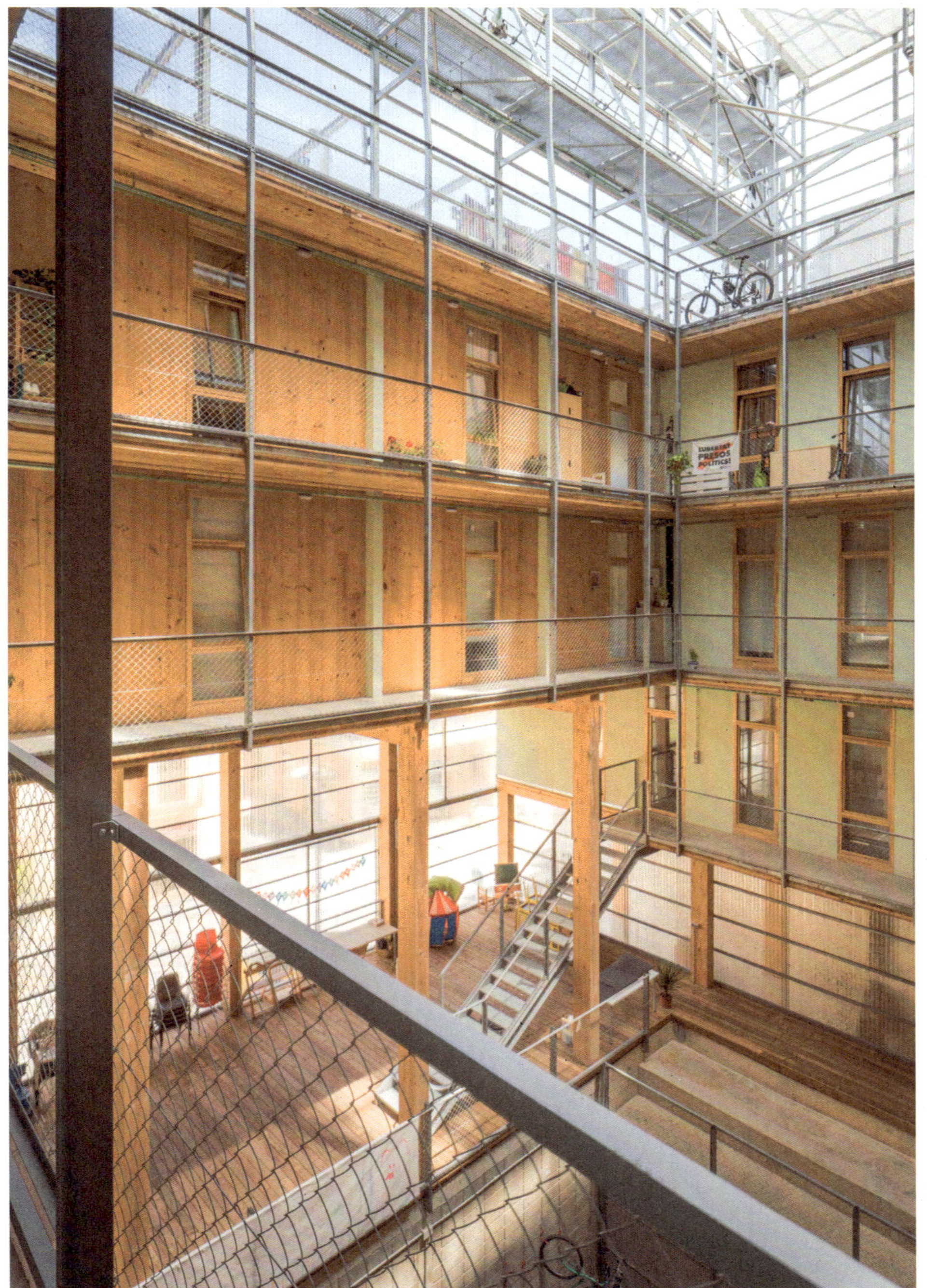

La Borda, Cooperative Housing, Barcelona, Spain. Designed by LACOL (Image: Lacol i Lluc Miralles)

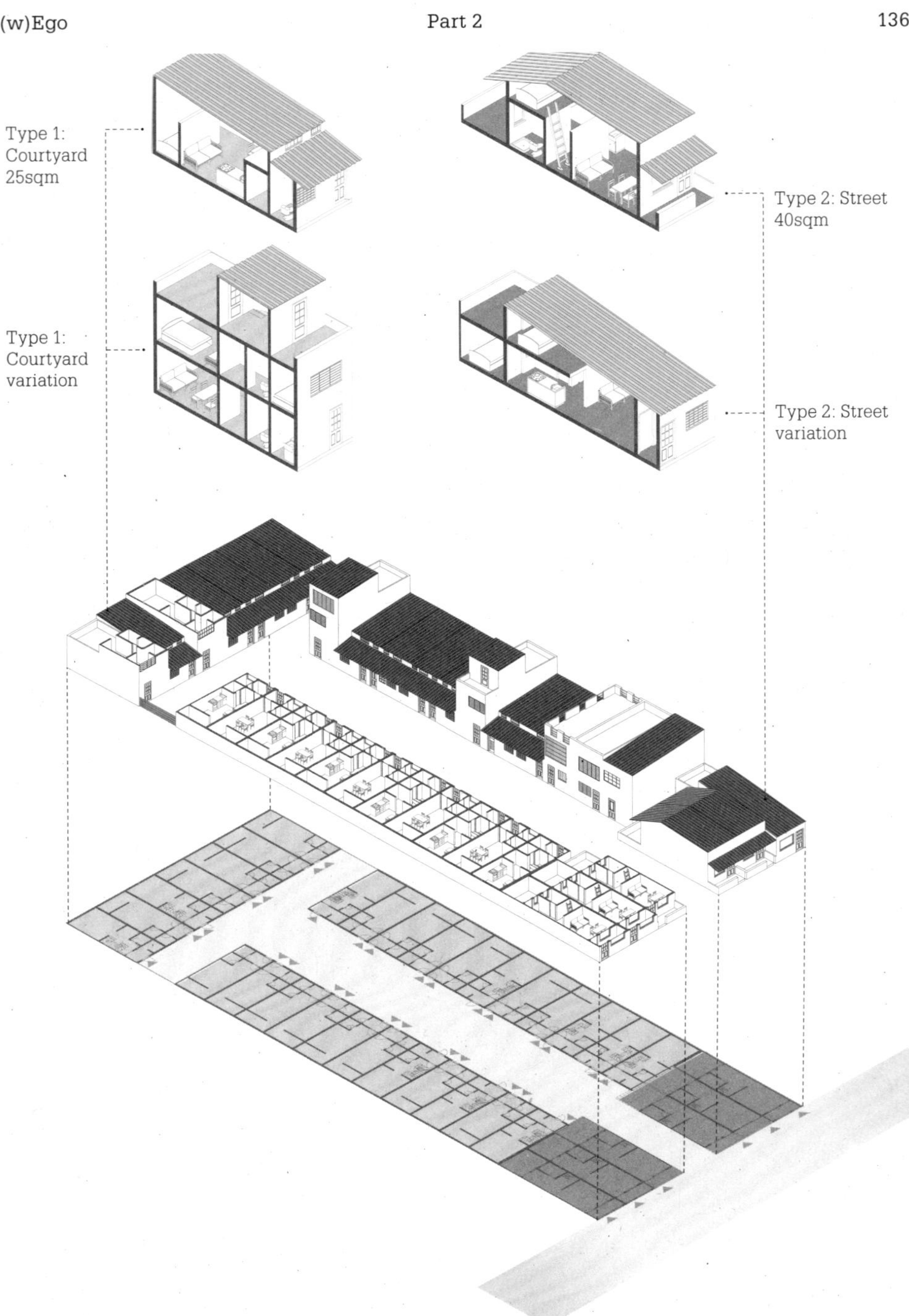

Axonometry of a cluster in the Charkop sites and services scheme in Mumbai, India (Drawing: Freya Crijns)

development in the mid-80s, showing that these schemes could work if public space worked. The top-down intervention in Aranya takes place at the level of infrastructure, securing what is going to remain forever.

Doshi designed a very sophisticated structure for the public space. Then users were given a sanitary core, from which to develop their homes over time according to their own capacity, skills and resources. Doshi designed a fully developed demonstration sector, to show how the completed housing and city would look like. This pilot was taken much further by the dwellers. Now it doesn't look anything like it used to, but the structure of public space remains, and that's what makes it an interesting case to study.

View of a cluster in the Charkop sites and services scheme in Mumbai, India (Photo: Nelson Mota)

JAF What should the 'future city' include?

NM You need diversity in many ways: different income groups, different topological approaches, a mix of typologies... As history abundantly shows, whatever monolithic approach you take, the chances are that it's not going to work.

It is also necessary to think of housing as part of a global system with infinite local variations. Architects should not be afraid of contributing to the design and development of systems that become attractive for developers, goverNM ents and users. Systems, for example, that create possibilities for cost recovery, limiting profits and engaging with multiple stakeholders and social groups with different aspirations in terms of housing. We need to seek better governance, better management processes and better design that promote diversity at all levels. But there's a big struggle ahead of us. In academia we should try and play a more engaged role in the whole process. Even if solutions are mostly political, I believe that there is a lot that we as designers and educators can do to make better future cities.

View of a street in Aranya township, Indore, India. Designed by Balkrishna Doshi (Photo: Rohan Varma)

MP.09
MP. 0563

No more sprawl, please

Interview with Paul Kuitenbrouwer
by Javier Arpa Fernández

Javier Arpa Fernández: What does your housing research focus on?

Paul Kuitenbrouwer: In our design studios, we always combine typological research with the way an intervention responds to its social and physical context. Recently, we conducted a studio on Dutch housing, where we studied historical experimental projects to see what made them innovative. We took those projects out of their context, studied them as typologies and then inserted their constituting principles into a smaller site. Students were asked to re-work the projects and to see how to transfer them to a different site. The original dwellings needed to undergo several modifications so as to respond to their neighbouring buildings and context.

Another design studio we set up, titled HIGH-RISE>LOW-RISE : Open Source Closed Circle in Parkstad Limburg, focused on a high-rise block which was meant to be demolished to make space for new buildings. We studied the possibility of dismantling it instead of tearing it down, recycling as many parts as possible and reusing them as starting points for new typologies.

The studio was an invitation not to build from scratch, but to reuse, refurbish and transform the existing. The studio built upon a request from a housing agency. It was really interesting to give this agency new insights to inform their approach. It also gave students new perspectives.

JAF The work you just described sounds like an invitation to reclaim the existing. Where would you locate the new homes necessary to satisfy the growing demand in countries like the Netherlands?

Intense Low-Rise, Groningen, The Netherlands. Green Dice, a proposal fcr intense small-scale housing (Jarmund/ Vigsnæs AS Arkitekter MNAL, Norway)

PK No more sprawl, please. You just have to go to Belgium or to the U.S. to see the consequences of living in an endless sea of houses. A total lack of complexity.

Years ago, West 8 called their master plan for Borneo Sporenburg 'a sea of houses'. But it was a limited sea of houses on a peninsula that needed density so that the project would be feasible. They designed it following the principles of a spatial experience that Amsterdam residents know well: the Jordaan district. The 6 m wide streets and the 11 m tall facades let everyone experience an urban feeling similar to the inner city.

Complexity works better than sprawl. This was already understood by the City of Groningen at the beginning of this century with their idea of intensity, also supported by Winy Maas, with Nick Verdonk as city architect. He came up with a plea for 'intense low-rise' typologies.

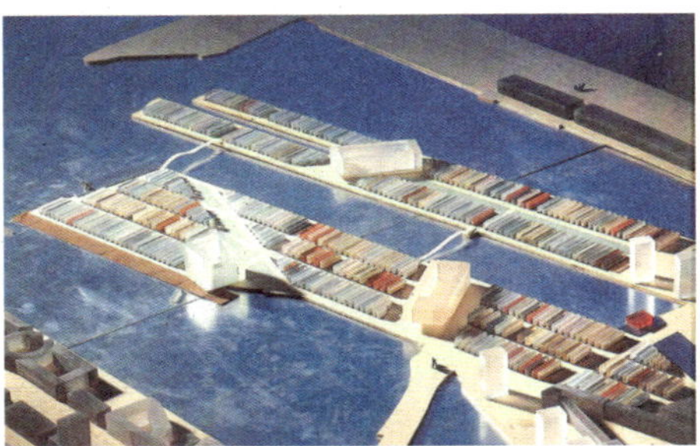

Een Zee van Huizen | A Sea of Houses by Brigitte de Maar

JAF How does 'intense low-rise' work?

PK Intense low-rise typologies are aimed at intensifying cities within the existing boundaries, not only in the central areas, but also in the suburbs. How can we intensify the existing? It is essential to avoid making monotonous housing areas and to introduce a functional mix of uses, at the scale of the neighbourhood, the urban block and the building. Intensifying the city makes the city work better. When people can find all amenities at a certain walkable distance, the city works. I do not mean to import the extreme density present in many Asian cities; it wouldn't work in the Dutch context. Still, there is quite some work to do in terms of intensification in the Netherlands.

Moreover, intensity allows us to respect the landscape, understood as a spatial and cultural term. I do not know precisely if we need 800,000, 1 M, or 1.5 M new homes in the Netherlands, but what I know for sure is that we should be keen on not relying on the remaining landscape to solve our housing needs. I think we should push the urban intensification agenda instead of relying on sprawl.

JAF What do you think the future of social housing in the Netherlands will be?

Intense Low-Rise, Groningen, The Netherlands. Green Dice, a proposal for intense small-scale housing (Jarmund/Vigsnæs AS Arkitekter MNAL, Norway)

PK The existence and permanence of social housing is strongly related to the way society is organized. Social housing policies result from the collective responsibility we have to allow people who do not have enough resources to access a certain basic quality of dwelling. When you liberalize everything, you lose that. Therefore, the survival of social housing as we know it requires that we all remain aware that a certain amount of solidarity is needed. If everything is left to individual responsibility, in accordance with the current liberal political stance, social housing will disappear.

I think it's also very interesting to look beyond the Netherlands. We have organized studio trips to Denmark to study collective housing. It seems that people there are more used to sharing than we are in the Netherlands. On the other hand, they are only sharing within a limited group, excluding everyone who is not part of it. It's interesting to see what to take from that.

Sharing versus possessing could lead to alternative financial models. But this is a complex choice. We prefer to concentrate on the issues that can really be studied within the design disciplines. We may be architects concerned about society, but we are not sociologists or economists.

JAF What are the topics that you would like to explore next?

PK Within the Chair of Public Building, I am currently exploring the concept of 'multiplicity'. Multiplicity in architecture aims to give buildings and building elements properties that make them less singular in function: more productive, more transformative and resilient. I think it's very interesting to see what this can mean for housing. The limits of flexibility in housing are related to the technical parts, the facade's performance, daylight and fresh air… and I am addressing these issues.

Multiplicity goes beyond the barrier of a certain typology, whether that is a public building or a housing block. Multiplicity is very important for the future at a moment in which sustainability is such a concern.

We should also go beyond the limits of the building and look at the scale of a city block, which has greater urban impact. As we know already, the separation between architecture and urbanism is not as strict as we once thought it was.

Let's move from the flexible object to the flexible block and to the flexible city.

Borneo Sporenburg, The Netherlands. Urban plan designed by West 8

Tools are only tools

Interview with Mo Sedighi
by Javier Arpa Fernández

Javier Arpa Fernández: What do you think of the Why Factory's Wego research?

Mo Sedighi: I realized a building in Iran with a similar approach. I designed the structure, and the future residents could determine the configuration of their homes according to their financial capacity. The project name was 'Housing for the Future' in Persian. There, a total of 12 users could purchase units of 40, 80 or 120 square metres. It was very interesting to see if they wanted a maisonette or a simplex, duplex, or triplex type. (w)Ego is more complex because you're looking at user desires from the very beginning. This is a very interesting approach.

JAF What is the focus of your research on housing?

MS In the experimental housing studio (2018-2019), we analyse the role of the architect, mainly in affordable housing projects for low- and mid-income residents, like the experiments undertaken in the 60s and 70s in the Netherlands. We also look at best practices not only in the urban Global North but also in urban Global South. We analyse, for instance, projects by Balkrishna Doshi or Kamran Diba: how did those architects develop the housing units? How did they cluster them together? How was the pedestrian precinct introduced and what was the impact on the urban community?

We try to identify the DNA of those projects, mainly from a typological point of view; we look into the socio-political and economic context of those realizations; we try to understand what triggered architects to experiment and we try to draw relationships with the current context. Then we focus on design experiments where students are invited to think

Shushtar-Nou in Iran. Designed by Kamran Diba in 1976 (Source: Iran's Cartographic Centre)

about many forms of dwelling disconnected from a specific site.

They base their design on an existing housing typology, then work on modes of grouping the units and finally develop the public circulation, from the scale of the housing complex to the scale of the neighbourhood. Only then do we introduce a context into which the prototype needs to fit. To a certain extent, we try to use the notion of 'typology transfer' as introduced by Emanuel Christ and Christoph Gantenbein. This is how our students start designing. It's not completely from scratch.

I believe in such 'type and typology transfer'. We can learn by copying from one context to another. Then we have to look into socio-political and cultural circumstances and add user participation. Without it, we cannot complete the project successfully and that's why the notion of (incremental) growth and change is very important. People should be able to appropriate, perceive and use their spaces according to their needs and wishes in order to produce long-lasting settlements. If residents have children, for example, they have to be able to add spaces or facilities to their homes. Otherwise they'll move out of the neighbourhood, looking for a new house to fit them. I think that by including the notion of growth and change, we can accommodate these needs through time.

JAF So you try to extract lessons from the past?

MS Yes, I do. In 1974 an international conference in Iran gathered many international architects of that time. Emerging practitioners from the East met with renowned architects from the West and elaborated together the guidelines for designing future urban communities. These recommendations were born as a reaction to the Modern principles, as a kind of continuation of a Team 10 movement. Jaap Bakema, Aldo van Eyck and many others were there. One of the key outcomes of this conference was the Habitat Bill of Rights, a CIAM-like Charter of Habitat with design guidelines and housing recommendations presented to the first UN conference on 'Human Settlements' that took place in 1976 in Vancouver.

I use those guidelines as a source of inspiration for the students and for myself as a designer, and I try to experiment with them in mind. At the same time, I try to incorporate ideas about the users' wishes, as well as ideas of growth and change throughout time.

For example, I designed a complex for 288 residents, where I employed a simple unit that I started to cluster together in a very simple way, with the central staircase. By just shifting the block in multiple layers, I could get a kind of stepped, set-back configuration. The idea was that users would have the opportunity to build or occupy these extra spaces as an extension of their homes. I employed Aldo van Eyck's notion of undefined spaces, yet another great example from the past, in order to let people be involved in spatial production at a later stage.

JAF Is this a public or private housing project?

MS It is public housing. It was funded by the government and designed and developed by myself together with a housing developer.

I do believe that architects can make a bigger impact on society if they work with developers rather than just

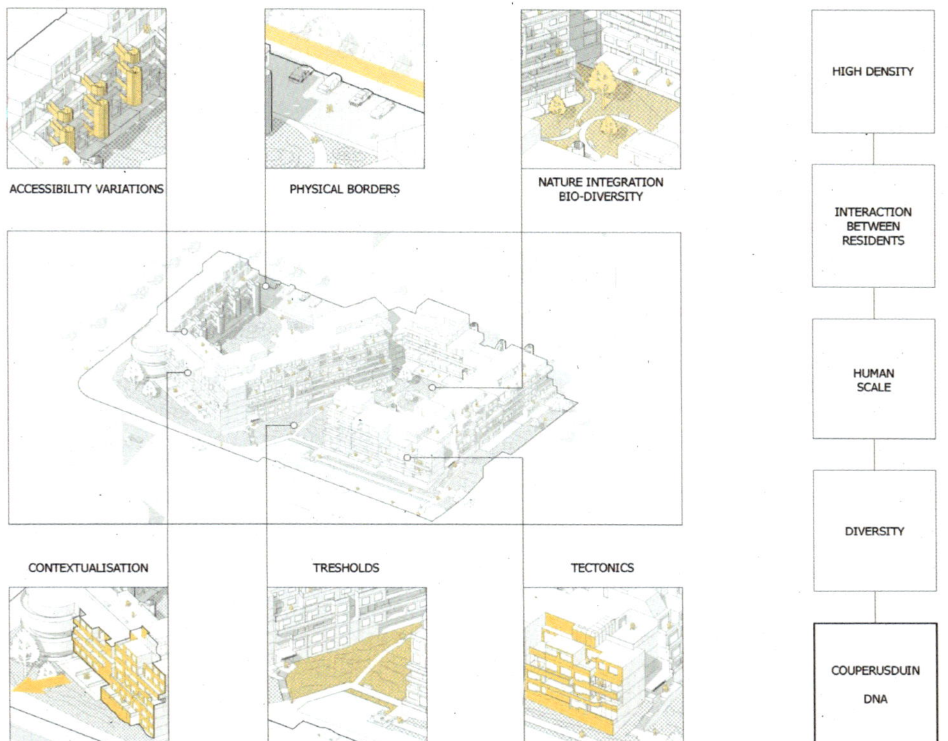

An example of experimental housing in the Netherlands: COUPERUSDUIN in The Hague, 197. Designed by Sjoerd Schamhart (Source: The analytical drawings of students)

handing over drawings to a contractor and supervising the process. That's why I work with developers. If I raise the density for the developer, making it more economically beneficial for them, I can have their attention. This way, I get more room for experimentation. In the project I mentioned earlier, the government approved 200 housing units and I raised that figure up to 288 units. Suddenly, I received the attention of the developer and the chance to experiment with user participation. This allowed me to be more innovative in the design process and to experiment with prototypes instead of producing standard blocks that are replicated endlessly.

288 Housing Complex, Teheran, Iran. Designed by Mo Sedighi (Photo: Mo Sedighi)

JAF Is this housing adaptable?

MS The project consists of a structure with some prefixed elements such as staircases and service installations, whereas the configuration of the floorplans of the units is customizable. Those small units are expandable but also changeable. It means that they can be horizontally connected and also vertically. Users could choose how they wanted to gain a bigger house.

JAF At the time we are having this conversation, the Netherlands is launching the 1M Homes Initiative. What do you think about it?

MS I think the government's plan is too ambitious. We first need to identify for whom we are going to build. I also think that we have to use the existing infrastructure, and build in the inner city. Let's build denser neighbourhoods, multi-storey apartments, typologies that fulfil the cultural and social needs of the users and incorporate innovation.

Let's seriously think about patterns of inhabitation and investigate typology. I believe in type and typology because they have translated the real needs of people throughout history. If you fulfil the wishes of users, you have definitely produced the 'right' typology. We cannot reinvent the wheel again and again. Architects have the benefit of looking at the built environment seeing what went wrong and what went successful. And then based on that they can come up with new types. I am not sure the government's 1M Homes Initiative is doing that.

An example of in-between realms as undefined spaces to stimulate self-expression, self-determination, and self-organization (Photo: Mo Sedighi)

JAF You're teaching your students to reuse, employ and apply existing types to different contexts. Where should we innovate, then?

MS When we are critical, we are being innovative because we are critically looking at what has been done, and we try to incorporate only what we think is still relevant for society. Rather than just copying and pasting or imitating, we are adding. We try to incorporate new needs, like sustainability. By critically thinking about the past, we can innovate for the future.

JAF What is your take on technology?

MS I always quote Louis Kahn: 'technology is just a medium'. I don't think that technology is the answer or the end. But of course, some new ideas could only be realized by new technologies. We have to use our current technology to design; otherwise, we are neglecting progress. I'm a fan of using new design tools to produce smarter cities that incorporate technology.

But technology shouldn't limit people or frame their thinking, as Richard Sennett argued in his book *Building and Dwelling*. Virtual reality tools, for instance, can help a client understand our design but it is just a means. Parametric design allows us to develop maybe 500 homes at once, but it doesn't mean that we have to limit ourselves to those 500 possibilities. For me tools are only tools.

JAF Are you optimistic about the future?

MS Yes, I'm optimistic. I think history proves that we can keep our hopes alive by looking to the future. If we compare our lives now with humankind one hundred years ago, there is a kind of nostalgia. I think people, generally, are happier nowadays than one hundred years ago. That's why I think in one hundred years' time we will be happier than today.

We are destroying our planet, but at the same time we are learning how to prevent the disaster. So I want to remain optimistic about the future.

Shushtar-Nou in Iran. Designed by Kamran Diba in 1976 (Photo: Mo Sedighi)

Current housing is not adaptable

Interview with Birgit Hausleitner
by Javier Arpa Fernández

Javier Arpa Fernández: What is your first impression of the (w)Ego research?

Birgit Hausleitner: I find the ideas of flexibility and adaptability really exciting, and I would love to see them applied to the urban scale too, as is the case with the Oosterwold project by MVRDV, providing a base framework, capable of adapting to needs that change: downsizing or upscaling.

JAF Do we need to do more about housing and adaptability?

BH I think we need to do more research and — very importantly — to communicate more about housing and adaptability. The Rietveld Schröder House in Utrecht, with its moveable walls, was a great point of departure. As a user, I need this changeability, to be able to move walls, for example. Our lifestyles and needs change throughout time, but our built environment remains fixed for the most part. Current housing is not adaptable and very little has been done in that respect by the design disciplines recently.

I think it's also very important how we as professionals communicate to users that the configuration of their home can change. It's important that we understand the ways in which users are satisfied, or not, with their dwellings and how we respond to new forms of living.

In Austria in the 1960s, for example, Roland Rainer developed the patio house settlement Puchenau in the vicinity of Linz, which was way denser than a typical Austrian single-family home neighbourhood. At the beginning, nobody wanted to actually buy a piece of land or a home there, because Austrians were not used to living in patio houses. In response to that hesitance, as a communication

1978 | **2003**

i3_Esquerra, Samper Sáenz, Urdaneta, Colombia / Colombia

i11_Aldo van Eyck, Holanda / The Netherlands

i12_Candillis, Josic, Woods, Francia / France

i8_Kikutake, Maki, Kurokawa, Japón / Japan

PREVI – Proyecto Experimental de Vivienda, Lima, Peru

1978 **2003**

◌16_Juan Reiser, Perú / Peru

◌20_Vier, Zanelli, Perú / Peru

◌7_Miró-Quesada, Williams, Núñez, Perú / Peru

3_Esquerra, Samper Sáenz, Urdaneta, Colombia / Colombia

PREVI – Proyecto Experimental de Vivienda, Lima, Peru

strategy, a small sample area was built to show future users what living there could feel like. It became a really successful project. Satisfaction is really high amongst residents and basically nobody moves out voluntarily. As I said, the question is how to actually communicate the qualities of adaptability.

Rietveld- Schroeder House Utrecht, The Netherlands

JAF How do you think adaptability can be exported from architecture to urbanism?

BH In order to translate adaptability to urbanism you need leeway, buffer spaces in the city where activities can extend or shrink. And this is not the case in many places. Adaptability in urbanism depends on how accessible a site is, how much space there is, who your neighbour is, etc. Adaptable urbanism is about being able to swap places and programmes, adjust sizes of units and how public or private a place is.

At the moment I work mostly on London. We did a lot of fieldwork in the last two years and it was really interesting to see how people adapt in this city. Adaptability happens often in the tiny leftover unbuilt places, where building parts are added or transformed. Often in the form of loft conversions to add more space to dwellings or offices, or transformation of ground-floor spaces which can allow adaptation in terms of programme.

In London, many former stables and service buildings in mews, back alleys and spaces inside building blocks have been transformed into dwellings. These dwellings happen to be a lot more comfortable in terms of noise than those along the main streets at the edges of the building blocks, as they are protected from traffic. You can feel the diversity of environmental conditions and the re-interpretation of the relations between form and the changing programme inside.

Puchenau Housing, Austria. Designed by Roland Rainer

JAF You give relocation of uses and users as examples of adaptable urbanism. Is demolishing a part of this?

BH I'm not totally against demolishing, and I think we need to be radical sometimes. For students it is at times really difficult to suggest more radical changes; they can be very anxious about demolition. Students tend to work only with leftover spaces and do not dare to demolish buildings or change block structures. I always ask them: What if Haussmann hadn't transformed Paris like he did? His boulevards connect the different parts of the city and add complementary environmental qualities to the network of smaller streets and alleys.

An interesting approach is also continuous transformation plot-wise, as we see in many neighbourhoods of Tokyo, for example, and in the Massena quarter in Paris, where Christian de Portzamparc proposed the structural independency of buildings as the most relevant precondition for continuous change and adaptation within the building block.

JAF How do you think ideas about adaptability can be applied to the context of the Global South?

BH I've worked a lot with students on Latin America, more precisely on the dense informal settlements of Lima, or Rio de Janeiro. We looked back at the experimental housing project PREVI built during the 60s in Lima, as a precedent, where we can see, decades after construction, how the residents adapted the buildings to their needs, building extensions and adapting it from the bottom-up in many ways. Another set of precedents are the housing projects by Elemental in Chile built since 2000: they provide base structures that can be further developed by the residents. For me, this is an interesting concept on the architectural scale, but questionable on the urban scale. Who is providing the base infrastructure? How can qualitative public space be organized? How can the adaptability of built forms be organized in neighbourhoods of higher density? How can we address the phenomenal population growth?

Municipalities try to solve these issues by growing vertically, but this often results in the loss of the direct connection between indoor and outdoor spaces, which is really important to let people survive, to grow food, for example. When you force low-income populations to live in high rises, you are not letting them look after themselves.

In places like Kowloon Walled City, where the idea of hyper-density was taken to the extreme, people ended up adapting, because they could find some indoor and outdoor vertical connections. Although a terrible example, it's an interesting case because people themselves could adapt. The question is, how do you design such a hyper-dense site that residents really want to inhabit?

I think we have to densify and densify way more. There will be many people on the move on the planet. They have to be accommodated somewhere. Involving people in the process and finding new forms and new urban models that are responsive to change are the key challenges, be it in the slums of the fast-growing metropolises of Latin America or in the wealthy midsize cities of Europe.

Kowloon Walled City in the 1990s prior to demolition, Hong Kong

Kowloon Walled City in the 1990s prior to demolition, Hong Kong

Better Together!

The Why Factory (TU Delft)

Tutors: Winy Maas, Felix Madrazo, Adrien Ravon, Arend van Waart

Students: Niels Baljet, Francesco Barone, Félix Borel, Charles Ducerisier, Lucile Dugal, Chun Hoi Hui, Tarryn Leeferink, Zichen Liu, Javier López-Menchero Ortiz de Salazar, Prokop Matej, Marek Nosek, Matteo Pavanello, Woo Soojung, Iason Stathatos, Wen Jun Tan, Olina Terzi, Loes Thijssen

Text by Adrien Ravon

There are housing solutions for all tastes within the realm of collective housing. Yet, the pursuit of the single-family detached home, the suburban dream, has led to the production of monotonous suburban landscapes that are endlessly repeated and far from dreamy. Growing private car use and increasing air pollution, high energy consumption, loss of habitat and dwindling water supply are just a few examples of the consequences of sprawl.

Density is an alternative to this model of sprawl and its dramatic impact – exacerbating climate change, land consumption and socio-economic disparities. However, under the pressure of the housing market to maximize profit, density has often resulted in a mere maximization of housing units inside a given envelope, leading to the production of low-quality standardized housing products.

Following design research into the individualization of high-rise urbanism, this experiment explores alternative densification models that can integrate the qualities of life in a village into dense, compact, and affordable interventions. Imagine that all the villas, detached houses and any other houses of your dreams could come together to create something more than they would on their own.

Inspired by our dream home experiment <'Dream Homes', pp 62-81> , we collected a set of 36 different volumes representing 36 different dream homes.

When separately displayed on a grid, they look alike: a series of detached houses placed next to each other.

But when they gradually are brought closer to each other in this model, stacked or compressed inside a smaller envelope, their uniqueness is revealed and their compatibility unlocked. How far can our dream homes be compressed, squeezed, jammed in, and interlocked with others, and still retain their essence?

We believe that densification can be a catalyser for the empowerment of individual dreams and the fulfilment of collective creativity. Living together in density doesn't necessarily mean a standardization of lifestyles.

On the contrary, density can lead to the endless emergence of responsive solutions that have a positive impact on our lives and planet, and that will keep challenging and evolving our current dreams.

This experimental model sequence explores the question, and sets the brief for the next chapter on dream homes, density, and how to negotiate the two through a multi-player video game.

The (w)Ego Game

The Why Factory (TU Delft)

Tutors: Winy Maas, Felix Madrazo, Adrien Ravon, Arend van Waart

Students: Niels Baljet, Francesco Barone, Félix Borel, Charles Ducerisier, Lucile Dugal, Chun Hoi Hui, Tarryn Leeferink, Zichen Liu, Javier López-Menchero Ortiz de Salazar, Prokop Matej, Marek Nosek, Matteo Pavanello, Woo Soojung, Iason Stathatos, Wen Jun Tan, Olina Terzi, Loes Thijssen

Guest Critics: Jeroen Zuidgeest, Ekim Tan, Huib Plomb

Text by Adrien Ravon

There are many possible dream homes, as many as the dreams of what makes a home. But how do those dreams coexist when placed next to each other, inside a predefined envelope? The (w)Ego Game explores the process of fitting many dream homes inside a conventional urban typology in a competitive but also playful and compatible way.

What tools are needed to make multiple dreams into a built reality? Video games already offer a huge range of participatory alternative versions of the world we live in. What if a video game could offer its players increased agency over their dreams... in real life?

Students developed a video game which allows a group of users to negotiate their desires in real time and in 3D. The game offers players a toolkit enabling them to replace the architect in the design of their dream apartment, resulting in a multitude of user-based design solutions. (w)Ego then integrates the competing desires, or egos, of each resident into a standard housing block. In this game, there are no winners or losers. The aim is to facilitate an equal degree of satisfaction in the fairest possible way.

Why a Game?

In 1997, MVRDV and Architect Bjarne Masterbroek co-designed the 'Double House' in Utrecht – a multi-story building shared by two families that had never met before but who needed each other to buy the plot. One could afford to buy 60 per cent of the plot while the other could purchase 40 per cent; one wanted to maximize direct access to the garden while the other wanted to maximize views of the surroundings.

Through a sequential process of negotiation and collective creativity, those different desires were put together in order to reveal something more than the clients' individualities. In search of a win-win solution, where each client would get the most out of this negotiation, the two architects became mediators of this process, and the clients became the real designers of their dream home, embracing density.

This dialectic is expressed in a diagram revealing the steps in the negotiation. The diagram is both a generative and communicative tool. It's like a turn-based game where one player does something and the other one responds. But unlike many games, there are no winners or losers in this process. Both apartments share some common spatial qualities, such as ample rooms, generous views and direct access to the ground floor – but in very different and unique ways. It proves that the party walls, just like individual desires, are something malleable and to be challenged in a context of urban density. The party wall thus becomes a generator of freedom that binds us together.

Taking the Double House diagram and our collection of 36 dream homes as a point of departure for a design brief, we set out to question the role of the architect in collective and participatory design. What if taking as many intermediaries as possible out of the design process would allow for more possibilities and empower future residents to become the true designers of their dreams?

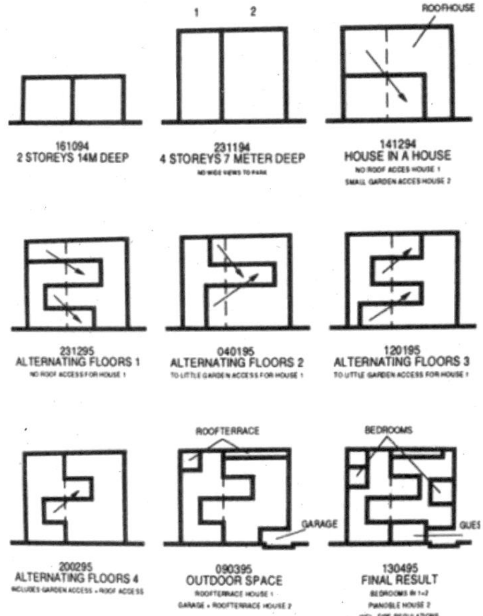

Double House Diagram, MVRDV, 1997

The Double House diagram is our point of departure. In this example, however, the negotiation process still involved two architects defending the wishes of their clients. How can we automate this facilitation process? Students started to explore a series of tools of engagement, able to facilitate a fair and creative self-mediation. The exercise was at first between random pairs. There was no referee, no middle man, no architect, only two individuals negotiating together.

Discussion appeared to be an obvious but valuable tool for reaching an agreement. Users would state what they wanted and then discuss it in order to find a consensus. 'If I have the window over here, you can have the living room over there', and so on. However, dialogue often led to very compromised solutions. In fact, those experiments mainly ended back at the first stage of the Double House diagram, where a straight wall would divide the plot into two straight extrusions. Puzzling in and out verbally was not enough to overcome the preconceived definition of a straight wall standing for a fair division.

The next experiment sought a more detailed level of negotiation. Students started to negotiate by sketching on paper – just like architects do – back and forth with their clients. Students sketched a part of the section, each at a time. This turn-based process was the first attempt to define some basic rules to enhance a fair, but spatially exploratory, negotiation. They decided to use gridded paper to define a collective format. Students would fill up the grid with one bit of their apartment at a time, placing needs and desires on the page. Each move would react to the previous one, using the resolution of the grid to refine, define and detail the boundaries of their dreams.

Conscious of the importance of the grid as a collective format, students decided to use a spreadsheet software as a sketching tool – like an online spreadsheet where you can co-edit a document. Excel became a tool to co-edit the housing block, cell by cell. The use of colours or annotation would help to define the importance of different amenities. One specific aspect of this experiment was to be able to overwrite and keep the negotiation running even after all the

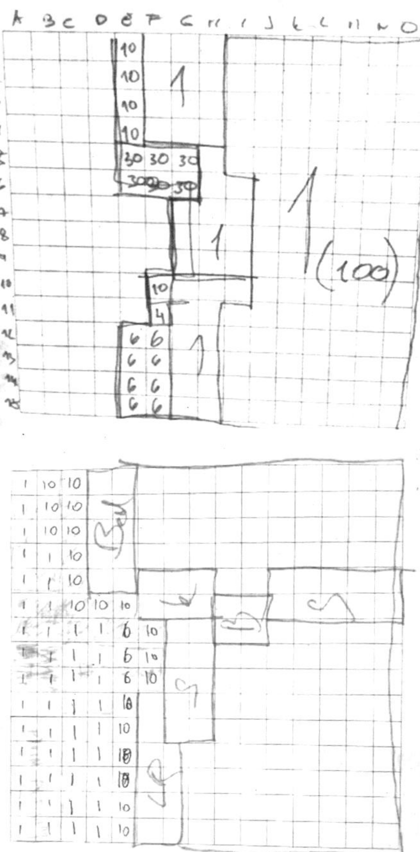

Samples of a negotiation process on paper

cells were filled, in a way that wasn't possible on the paper grid. With digital spreadsheets, users could change their mind, try other solutions, refine some parts, and re-negotiate again and again.

Learning from our previous experiments, we identified a need to address floorplan and section drawings simultaneously in order to engage a three-dimensional negotiation. The next experiment therefore took place in a 3D modelling software environment that could divide a three-dimensional slab into a series of voxels (3D pixels):

one step closer to a digital and immersive environment.
This series of exercises led us to define the premise for the development of a generic tool that could help users build a digital version of their ideal housing block. We learnt about the need for establishing clear rules, and kept the grid as a collective format; we understood the importance of negotiating in three dimensions and with a certain degree of detail; we saw the potential of co-editing simultaneously and overwriting over time; we reflected on the role of abstraction, embodied by voxels, that would become our unit of measurement.

We next decomposed the process of negotiation and its complexity into scriptable steps, to be translated into a computer program. This led us to conduct an experiment that would become the core of our research: a spatial investigation of conflicts embodied in a video game, where several users would be able to co-edit their housing block simultaneously and negotiate over time.

Negotiating through discussion led to over-compromised results. Sketches became too complex, unreadable and fixed. The online spreadsheet became too slow and lagged as it accommodated changes from a large number of participants. 3D modelling required specific skills and therefore reduced the number of potential participants. How could a gaming environment overcome the challenges of speed, responsiveness, details and changeability while enhancing interactivity with the program, and thus between users?

The principle of a game is to be organized according to a set of rules and a collective framework in order liberate the various actions of participants so as to compete or cooperate. In the field of participatory architecture and urbanism, games are sometimes used by municipalities, citizens, and developers. City gaming is a method that has been implemented in real-life problem solving and as a decision-making process with multiple stakeholders, negotiating needs and perspectives as diverse as those of activists, residents, politicians and developers, interacting with each other in real time. This approach has been developed for over a decade by Dr Ekim Tan of Play the City[8], whose successful series of bespoke games for municipalities, policy makers, researchers, community groups and developers invite us to take games seriously as an inclusive tool for making cities.

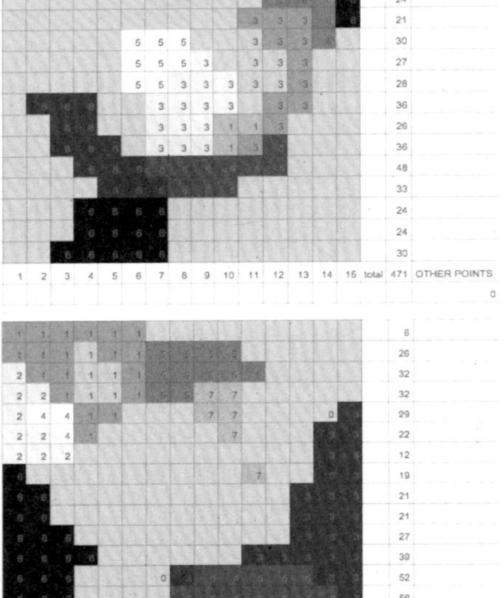

Samples of a negotiation process on a digital spreadsheet

Inspired by Ekim Tan's participatory approach to negotiating the fabrication of the city, we explored how gaming could enable users to engage with and take control of the design of their own dream homes in a collective context. Games simultaneously offer learning and engagement, bringing users into the design process at the start of a project rather than offering passive or one-off ways to contribute to top-down decisions.

Real-time game session with two users

Our ambition was to design a video game in which all characters could interact simultaneously and play their egos. In (w)Ego, players are not just clients. They are fully engaged, immersed and responsible for the design of their dream. Together, players build a relation of trust towards the game and towards each other. This process gives a clear and transparent view of the negotiations and their implications. In (w)Ego, any and all decisions have an immediate effect on the spatial configuration of the plot.

In this playful approach, players were invited to be selfish. Students were immersed in this real-time process of negotiation, which became increasingly direct – as if the act of 'playing' were unlocking some constraints in their interactions. Moves became more precise; they needed to let go of some things and defend others. The responsive game helped each player to order their priorities and understand where they should put their focus. As a process, negotiation games help participants to learn more about themselves.

The iterative process of gaming allows players to negotiate back and forth, iterating solutions and learning to work with their neighbours, even in a selfish way. An intertwined, solid and indefeasible set of relations emerge – becoming the ground for a collective, three-dimensional design. Within the limitations of the slab, and of the game, egos coagulate and solidify into the collective dream.

For more than a decade, our design studios briefs have been setting up the frame for collective production, within which each student finds their own role in the studio – contributing towards the production of a collective output. Inspired by professional game design workflows, this brief invited students to define a series of tasks and responsibilities for the development of the (w)Ego game. Some took care of the user interface, others developed the narrative, yet others focused on rules, or game modes, modelling, graphics, characters definition, etc. Together, they developed a functioning game where all 16 students could play simultaneously and responsively. This process became an opportunity to reflect on our pedagogy: how to enable a sense of freedom and self-expression within the collective format of a studio design brief.

Real-time game session with 16 users

Egos At

Students were invited to seek out and create extreme characters, personalities and egos. They then took on the role of their characters and identified with their personalities and needs as they negotiated space for them in the game. From tempered and normative to exuberant and megalomaniac, a variety of user profiles were formulated, reflecting a range of economies, lifestyles, passions, tastes and personalities.

Characters were inspired by real and fictional personalities. The exuberance and egos of these clients were deliberately exaggerated in order to stress the negotiation process with extreme, seemingly incompatible desires. In this experiment, teenagers, activists, musicians, elderly people, artists, billionaires, academics, yogis, and funambulists would have to play, negotiate and cooperate. This disparate collection of user profiles generated some absurd but fruitful situations for the game to solve. Differences between egos would become the mortar for binding them together.

The (w)Ego Game aims to accommodate this cacophony of egos in a 2.0 version of a co-op. It does this by facilitating cooperation between profiles with divergent rhythms and activities through gaming. The video game provides an equitable framework for the self-orchestration of this seemingly impossible puzzle.

Students modelled a collection of dream homes inspired by these different characters and their spatial requirements. This dream home collection became the spatial embodiment of their corresponding ego – a house where they could truly be themselves.

The Zen House, the Stretching House, the Single Family Detached House, the Lazy House, the Platforms, the Stack, the Loop, the Container House, the Add-on, the Jungle Gym, the Stage, the Bookshelf, the Cave, the McMansion, the Russian Doll, the Jumping Castle... Each home presents unique qualities and specific spatial organizations. Character traits were expressed by the shape, volume, footprint, height, view, exposure, sunlight, circulation and distribution of amenities.

Can we quantify how egoistic these individual homes are? First of all, there is a possible distinction between basic needs, common to everyone (such as kitchen, bathroom, bedroom) and spaces that cater to desired activities, specific to each user (such as a bowling alley, meditation space, playground, etc.). By measuring the ratio of space dedicated to needs and to desires, it becomes possible to measure the proportion of ego embodied in every dream home. This ratio will later serve as a base to compare the results of the negotiation in terms of satisfaction.

In this experiment, dwellings are not measured in square metres but rather as volumetric entities: in cubic metres. This encourages players to explore three-dimensional spatial arrangements and unlock new ways of living in compact environments. Split levels, mezzanines, ladders, vertical apartments, duplex and triplex arrangements or even an apartment with just a 1 m2 footprint are all part of an answer to the scarcity of developable surface area in cities.

The Minimalist

The Funambulist

The Normcore

The 'Dude' Lebowski

The Hangouter

The Stacker

The Rollercoaster Addict

The Prepper

The Collectioner

The Yamakasi

The Guitarist

The Bibliomaniac

The Artist

The Mansioner

The Meditative One

The Kid

The Photographer

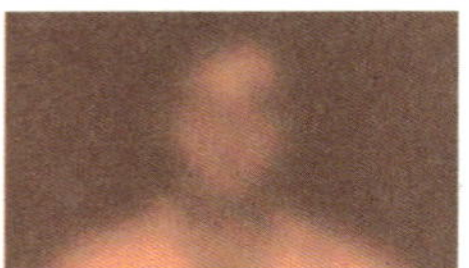

The Minimalist

The dream of the Minimalist is to live on a giant and continuous tatami – an empty space to sleep, eat, work, practice judo and meditation.

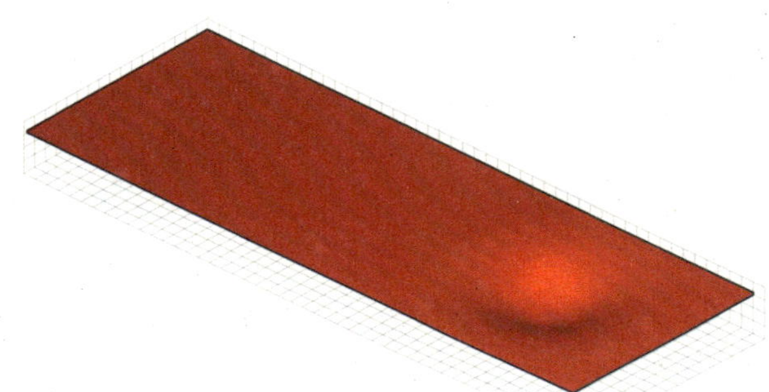

The Zen House

Volume: 2,200 m3
Width: 34 m
Length: 75 m
Height: 5 m
Roof area: 2,700 m2
Facade area: - m2

The Funambulist

The Funambulist wants to live in a house where he can climb around and walk on wire. The house therefore has to stretch to provide enough length for his desired activity.

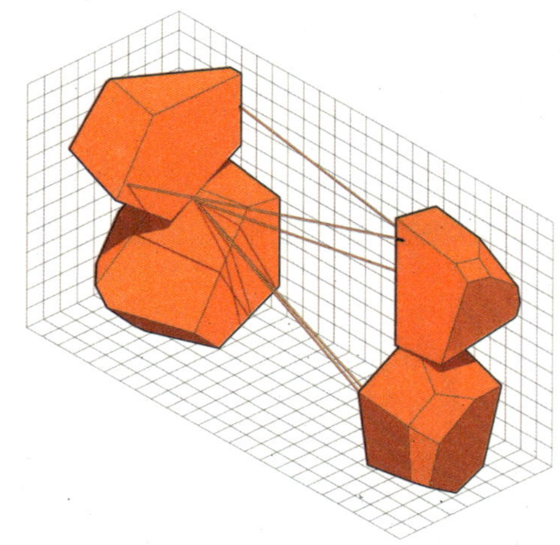

The Stretching House

Volume: 342 m3
Width: 7.5 m
length: 7.5 m
Height: 21 m
Footprint: 56 m2
Roof area: 41 m2
Facade area: 31 m2

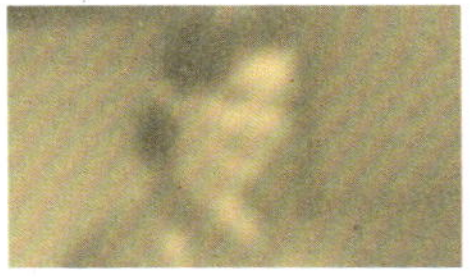

The Normcore

The dream home of the Normcore resembles a traditional detached house that can typically be found in suburbs. It has a garden, some basic amenities and a pitched roof.

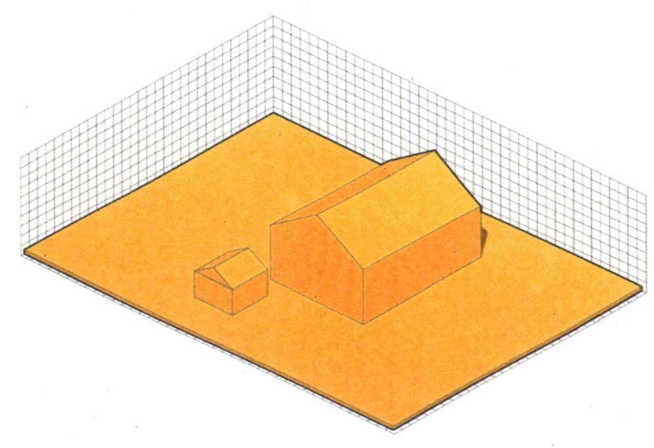

The Single Family Detached House

Volume: 539.5 m3
Width: 35.5 m
length: 51.5 m
Height: 10.5 m
Footprint: 1,837.6 m2
Roof area: 1,849 m2
Facade area: 210 m2

The Dude

The Dude is lazy and spends a lot of time at his place or playing bowling. His dream home therefore consists of a big room acting like an elevator and a personal training bowling alley.

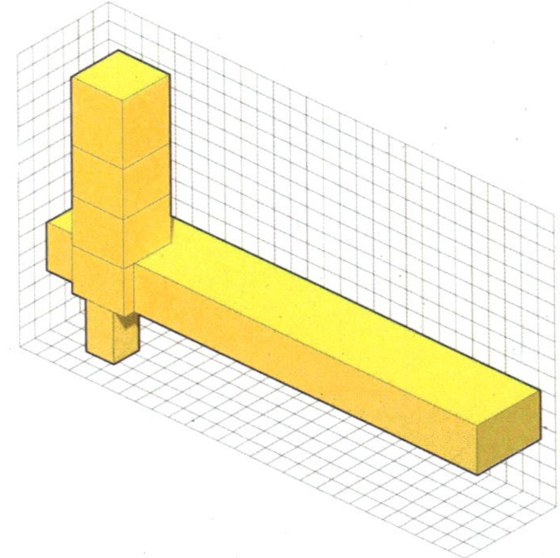

The Lazy House

Volume: 660 m3
Width: 6 m
Length: 24 m
Height: 15 m
Footprint: 24 m2
Roof area: 84 m2
Facade area: 320 m2

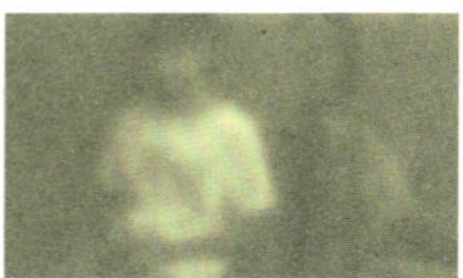

The Teenager

The Teenager loves to hang out. His dream home is made of many platforms to meet with his friends. His desire is to spread out those platforms in different positions and heights in the slab to generate maximum space, access and visibility.

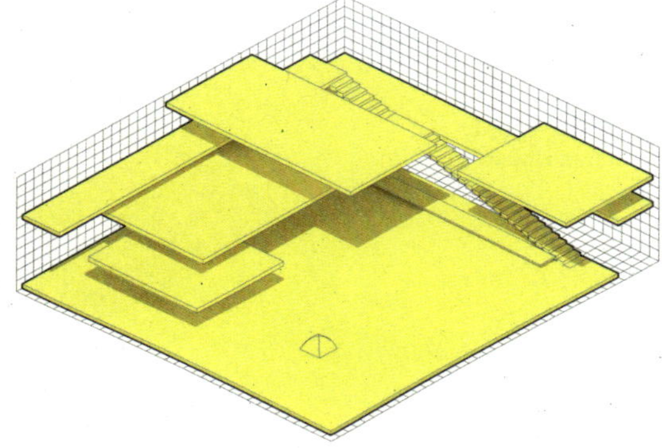

The Platforms

Volume: 410 m3
Width: 40 m
Length: 40 m
Height: 11 m
Footprint: 1,600 m2
Roof area: 200 m2
Facade area: 2,400 m2

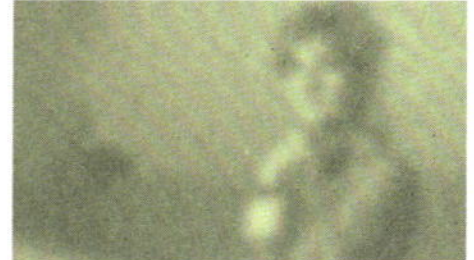

The Stacker

The Stacker wants to work and live in the same place. Key ordering principles include a direct entrance sequence, large voluminous space and bright airy interiors.

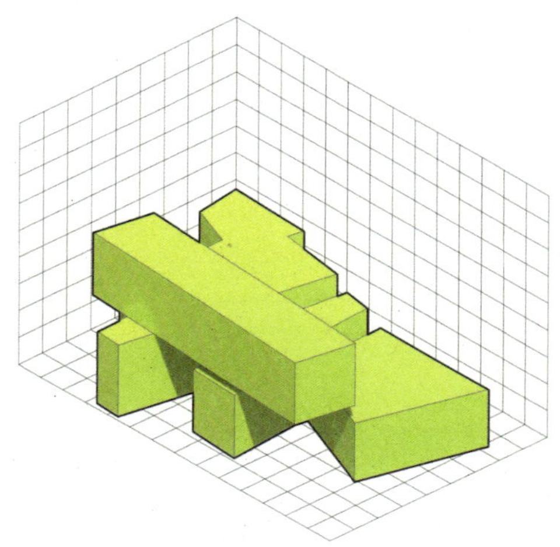

The Stack

Volume: 310 m2
Width: 10 m
Length: 15.7 m
Height: 6.2 m
Footprint: 162 m2
Roof area: 105 m2
Facade area: 541 m2

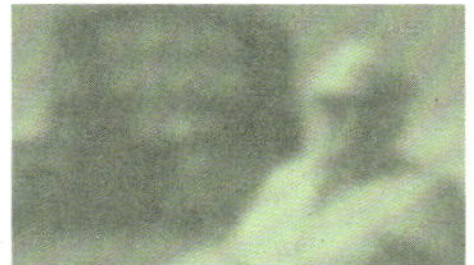

The Rollercoaster Owner

Can one own and live in a roller coaster? This is the dream materialized in the looping house. Here, all amenities are reachable along a continuous track looping up and down, left and right throughout the dwelling unit.

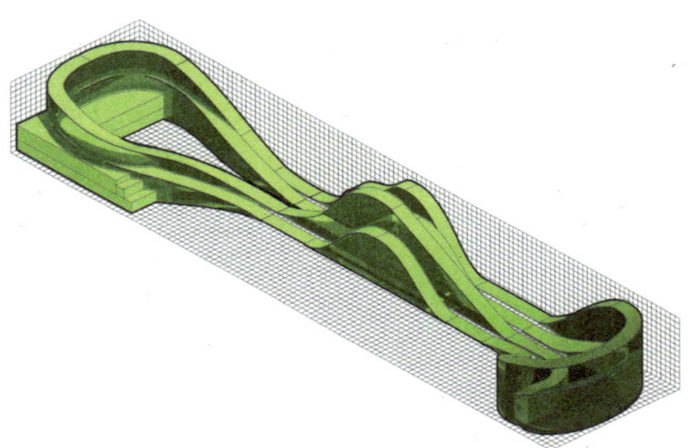

The Loop

Volume: -
Width: -
Length: -
Height: -
Footprint: -
Roof area: -
Facade area: -

The Prepper

The Prepper grew up in the Bomb Shelter era, and that mind-set just never wore off. His dream home acts as a bunker. It is a compact house, made of different combinations of containers. All amenities should be accessible quickly and be condensed around the living area.

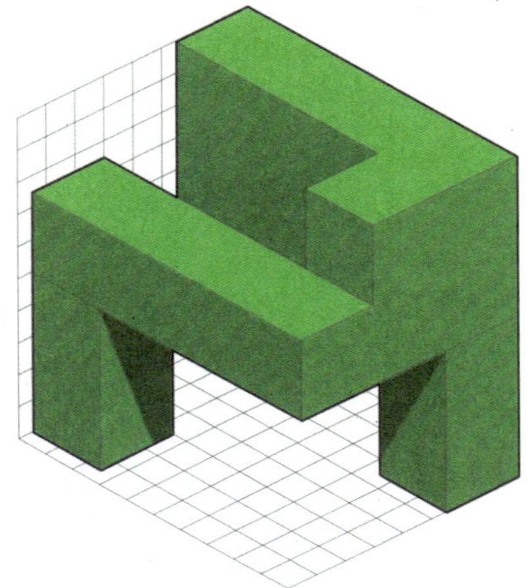

The Container House

Volume: 410 m3
Width: 9 m
Length: 12 m
Height: 15 m
Footprint: 108 m2
Roof area: 105 m2
Facade area: 541 m2

The Collector

The Collector loves doing many activities. His dream home is therefore a house with a specific room for each activity he would like to perform. This house is fragmented. It has many small rooms. The main principle of organization is to incrementally add on rooms next to each other.

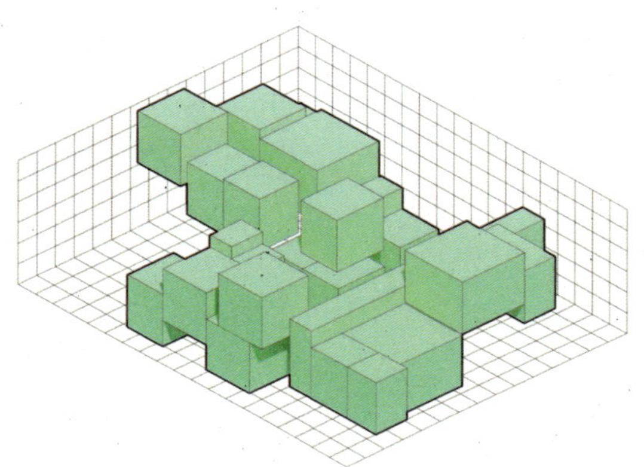

The Add-on

Volume: 596 m3
Width: 21 m
Length: 22 m
Height: 4 m
Footprint: 215 m2
Roof area: 217 m2
Facade area: 416 m 2

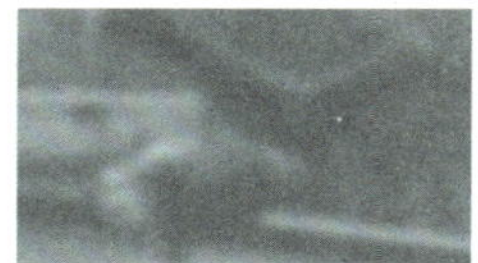

The Yamakasi

The Yamakasi loves to move and exercise. His passion is urban parkour and his dream is to perform inside the apartment. The house and rooftop consist of diverse configurations of boxes for different parkour activities: jumping, climbing and performing 'free-urban-flow' at home.

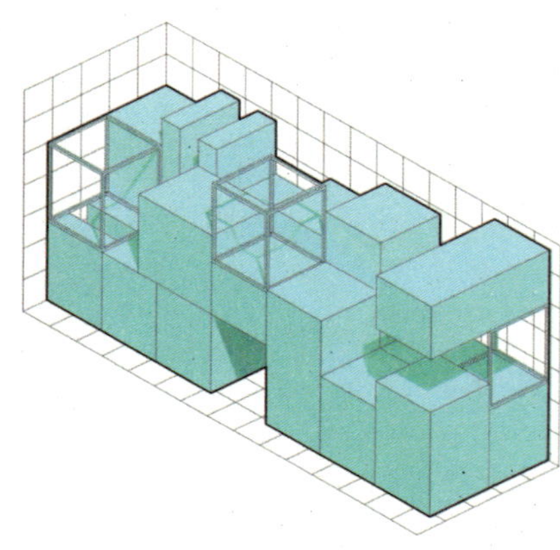

The Jungle Gym

Volume: 1,050 m2
Width: 5 m
Length: 17.5 m
Height: 12 m
Footprint: 150 m2
Roof area: 143 m2
Facade area: 541 m2

The Guitarist

The Guitarist enjoy making loud music and performing for his friends. The private realm of the house is suspended, to allow greater volume for semi-public functions such as exhibitions, performances and parties. His dream home takes the shape of a megaphone, acting like a stage towards the street.

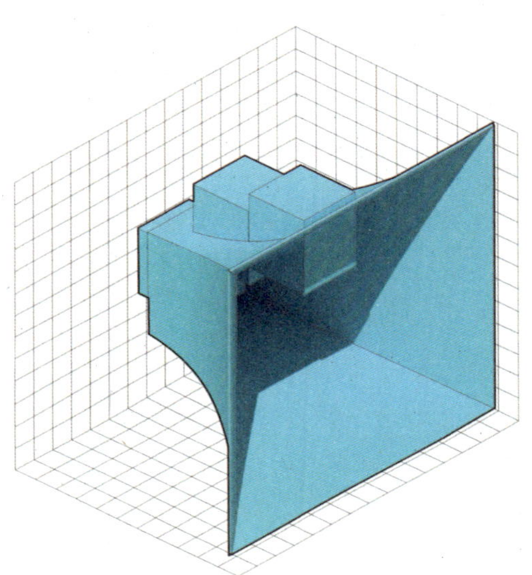

The Stage

Volume: 885 m3
Width: 21 m
Length: 14 m
Height: 9.2 m
Footprint: 294 m2
Roof area: 241 m2
Facade area: 115 m2

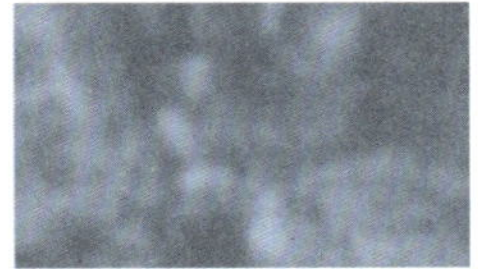

The Bibliomaniac

The Bibliomaniac has filled her flat to the brim with thousands of newspapers, magazines, books and stamps. As the collection grew, the Bibliomaniac started to stack around her. The Bibliomaniac's dream home would be an infinite spiralling bookshelf that could serve as the perfect library.

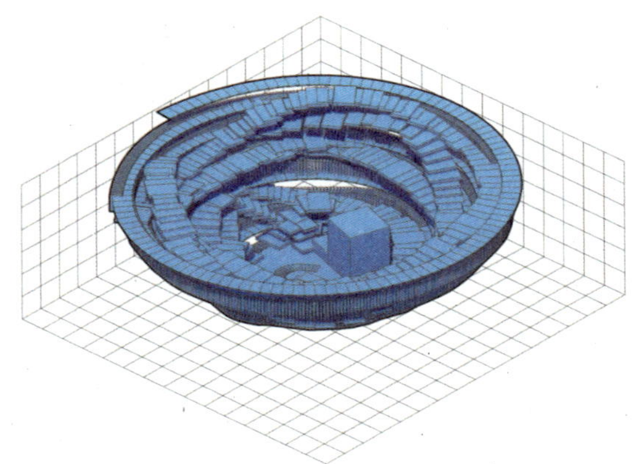

The Bookshelf

Volume: 104 m3
Width: 17 m
Length: 16.6 m
Height: 6 m
Footprint: 283 m2
Roof area: 1,019 m2
Facade area: 41 m2

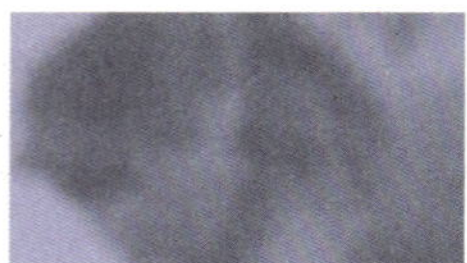

The Artist

The Artist would love to live entirely in his own gallery space. It's like a cave for him. He has an extravagant desire for space. His house is an adaptable frame structure that can fold within itself. It is a spacious, adaptable open space for his creative flow.

The Cave

Volume: 13,800 m
Width: 90 m
Length: 90 m
Height: 28 m
Footprint: 8,100 m2
Roof area: 12,600 m2
Facade area: 6,500 m2

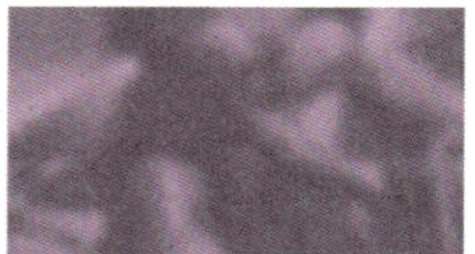

The McMansioner

The McMansioner dreams of living in an oversized home far bigger than one's needs. The home is conceived in four layers: one for cars and games, one for sports, one for relaxing and one for a quad biking track.

The McMansion

Volume: 800 m3
Width: 5 m
Length: 20 m
Height: 12 m
Footprint: 100 m2
Roof area: 260 m2
Facade area: 418 m2

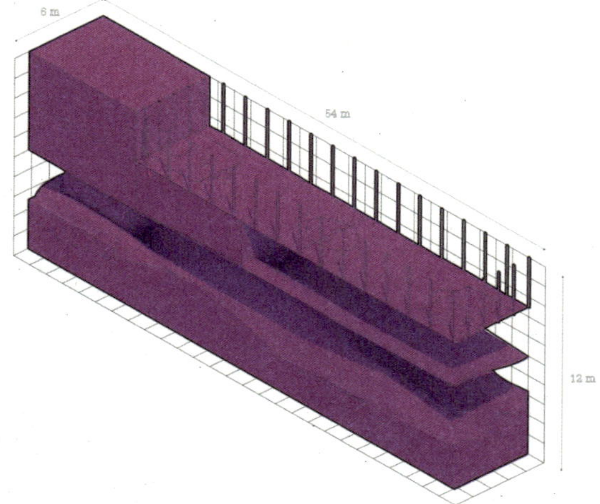

The Meditative One

The Meditative One practices transcendental meditation. His house is composed of three main volumes, each of which corresponds to different uses but also to different levels of privacy. The biggest volume includes the two others.

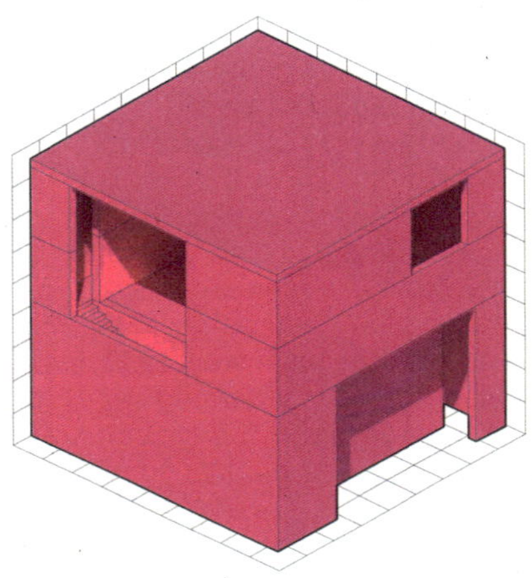

The Russian Dolls

Volume: 1,000 m3
Width: 10 m
Length: 10 m
Height: 10 m
Footprint: 100 m2
Roof area: 100 m2
Facade area: 400 m2

The Kid

The Kid loves to constantly change environments in order to play. His dream home is an infinite space for playing. It looks and is organized like a jumping castle, with different rooms for playing. The Kid can go from one room to the other by jumping around or crawling.

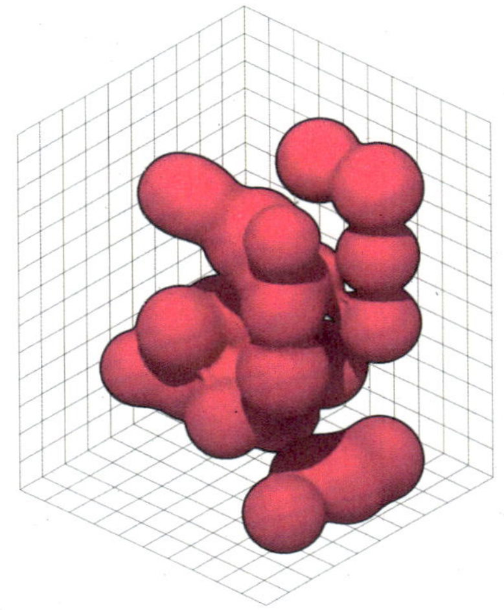

The Jumping Castle

Volume: 785 m3
Width: 5 m
length: 5 m
Height: 25 m
Footprint: 108 m2
Roof area: 13 m2
Facade area: 854 m2

Meet Your Neighbours

Within a collective envelope that is finite and rigid, what is the right density to set for this experiment? A desktop study based on comparing different urban housing densities from cities around the world gave a first indication. For example, a game density based on Kowloon Walled City in Hong Kong would be very different from one taken from the Eixample District in Barcelona, or Borneo Sporenburg in Amsterdam, Brooklyn in New York, Broadacre City, Boston's residential fabric or a typical block in Brasilia. We also calculated that the total volume of all dream homes previously defined by students was way too big to fit a typical housing block envelope from any of those examples.

By reducing the total volume of the dream homes by 25 per cent, we reached a volume comparable to an average housing block, setting players the challenge of achieving this degree of compactization through collaboration. Players would have to compromise and negotiate in order to fulfil their dream as much as possible. This reduction of the size of the envelope led to a collective framework emphasising the need for negotiation. When egos are situated closer to each other, the space for negotiation becomes more restricted, while the potential for both conflict and cooperation increases.

The game could be applied to any architectural or urban form – anywhere from a tower, perimeter block or slab to a neighbourhood or city layout. Building on previous experiments and inspired by the MVRDV's Double House in Utrecht, we decided to focus on a vertical slab of 39.6 × 4.8 × 39.6 m, translated into voxels (three-dimensional pixels) of 0.6 m3 – our digital unit of measurement. For the sake of the experiment, the slab had no specific context. It could have views and daylight on both sides. The slab works as a condensed representation of the choices presented in an urban context: you can either be on a corner, high up, well connected in the middle, or have the most access to the ground. But, unlike on Pinterest, you cannot have all of these at once. In this sense the slab is closer to the reality in the city than the dream home collages in chapter 2.3. Its shallow depth makes the negotiation process easily readable from both sides. With these parameters in place, we set out to negotiate how the dream homes could best fit within this envelope.

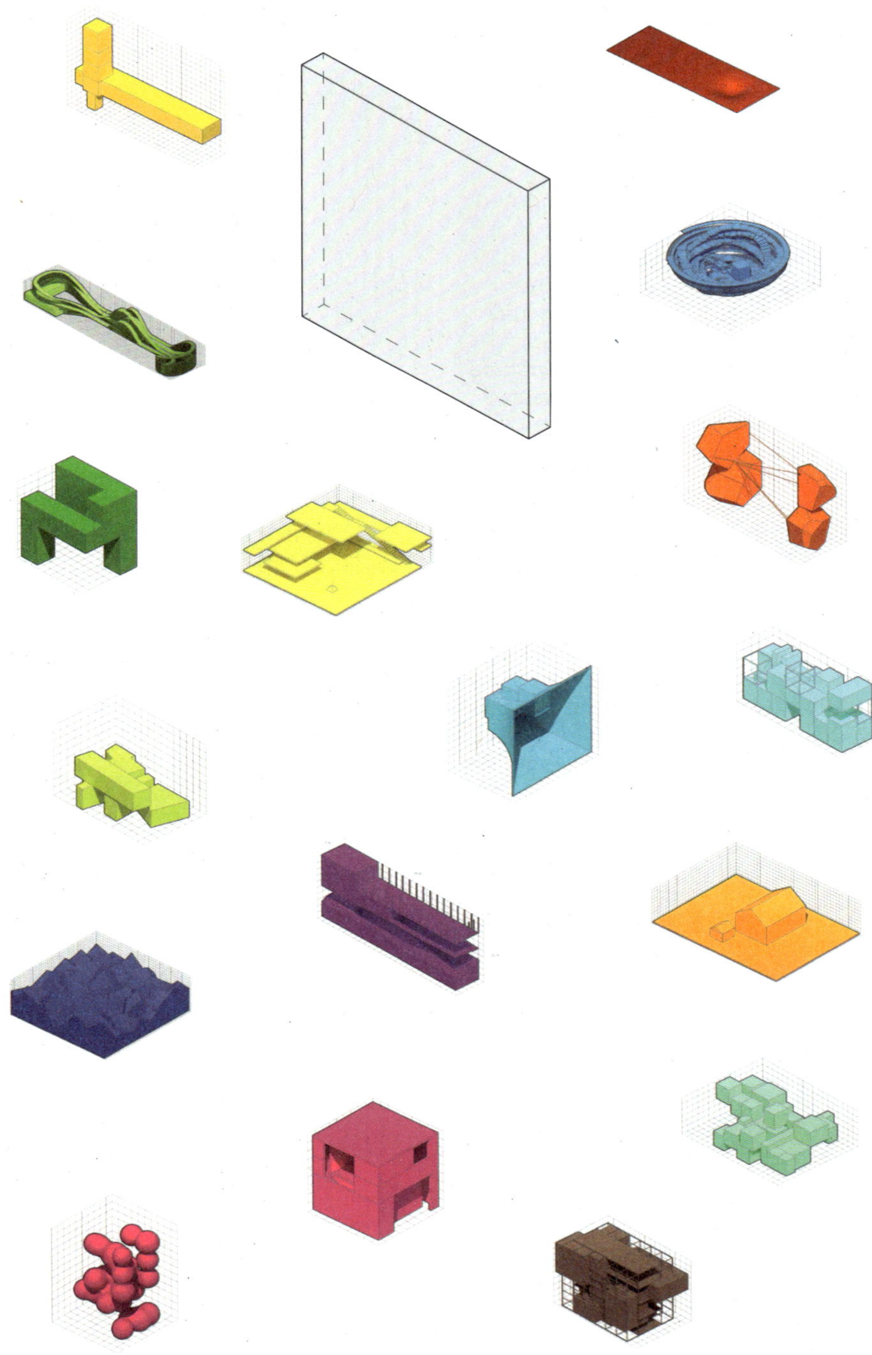

Four Scripted Games

A set of four different games were scripted: the Blind Game, the Strategic Game, the Automaton Game, and the Trading Game. Each highlighted one specific aspect of reality. Four different teams of scripters competed in order to discover which algorithm would give the most satisfying and unexpected results. This led to an effort to decompose the process and puzzle out collective housing design issues through a set of rules – such as regulations, economical constraints, physical awareness of surroundings – applied to the game with a certain level of abstraction. Fire escape routes, mechanical, electrical matters such as plumbing, pipes and cables and accessibility would come in a second phase of the game. This level of abstraction, emulating real-world urban situations, allowed us to focus on one aspect of reality, to maximize it and implement the successful solutions.

The four games provide a broad-spectrum approach to gaming as an urban design tool. By generating more than one approach, we were able to gain valuable insight into how different players reacted to the different priorities, limitations and scenarios.

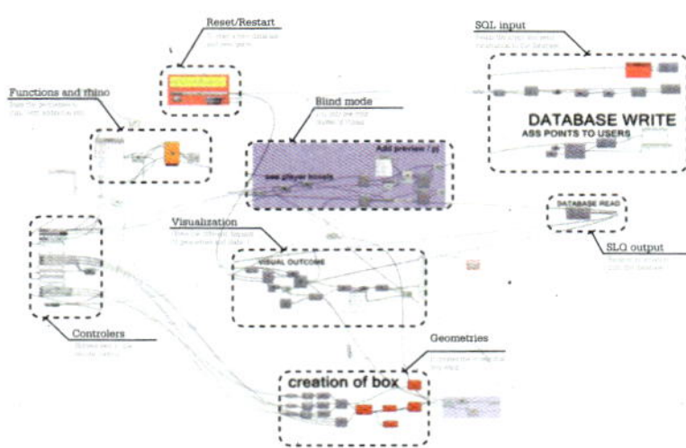

Grasshopper Script of the Blind Game

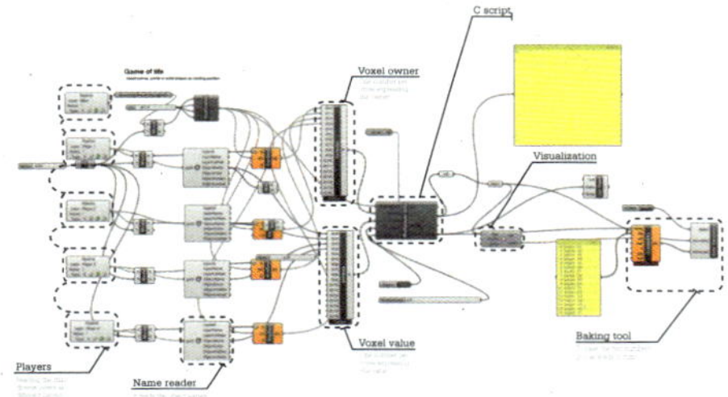

Grasshopper Script of the Strategic Game

Grasshopper Script of the Automaton Game

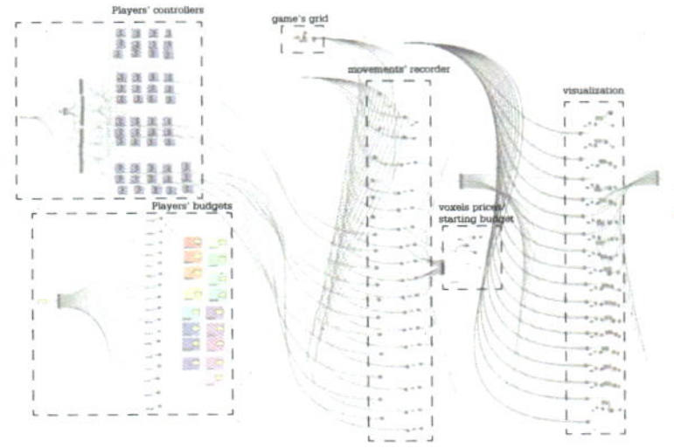

Grasshopper Script of the Trading Game

The Blind Game

The Blind Game is based on some information about your opponent that is missing. In this game, needs and desires are placed voxel by voxel, not knowing what kind of facilities your neighbours are placing next to you. This supports a fair negotiation based on co-creation, co-design, competition and collaboration without knowing the missing information.

1 Players pick an avatar and start playing for their dream home.

2 Players choose a function, specify the dimensions, place voxels in the slab and freeze the desired space.

3 The negotiation occurs in 6 blind turns.

4 Players expand their house by two functions per turn. Once a player has claimed some voxels, those disappear from the usable grid, so no overlapping is possible.

5 During the game, player can only see what they produce (their voxelated apartment). Motivations for expansion are therefore entirely selfish.

6 Only once the game is over, players discover their neighbours and the configuration of their apartments in relation to others'.

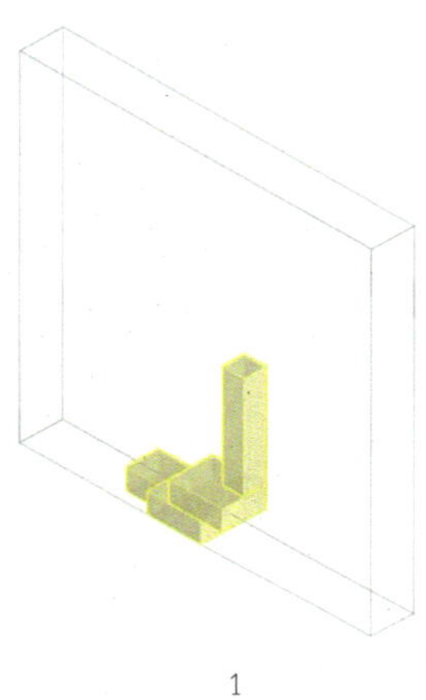

1

2

3

4

5

6

Blind Game Evolution

Dream Home	Step 1	Step 2	Step 3	Step 4	Access
	20%	46%	56%	66%	63%
	35%	46%	78%	86%	85%
	27%	36%	55%	57%	57%
	26%	37%	46%	51%	50%
	26%	52%	83%	84%	83%
	25%	43%	72%	88%	86%
	26%	37%	46%	51%	48%
	25%	41%	70%	71%	

Evolution of the degree of satisfaction per user during a Blind Game session

Blind Game Evolution

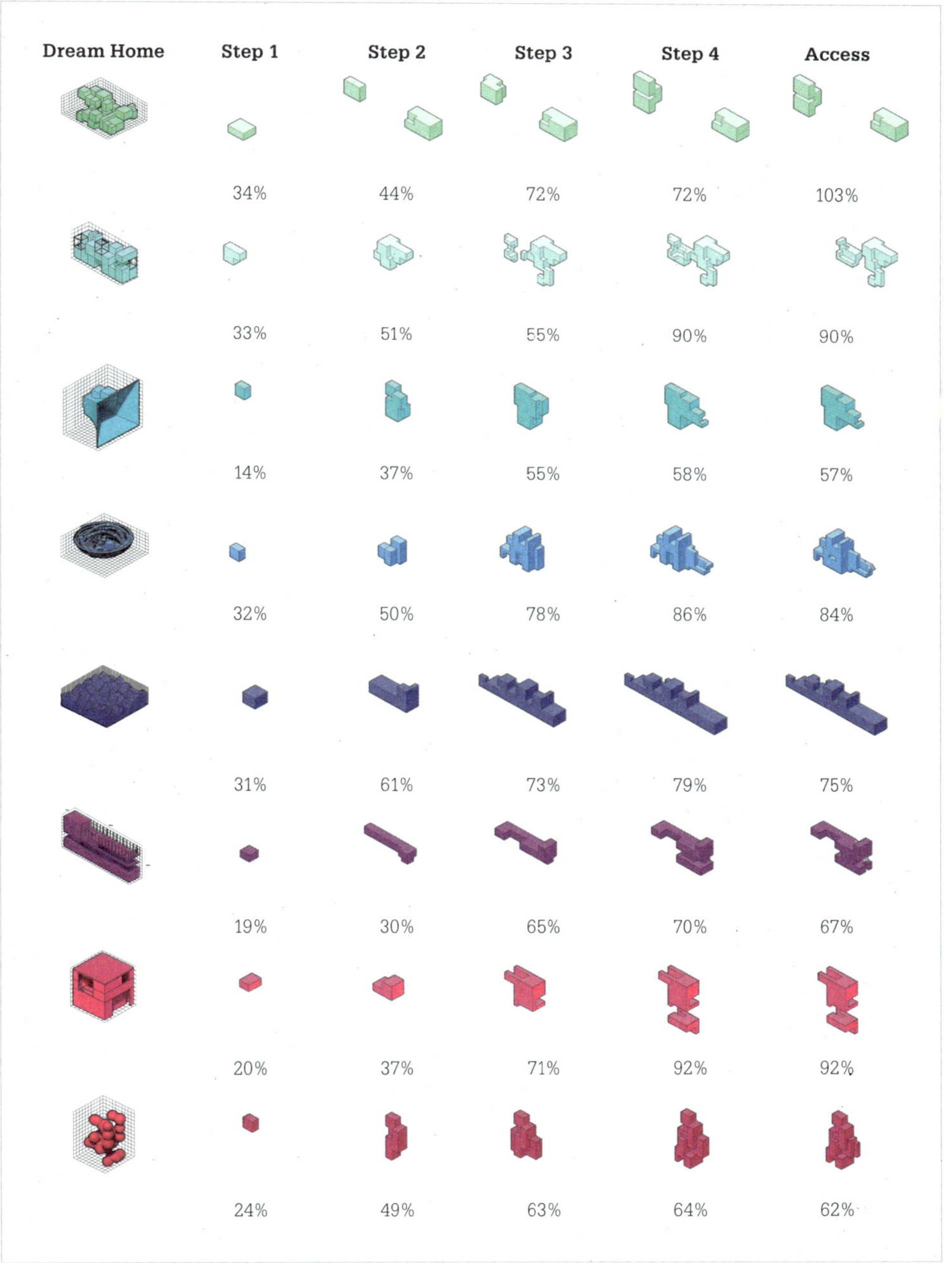

Dream Home	Step 1	Step 2	Step 3	Step 4	Access
	34%	44%	72%	72%	103%
	33%	51%	55%	90%	90%
	14%	37%	55%	58%	57%
	32%	50%	78%	86%	84%
	31%	61%	73%	79%	75%
	19%	30%	65%	70%	67%
	20%	37%	71%	92%	92%
	24%	49%	63%	64%	62%

Evolution of the degree of satisfaction per user during a Blind Game session

The Strategic Game

The Strategic Game is a more direct approach to cooperation: players can see what others are doing and negotiate with them. The speed of the game requires users to think strategically and quickly about the importance of certain spaces.

1 Each player picks an avatar and starts playing for their dream home.

2 The game requires a phased approach. Players have three minutes per round, six rounds in total.

3 The ability to see and battle their opponents in real time allows users to engage in disputes and negotiations over space, view, position.

4 In order to win, each party needs to formulate or adapt a strategy – for example, where to start within the envelope, or to surround or block your neighbour in order to save some space for yourself.

5 Voxels have different values, depending on their importance to you (needs versus desires); voxels with higher value can overwrite voxels with lower value.

6 Players can occupy empty voxels or claim their neighbours' voxels when their need is greater; the puzzle constantly reshuffles until the time is up.

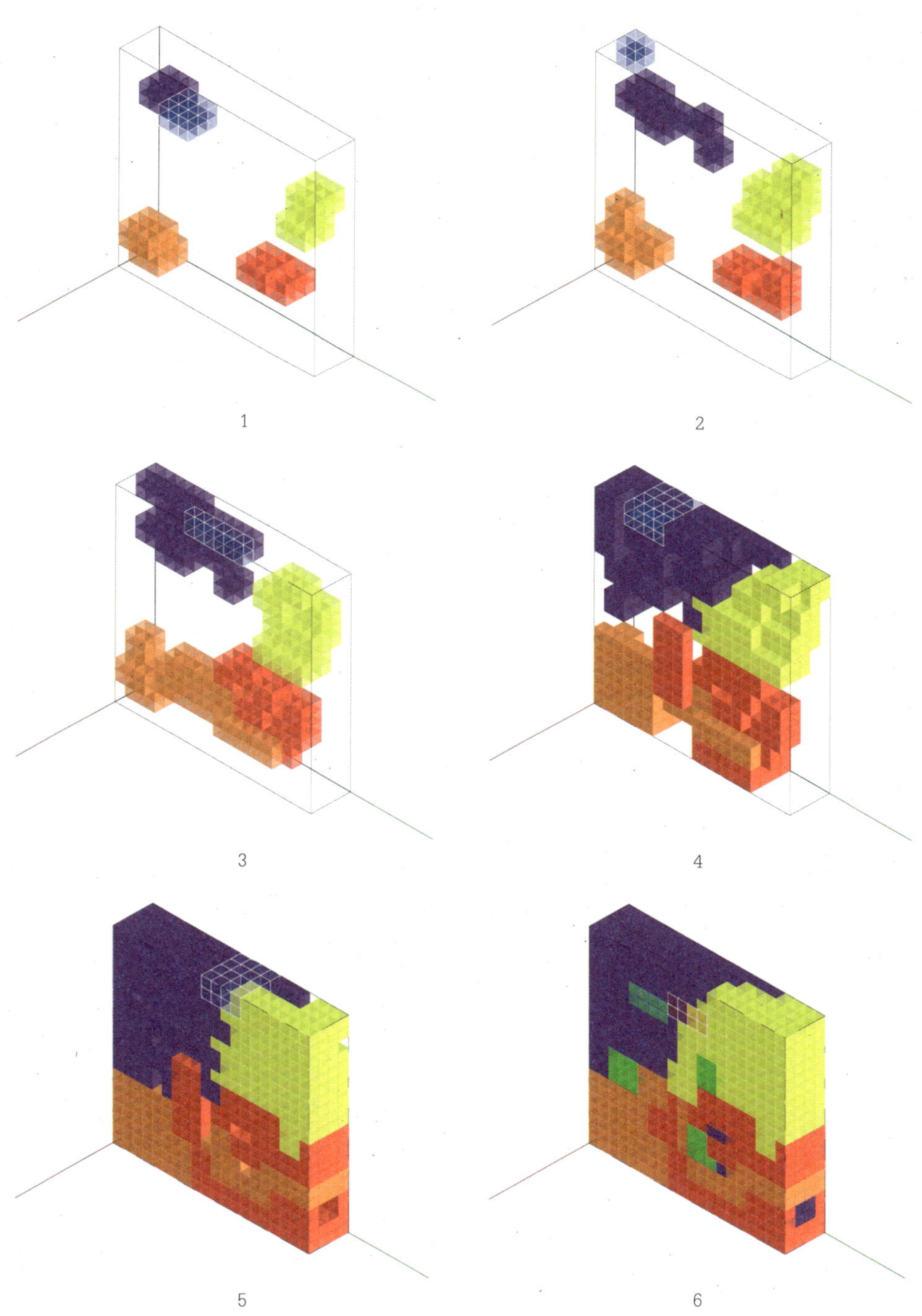
1
2
3
4
5
6

Strategic Game Evolution

Dream Home	Step 1	Step 2	Step 3	Step 4	Access
	43%	46%	37%	42%	42%
	41%	49%	54%	56%	51%
	67%	64%	68%	67%	61%
	16%	20%	22%	33%	30%
	27%	43%	54%	70%	65%
	76%	84%	95%	93%	90%
	31%	37%	38%	32%	31%
	24%	49%	84%	77%	77%

Evolution of the degree of satisfaction per user during a Strategic Game session

Strategic Game Evolution

Dream Home	Step 1	Step 2	Step 3	Step 4	Access
	39%	51%	57%	85%	78%
	12%	8%	11%	16%	15%
	22%	35%	34%	47%	45%
	43%	71%	68%	76%	74%
	82%	79%	76%	82%	79%
	37%	43%	42%	46%	43%
	28%	27%	34%	31%	31%
	28%	39%	38%	36%	35%

Evolution of the degree of satisfaction per user during a Strategic Game session

The Automaton Game

The Automaton is a self-generative game based on cellular automata – a mathematical model based on simple rules governing cell replication and destruction that is commonly used to model complex systems composed of simple units. The Automaton is fascinating. Players watch the game evolving and patterns emerging. Does the computer 'get it'? And – stranger – do its algorithms know you better than you know yourself?

1 Each player picks an avatar and starts playing for their dream home.

2 Players need only specify the initial position of their dream home.

3 Players pre-assign specific values to their voxels.

4 Once all the players are ready, the game can start.

5 The game consists of a finite grid of cells and a finite number of states. Each cell is surrounded by neighbouring cells that influence each other.

6 No further input is required. The algorithm does the work.

1

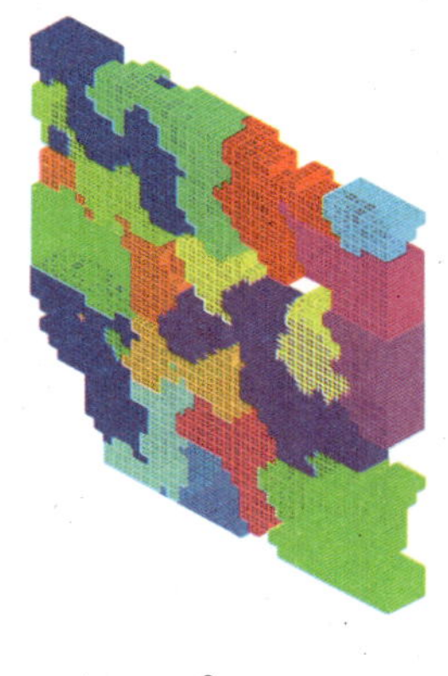

2

3

4

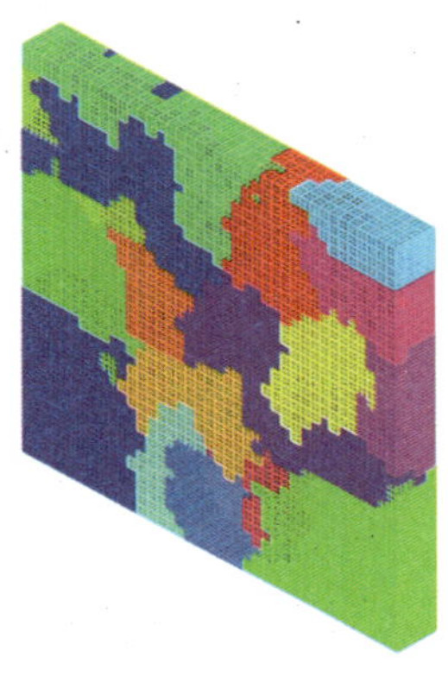

5

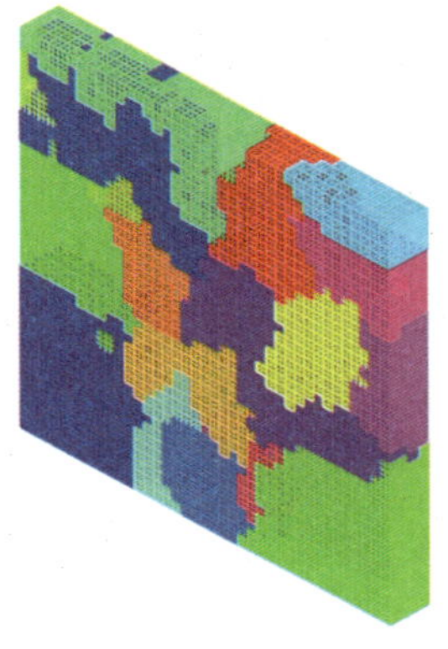

6

Automaton Game Evolution

Dream Home	Step 1	Step 2	Step 3	Step 4	Access
	55%	72%	74%	75%	72%
	41%	58%	63%	54%	48%
	27%	50%	50%	47%	43%
	41%	68%	62%	57%	55%
	40%	57%	52%	61%	32%
	93%	160%	162%	166%	134%
	29%	59%	61%	62%	53%
	74%	119%	123%	120%	120%

Evolution of the degree of satisfaction per user during an Automaton Game session

Automaton Game Evolution

Dream Home	Step 1	Step 2	Step 3	Step 4	Access
	48%	72%	61%	63%	51%
	25%	55%	57%	59%	46%
	26%	41%	41%	41%	33%
	75%	126%	128%	123%	101%
	64%	104%	110%	112%	104%
	53%	83%	86%	88%	73%
	41%	62%	58%	57%	52%
	48%	75%	62%	61%	58%

Evolution of the degree of satisfaction per user during an Automaton Game session

The Trading Game

In this version of the game, economical value is introduced to the negotiation. Players can accumulate space and then sell or rent it out when they no longer need or use it. The trading process can be endless and is therefore limited by a timer.

1 Each player picks an avatar and starts playing for their dream home.

2 Voxels are assigned a value depending on their orientation and position in the slab. A voxel with more daylight and better views would have a higher value.

3 With this financial framework in mind, users consider the implications of each of their actions for their budget.

4 Players choose a function, specify the dimensions, place voxels in the slab and freeze the desired space.

5 After a few rounds, players can start trading their space with their neighbours.

6 The price of all the extra space is based on demand and all users operate on equal and fixed capital.

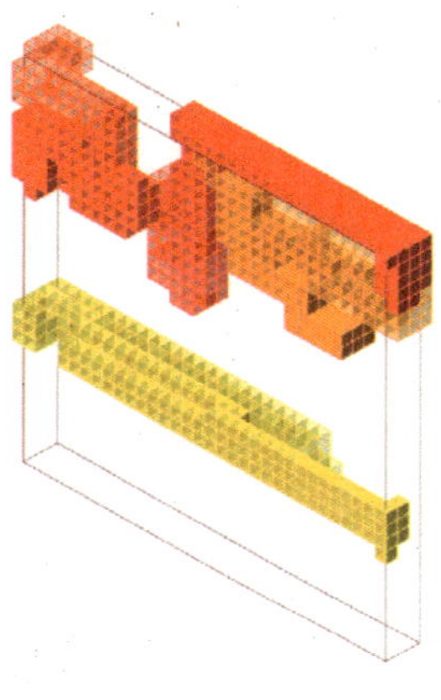

1

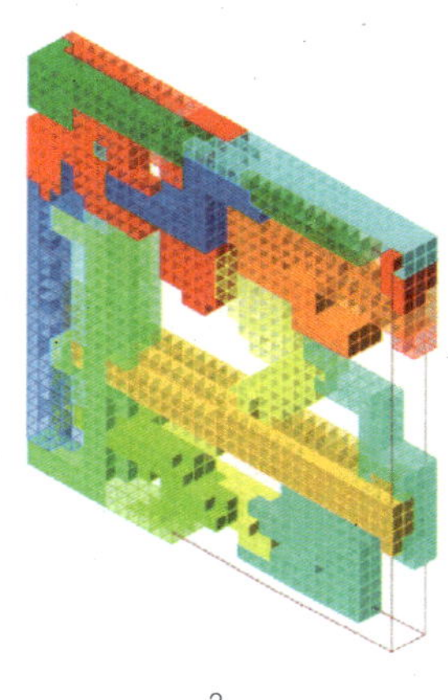

2

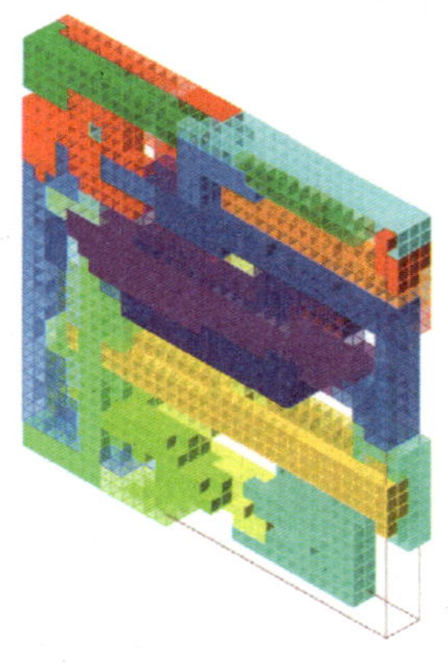

3

4

5

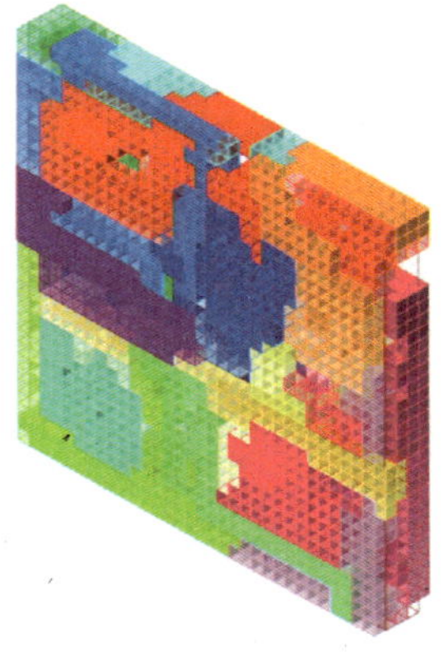

6

Automaton Game Evolution

Dream Home	Step 1	Step 2	Step 3	Step 4	Access
	83%	80%	89%	83%	80%
	60%	58%	60%	52%	52%
	65%	66%	56%	48%	48%
	68%	71%	80%	79%	75%
	76%	75%	92%	86%	85%
	77%	91%	82%	98%	98%
	74%	71%	72%	85%	81%
	110%	117%	84%	88%	88%

Evolution of the degree of satisfaction per user during a Trading Game session

Automaton Game Evolution

Dream Home	Step 1	Step 2	Step 3	Step 4	Access
	88%	93%	99%	118%	111%
	61%	54%	55%	46%	46%
	68%	68%	72%	86%	81%
	95%	92%	114%	105%	97%
	107%	115%	63%	79%	64%
	58%	55%	43%	57%	54%
	67%	61%	65%	67%	64%
	87%	100%	84%	62%	62%

Evolution of the degree of satisfaction per user during a Trading Game session

Evaluation Criteria

In the (w)Ego game, there are no genuine winners or losers. Participants are egoists: they are not trying to defeat their neighbours but just seeking for the best for themselves. When the game is over, some will do better than others, getting closer than others to the desires of the user they represent.

The (w)Ego Game incorporates a scoring system, able to combine and compare different criteria, such as size, shape, program, room configuration and size, height, length, orientation, position in the slab, as well as overall degree of satisfaction.

This set of criteria can be divided into two categories: those referring to the housing unit itself as a singular element abstracted from context, and those referring to units within a context (position in the slab and amid other neighbours).

All the houses are evaluated in a systematic way. But what if a player cares more about the length of their house than about its volume, while another participant would give more importance to the position in the slab, than to the size of their apartment? Another feature was therefore added: the possibility to assign a specific hierarchy to those criteria based on their subjective relevance. This ranking, varying from one user to the other, enabled us to translate the user's satisfaction in a more personal way. Dream houses are no longer objectively comparable, but contextualized amid the player's real desires.

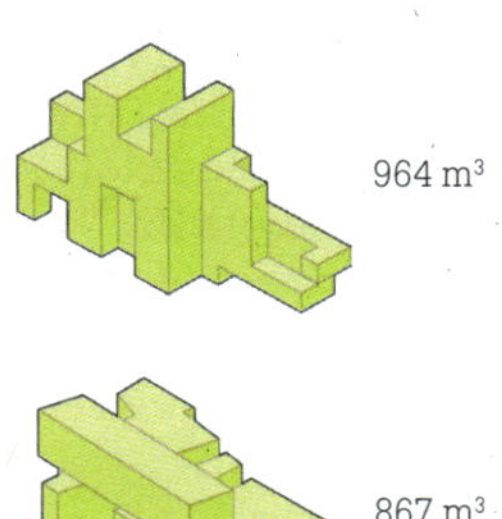

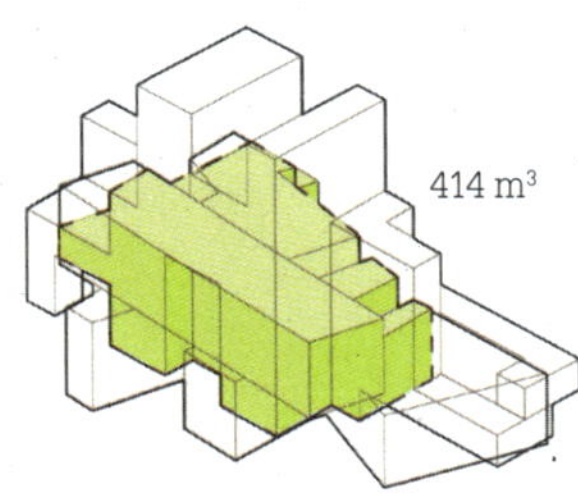

Volume

The volume of the resulting unit is one of the main factors that affect user satisfaction. Its value is based on a ratio between the initial amount of cubic metres envisioned in the dream home and the volumetric outcome of the game.

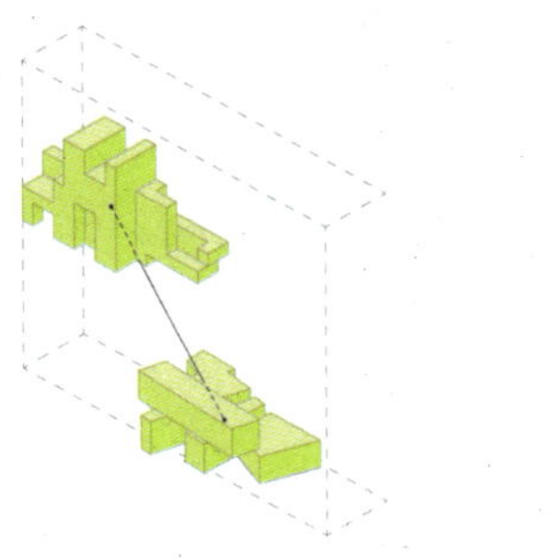

Shape

By overlapping and comparing the shape of the initial dream home and its outcome, it is possible to evaluate the house deformation.

Position

The location factor considers the difference between the initial desired location in the slab (access to the ground floor, corner, top corner, middle) and the one resulting from each game session. The smaller the difference the better the score.

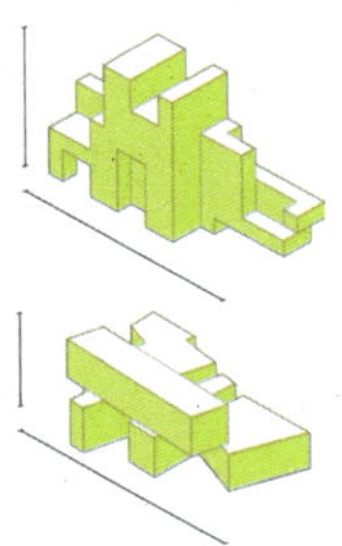

Dimensions

Here we compare the ratio between width, length and height of the desired house and its outcome. This gives a score and ratio relative to the overall dimensions.

The Results

The four games ended in different ways. Some could go on and on, like the Trading Game, others would exhaust themselves, while some had to be constrained by turns and a timer. But the end results were far from the only outcomes. The different game sessions generated a vast collection of typologies at each turn. We needed a method to systematically monitor and evaluate the results and evolution of each dwelling, the level of satisfaction of each resident, and the balance of overall satisfaction with the collective housing.

At the end of each turn, we took snapshots of the results in order to evaluate their outcomes. This freezing act allowed us to get a sense of the overall degree of satisfaction and the collective success of each negotiation. It became possible to compare them and look at the strengths and weaknesses of each process for each dream, at comparable moments in the game.

Collecting data became part of the learning process. The monitoring could systematically be applied to a large pool of users and help to make a more in-depth analysis. In addition, immediate feedback, enhanced by some quantitative and qualitative information, helped users to understand the implication of their actions in the game. Repeat games furnished users with a sense of where to start, how to place needs and desires strategically, which voxel to conquer first, and other tactics.

With user feedback it became possible to observe different speeds and degrees of complexity at play, the differences between man-made decisions and automatization, the role or need of additional discussion during the game sessions, as well as perspectives on which game was the most successful, the most entertaining, or in need of most refinement. This led us to reflect on potential additions to the games. How could we script a process that could offer all players 100 per cent satisfaction?

Collection of results from different game sessions

Blind Game Results

75%

SATISFACTION

Overall degree of satisfaction after a Blind Game session

Strategic Game Results

53%
SATISFACTION

Overall degree of satisfaction after a Strategic Game session

Automaton Game Results

65%
SATISFACTION

Overall degree of satisfaction after a Automaton Game session

Trading Game Results

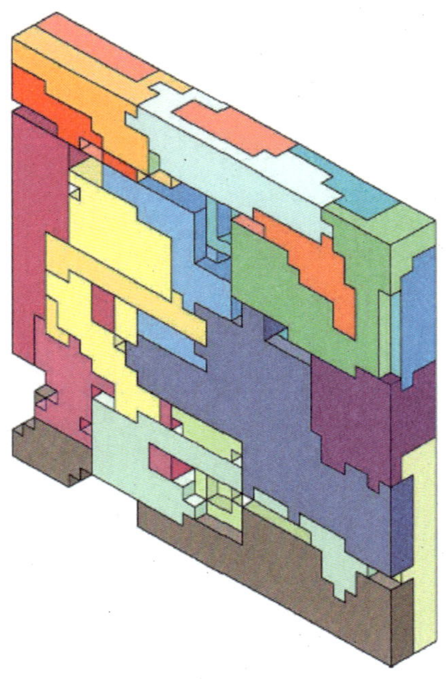

72%
SATISFACTION

Overall degree of satisfaction after a Trading Game session

The Blind Game Results

Overall, the imposition of spatial restrictions led to compact yet still diverse versions of dream homes distributed across the slab in a balanced way. Of the four games, the Blind Game gave the best results in terms of how the outcome matched the pre-game dream home. This is before taking into account player testimonies that recognize some deviations from the original dream as particularly successful, as in The Zen House or The Russian Doll. In this game, the character traits of each user were most recognizable, and the process of negotiation – achieved without direct interaction with others – was felt by players to be the most understandable.

The Zen House

The Stretching House

The Normcore

The Lazy House

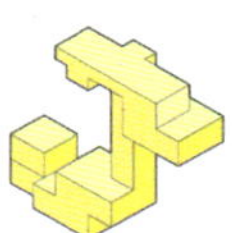

The Platforms

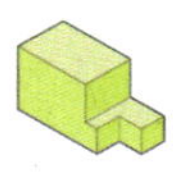

The Stack

The Loop

The Container

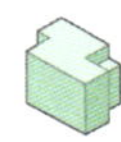

The Add-On

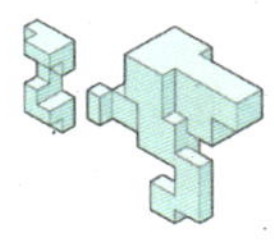

The Jungle Gym

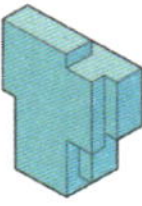

The Stage

The Bookshelf

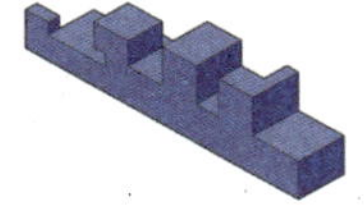

The Cave

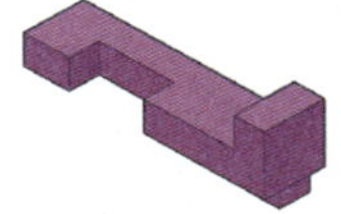

The Mansion

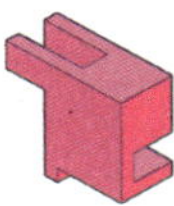

The Russian Doll

The Jumping Castle

Blind Game Results

The Zen House

User: The Minimalist
Home: The Zen House
Desired activities: a giant tatami
Area: 75 m2
Volume: 282 m3

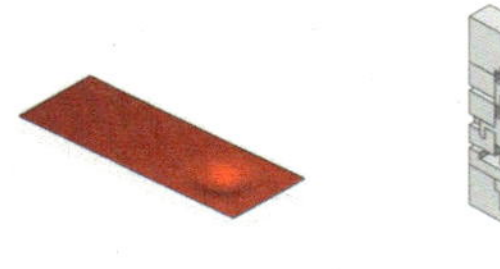
Dream Home Version

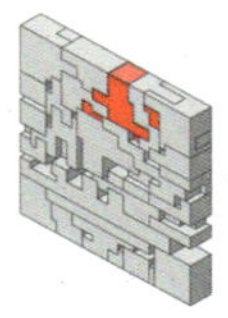
Resulting unit

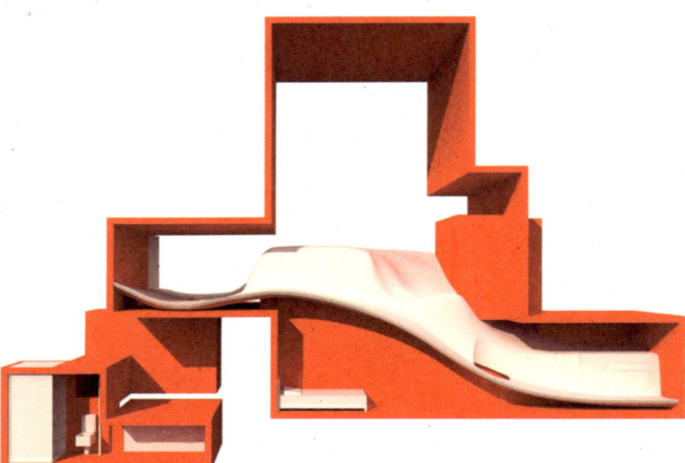

63%
SATISFACTION

The dream of The Minimalist was to have a house with a giant flat tatami. This version keeps the same principle of organization. But instead of a flat and continuous tatami, the negotiation process led to a new topography. The multilevel tatami doubles as circulation throughout the whole apartment, connecting different functional entities. All domestic activities are placed under this blanket, while the upper part remains dedicated to meditative space. The ceiling has been usefully deformed by the negotiation process with the neighbours; in the centre of the apartment, a generous volume provides a perfect place to meditate.

Blind Game Results

The Stretching House

User: The Funambulist
Home: The Stretching House
Desired activities: Climbing and funambulism
Area: 144 m2
Volume: 333 m3

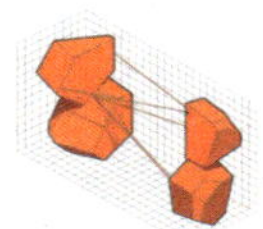

Dream Home Version

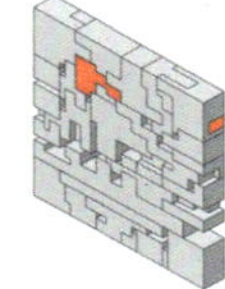

Resulting unit

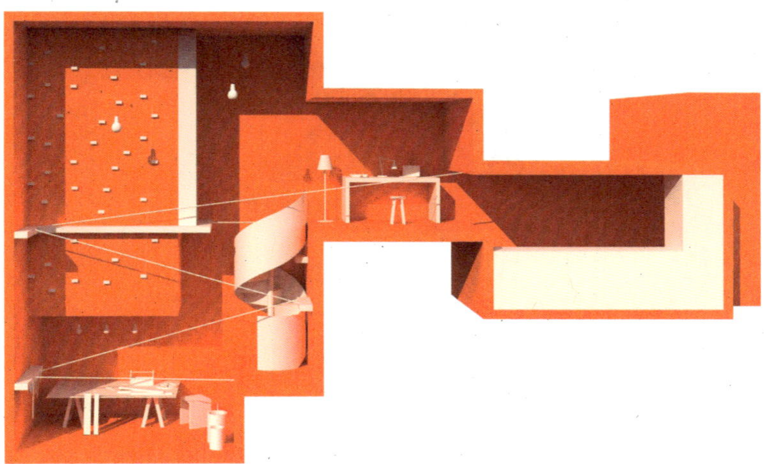

85%
SATISFACTION

The Funambulist wanted to live in a house where he can climb and walk on a tightrope. The house therefore had to stretch to provide enough length for the desired activity. He didn't need traditional circulation. In this game, he got a satisfaction level of 85 per cent. The house stretches through the slab, providing the required length for his activities. There is no traditional circulation, making the apartment inaccessible to anyone else but him. The house is not one long line but rather a multilevel space, with gaps and a corridor of different heights through which he can climb, crawl and balance.

Blind Game Results

The Normcore

User: The Normcore
Home: The Single Family Detached House
Desired activities: Attic, garden
Area: 115 m2
Volume: 430 m3

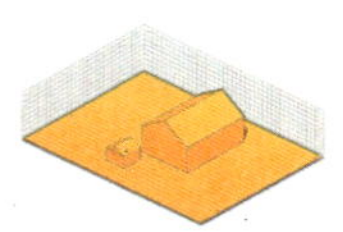
Dream Home Version

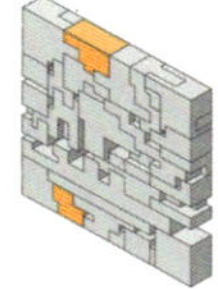
Resulting unit

57%
SATISFACTION

The dream home of The Normcore was a traditional detached house. It would have a garden, basic amenities and a pitched roof. After negotiation with the neighbours, the house was unexpectedly reconfigured. At the moment when the game stopped, the house was separated in two disconnected entities. She didn't manage to negotiate an adequate level of private access during the game session. The garden is now part of the attic, up in the slab, and the rest of the amenities stand on the ground with a direct connection to the street. Half of the pitched roof remains, composing a stylistic environment and shielding half of the house with the privacy of a garden. The relatively low degree of satisfaction is mainly due to an initial oversized desire for a very large plot.

Blind Game Results

The Lazy House

User: The Dude
Home: The Lazy House
Desired activities: Bowling alley and elevator
Area: 144 m2
Volume: 341 m

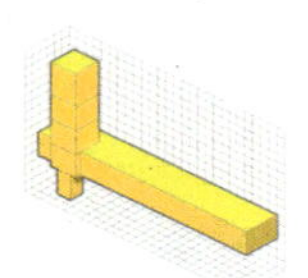
Dream Home Version

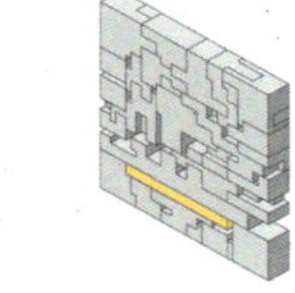
Resulting unit

50%
SATISFACTION

The dream of The Dude was to have a bowling lane with an elevator to access different amenities without any effort. Yes, he's Lazy. For him, the challenge was to ensure enough length for the bowling alley. After this negotiation, he managed to keep the initial L-Shape. The Lazy House is way smaller than what he envisioned, but its length and height still allow for all of his desired activities.

Blind Game Results

The Plateforms

User: The Teenager
Home: The Platforms
Desired activities: Platforms and plaza
Area: 104 m2
Volume: 515 m3

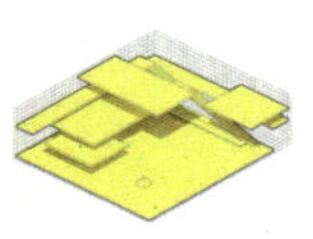

Dream Home Version

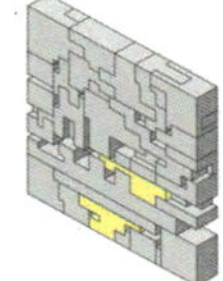

Resulting unit

83%
SATISFACTION

The dream home of the Teenager would be made of many platforms to meet with friends. In a way, it is an attempt to bring a sense of public space inside the housing slab. For him, platforms are a place to meet, discuss, and debate. After the Blind Game session, the vertical distribution of horizontal platforms was close to his original design. He managed to fit several platforms interlocked in between other players' apartments and distributed by a vertical core, following a strategy of stretching without detaching. This appears to be a valuable solution for fitting one continuous space inside the slab.

Blind Game Results

The Stack

User: The Stacker
Home: The Stack
Desired activities: Domestic space, working space, exhibition space
Area: 114 m2
Volume: 351 m3

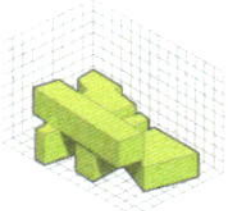
Dream Home Version

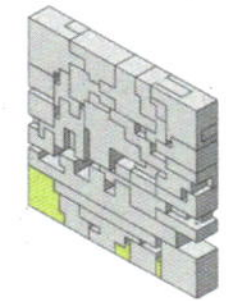
Resulting unit

86%
SATISFACTION

The Stacker wants to work and live in the same place. Her dream was to pile up spaces for different sets of activities – living, working and exhibiting. Instead of stacking, the game ended up scattering those nuclei throughout the slab. But that doesn't matter. Those different parts will later be connected by a semi-public street. In a way, it helps to separate work and living while remaining in the housing slab. The exhibition space is the largest. Actually, this collection of spaces could evolve, be shared, exchanged and reshaped as one's needs and desires change…

Blind Game Results

The Loop

User: The Roller Coaster Owner
Home: The Loop
Desired activities: Roller Coaster
Area: 92 m2
Volume: 428 m3

Dream Home Version

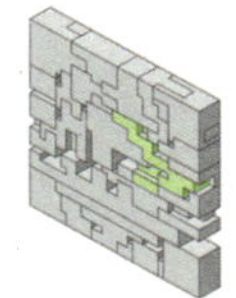
Resulting unit

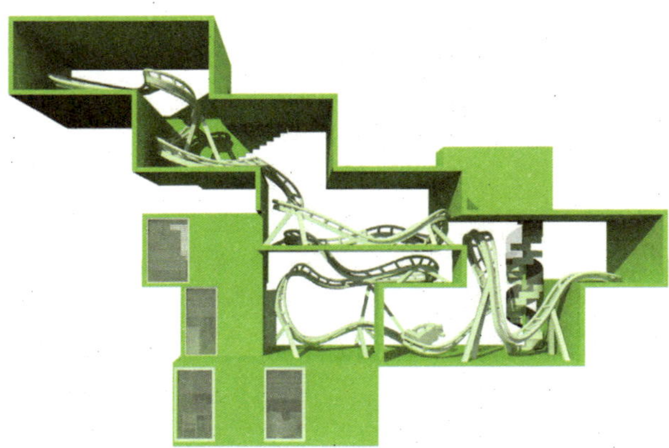

48%
SATISFACTION

How could one fit a roller coaster inside an apartment?! Throughout this process of negotiation with the neighbours, the Roller Coaster Owner had to compromise on scale in order to fulfil her dream. The roller coaster is way smaller than the one she wanted, but still manages to loop through the whole apartment, connecting different amenities. It was the only way to fit a looping roller coaster inside the slab. Sometimes, you need to compromise.

Blind Game Results

The Container House

User: The Prepper
Home: The Container House
Desired activities: Containers, storage
Area: 92 m2
Volume: 428 m3

Dream Home Version

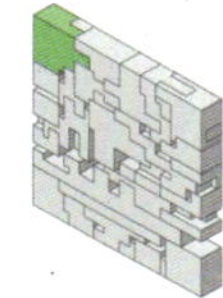

Resulting unit

71%
SATISFACTION

The result is not as spacious as the Prepper had hoped, but it does everything he needs it to do. All amenities are compressed and merged together, distributed on split levels. Kitchen, bedroom and living room are compacted together and merged in the same volume. A compact, easily defensible space is what the Prepper wanted, but perhaps it doesn't have to stay this small.

Blind Game Results

The Add-On

User: The Collector
Home: The Add-on
Desired activities: Yoga, painting, piano, photography, reading, etc.
Area: 115 m2
Volume: 544 m3

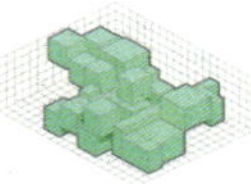

Dream Home Version

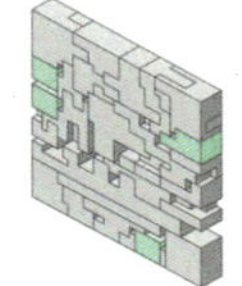

Resulting unit

103%
SATISFACTION

The Collector loves doing all sorts of activities. His desires in terms of space are rather modest compared to other neighbours. Here he has managed to get more volume than initially desired, and so got the highest satisfaction score of this game. The apartment is compact, easy to keep free of clutter, and has everything he needs in it. However, because of (or thanks to) another neighbour, the spaces and their functions have been separated in two, while still keeping direct indoor access. This means that he can live and work in two distinct, acoustically separated spaces in the same studio, opening up possibilities he hadn't envisioned.

Blind Game Results

The Jungle Gym

User: The 'Yamakasi'
Home: The Jungle Gym
Desired activities: Parkour gym
Area: 68 m2
Volume: 250 m3

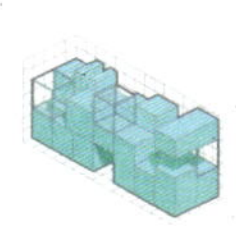
Dream Home Version

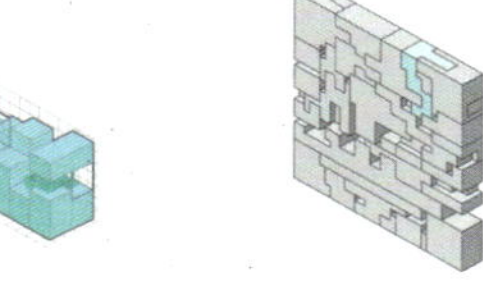
Resulting unit

90%
SATISFACTION

The Yamakasi loves to move and exercise. His passion is urban parkour and his dream was to perform inside his apartment. Throughout this negotiation, he has managed to define a dynamic, semi-urban interior. The vertical organization allows him to climb on the wall, jump across to other spaces and perform a range of movements for exercising and exploring. He actually was the only player trying to connect to the rooftop. He claimed it, but thinks it could be a shared terrace. Neighbours will have to visit him to access it. Despite the fact that the apartment is split into two, he got a high level of satisfaction, probably because of his rather reasonable demand for surface area and his specific interest in challenging spatial sequences.

Blind Game Results

The Stage

User: The Guitarist
Home: The Stage
Desired activities: Amplified stage
Area: 48 m2
Volume: 284 m3

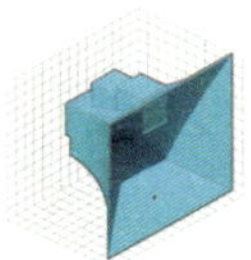

Dream Home Version

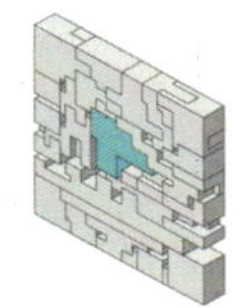

Resulting unit

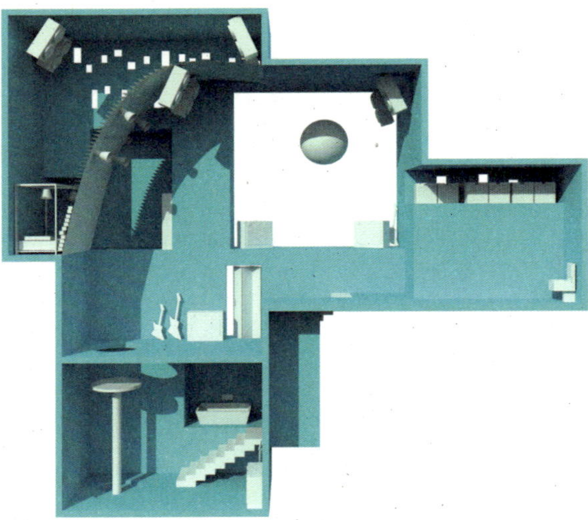

57%
SATISFACTION

The Guitarist plays heavy metal guitar. He loves to make noise. He wanted his house to look like a megaphone. The result is close to his desired shape, opening up towards the facade to spill sound into the city. Most of the private amenities are concentrated in the top left corner of the apartment, leaving enough space for private concerts and performances. From the stage, he can see his public, both inside the apartment and in the street. However, his degree of satisfaction is rather low, not because of the distribution or function, but because of the huge volume he originally dreamt of.

Blind Game Results

The Bookshelf

User: The Bibliomaniac
Home: The Bookshelf
Desired activities: Collection of books
Area: 96 m2
Volume: 378 m3

Dream Home Version

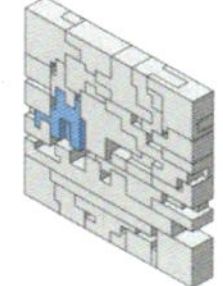

Resulting unit

84%
SATISFACTION

The dream of the Bibliomaniac is to live in a perfect library. However, the resulting house looks more like that of an academic who is in the midst of writing a thesis. Far from achieving a perfect display of her book collection, she discovered new ways of organizing books and amenities. Piles of books curate the different activities inside the apartment and offer new ways of managing a collection, revisiting its purpose and the possible shapes it can take. She only got a third of the space she thought she needed, but her dream has been met: her house is all bookshelf!

Blind Game Results

The Cave

User: The Artist
Home: The Cave
Desired activities: Studio and gallery
Area: 167 m2
Volume: 629 m3

Dream Home Version

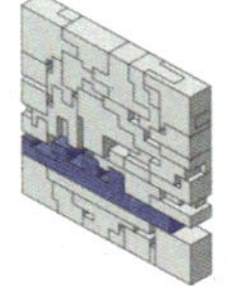
Resulting unit

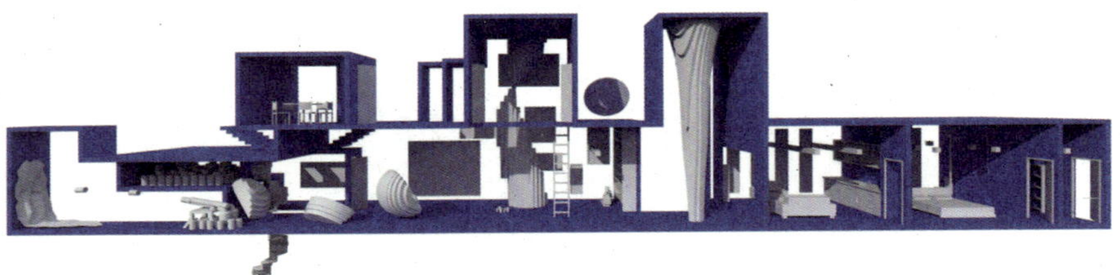

75%
SATISFACTION

The Artist loves to live in his gallery space. It's like a cave for him. He started out with an extravagant desire for space. His dream studio was 2,500 m2 distributed on a square of 50 by 50 metres. Those dimensions were obviously impossible to fit inside the slab depth of only three metres. The resulting apartment is actually 1/25 of the desired space – but it is still special. It is the longest in the whole slab, with a succession of spaces covering 167 m2 arranged on a single level. The height of the ceiling has been negotiated with other neighbours to obtain the maximum volume, and a range of lighting conditions for his studio.

Blind Game Results

The Mansion

User: The McMansioner
Home: The McMansion
Desired activities: Swimming pool, football field, garage, theatre, quad track
Area: 92 m2
Volume: 367 m3

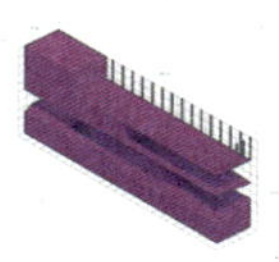
Dream Home Version

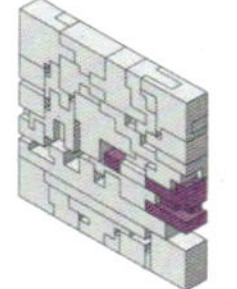
Resulting unit

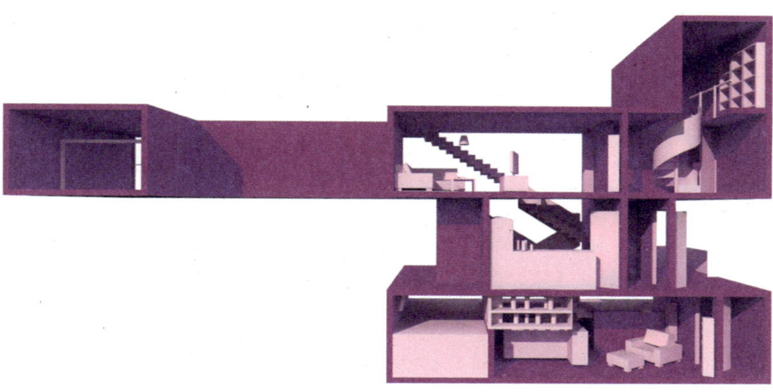

67%
SATISFACTION

Far from the traditional image of a mansion that the McMansioner aspires to, the house offers less than a third of the surface area he wanted. The amenities he dreamt of, such as a swimming pool and a football field, have been reduced to the scale of a bathtub and a single goal cage. He's not that pleased. If he reduced his ambitions, would he find greater satisfaction? In other words, is it absurd to desire living in a mansion in an urban environment?

Blind Game Results

The Russian Doll

User: The Meditative One
Home: The Russian Doll
Desired activities: Meditation room, filming studio
Area: 98 m2
Volume: 310 m3

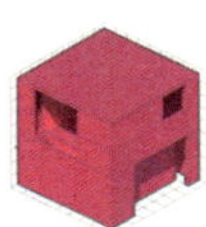

Dream Home Version

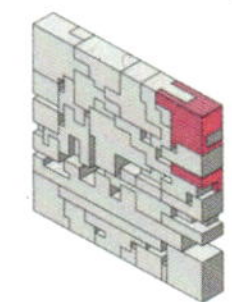

Resulting unit

92%

SATISFACTION

The results of the Blind Game made The Meditative One discover some unforeseen solutions. His goal was to achieve a certain degree of compactness, and he wouldn't have expected that splitting rooms and activities into different volumes (a studio and meditation space) could help him to clear his mind. Here again, work and domestic activities are spatially disconnected and provide more satisfaction than his preconceived idea of nesting one space within the other. He has to leave his apartment to go from one room to the other, but spatially dissociating activities gives him added peace of mind. Additionally, one space is at the top of the slab, so he can enjoy full daylight for his living and meditative activities, while his studio remains at the bottom, protected from direct sunlight.

Blind Game Results

The Jumping Castle

User: The Kid
Home: Jumping Castle
Desired activities: Trampoline, inflatable pool, hammock
Area: 46 m2
Volume: 323 m3

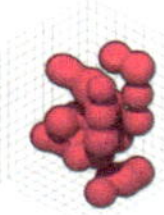

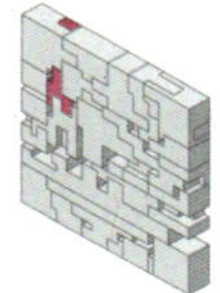

Dream Home Version

Resulting unit

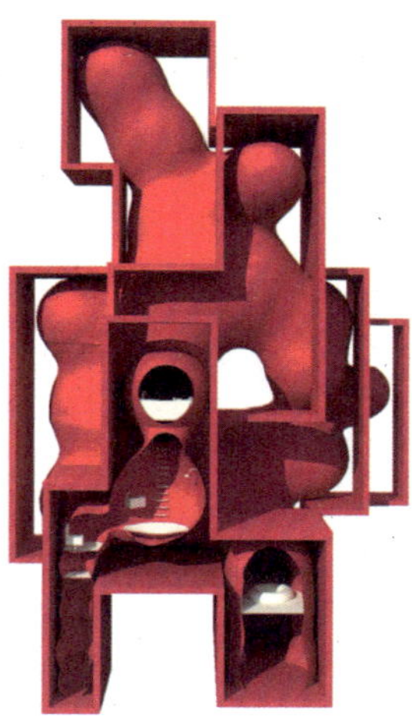

62%
SATISFACTION

This version of the Jumping Castle offers diverse spaces. That was one of The Kid's main desires. Here he can go from one playground to the other by sliding or bouncing through a blobby interior. The overall house is smaller than he originally envisioned, but all of his basic needs are met, clustered at the base of the apartment. The rest, a kind of inflatable organization expanding vertically, is for play. The rigidity of the voxels was an awkward fit for the free form of his desires, leaving a lot of leftover or undefined spaces that he's not very satisfied with. These show some of the limitations of this version of the game, and reveal the need for refining the resolution of the negotiations to accommodate more and more flexible desires.

(w)Ego Access

In the (w)Ego game, users only focus on their individual desires, without any restrictions apart from ego clashes with their neighbours. Taking egoism to the extreme meant putting aside the presence of common facilities or circulations for the time being. There was no core, no stairs, no elevator involved in the negotiation. Access, fire escapes, and mechanical, electrical and plumbing installations would come in a second phase of the game – as a post edit of the negotiation.

How would the residents reach their homes? On average, circulations take 15 per cent of the area in a collective housing building. We wanted to challenge the modern organization of housing circulation, with a bottom-up approach. A second phase of the game therefore incorporates the freedom of choice for each resident to define their access. A network of stairs, water pipes, electrical wires, would emerge from a multitude of individual desires. Infrastructure would follow everyone's needs and desires, connecting and going around the settled dream homes.

An add-on to the four different games was developed in order to provide access for each resident. The script was based on three goals: finding the shortest path for each resident between the block's entrance and their home; avoiding removing occupied voxels, trying to maximize the use of leftover spaces. An optimizer tested different possible routes to find the shortest route in accordance with each resident's desire.

1. Input outcome of the negotiation process.
2. Connect entrances.
3. Find shortest path.
4. Maximise the exploitation of empty voxels.
5. Avoid voxels occupied by basic needs (such as toilet, kitchen, bedroom, bathroom).
6. Optimize route.

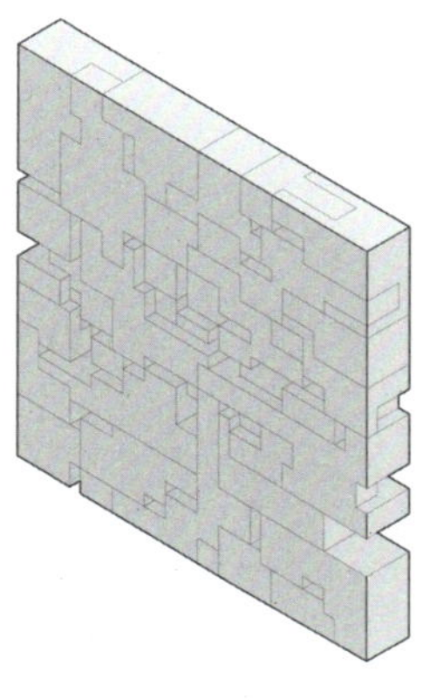

1

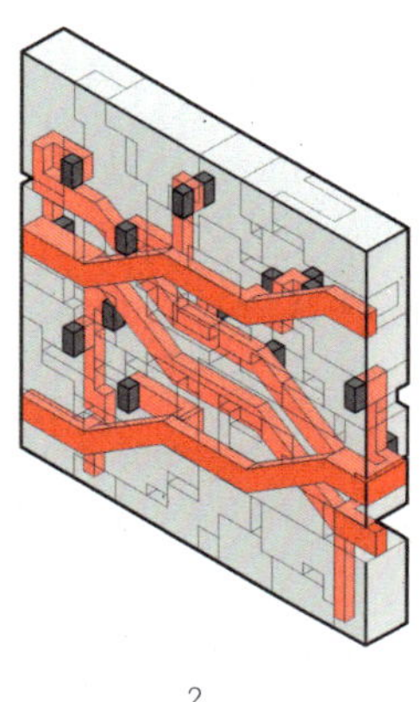

2

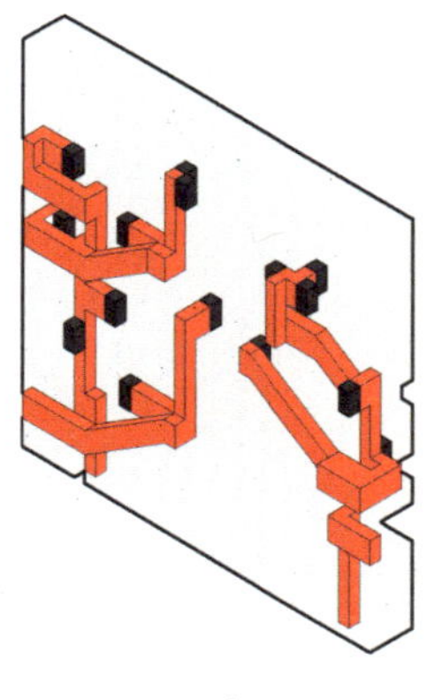

3

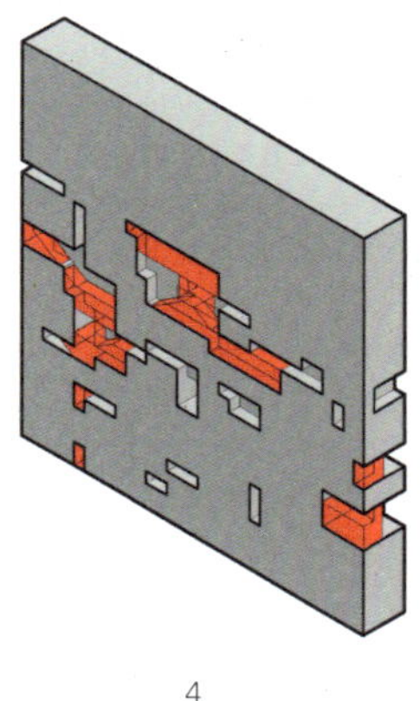

4

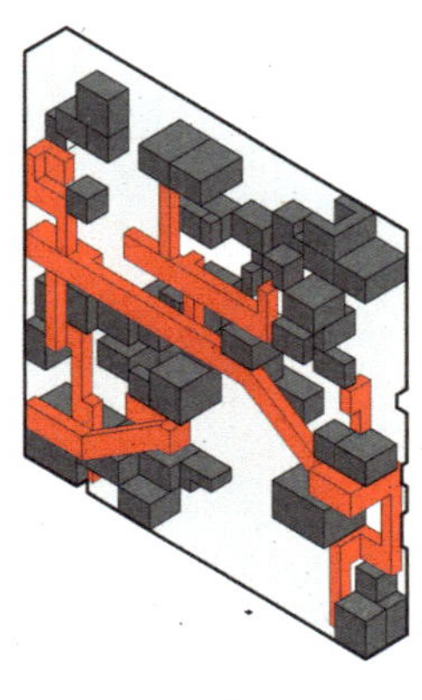

5

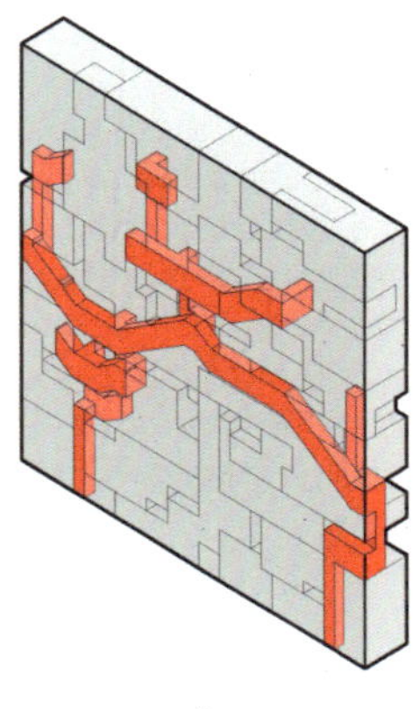

6

This Is It!

When all the pieces of this puzzle come together, an image of a lively, diverse, intense and compact community is revealed. Multiple lifestyles coexist, enhancing curiosity about others. (w)Ego starts from the user and ends with the collective. It is made by and of its residents' craziest fantasies, their unique fascinations and their differences. (w)Ego is about living in a dwelling that embodies one's desires in the density of a city. The facade acts like a section, revealing the interconnectedness and diversity of the homes that make up the slab, and a range of lifestyles and desires reminiscent of any piece of city fabric.

This model shows a frozen moment in which the villa, the loft, the studio, the penthouse, the duplex, the triplex, the tower, the panorama house, the playground and the concert space are so imbricated that they become one single entity. The materialization of (w)Ego assumes that the community, once mutually satisfied with the negotiation process, decides collectively to build this outcome.

The overall degree of satisfaction in the results gathered here is quite high. The spaces are smaller than expected but offer unique and unexpected spatial qualities, some of which have expanded the dreams and routines of their users. Adding furniture and details to our model (overleaf) helps to reveal those spatial qualities and expand the potential for curiosity, for exchange, for shared activities, play, working, and living together. (w)Ego comes alive.

Implementation test

The (w)Ego Slab

Through this experiment we have been exploring the role of gaming in designing solutions and processes that unlock residents' creativity. The observations captured in this chapter emerged during the conception of the game and the game design sessions, and have been key to reflecting on and questioning the potentials and limitations of (w)Ego.

(w)Ego is a learning process, just like becoming skilled at any game. A certain degree of trust and also a certain acceptance of losing control is required. Trust in the rules, trust in the game, trust in each other and trust in the computational model have all been challenged during the game sessions. Can we cheat? Is the programmer of the game the systematic winner? Is it possible to win at all? What happens if I do nothing? What if I prefer to team up? Can we share, and can that improve social and civic relationships? Can sharing, or other rules, enable people to be more creative, more curious, more innovative and more social? How does sharing enhance trust and communication towards each other? Does it change culture? Does it change society? And what about the dangers of the collective? Can sharing limit my dreams? How fair is (w)Ego? How can we reach equal or 100 per cent satisfaction for everyone? Is (w)Ego cheaper than other housing models, or more exclusive? Could it enable access to housing? Could it be used to train future generations to design their lives together?

We started our experiment by focusing on a negotiation between two neighbours. This allowed us to restrict the level of complexity at play, so that we could decode the rules, challenges and dynamics of negotiation. Once a set of rules operable for two users were established, the model became scalable to a large number of users. The only limitation was the computational power of our computers. At this stage we could dream big: What would a city look like if all its citizens were involved in its design through the principle of (w)Ego?

This exercise didn't try to fix a solution, but rather to set up the conditions for the unexpected to happen. New typologies were invented by the game itself, and players witnessed the malleability of their own dreams, informed and deformed by the collective. Design had been set aside for maximum empowerment. In the last games that were produced, players had a level of control comparable to a video game: they could go up, down, conquer space, fight and select one thing over another. All of these tools are not necessarily design tools, but they led to unexpected designs and spatial solutions that would have been impossible to preconceive. Roles in (w)Ego were completely shifted from the norm, leaving the figure of the spatial designer out of the process.

We also speculated about what would happen if we could develop the Automaton Game to a point where future residents could fill in a questionnaire, press enter, and wait for the software to generate an appropriate dream of a home. A refined version of the Automaton Game could redefine the market and profession as we know it, as well as the way we teach architecture. Would such a tool rarefy the role of the architect to the point of questioning whether it should exist at all, or might it open up opportunities for creating (and working out how and where to build) an ever more personalized, satisfying and responsive residential architecture?

Longitudinal section of the Blind Game result

Longitudinal section of the Blind Game result – part 1

Longitudinal section of the Elind Game result – part 2

Physical model resulting from the Blind Game, scale 1:50

View of the physical model resulting from the Blind Game, scale 1:50

Building (w)Ego

The Why Factory (TU Delft), MVRDV for Dutch Design Week 2017 and Shenzhen Architecture Biennale 2017

Research and concept design: The Why Factory (TU Delft)
Definitive design and construction drawings: MVRDV

Text by Adrien Ravon

Every autumn, the city of Eindhoven turns into an international stage for design, hosting 350,000 visitors during Dutch Design Week. In the context of Winy Maas' ambassadorship for the 2017 edition, The Why Factory and MVRDV collaborated to bring the (w)Ego research to life on the streets of Eindhoven. For nine days, visitors were invited to climb through, sit on, lie down in and experience a 1:1 model of the (w)Ego House. The nine-metre high slab block was made up of nine unique units, each fulfilling the egoistic demand of its imagined inhabitant. When squeezed together, the collection of rooms become more than a sum of egos: they are structurally interdependent and, collectively, can offer something more to their host city.

Later that year, the (w)Ego House was built again for the Shenzhen Biennale, held in the urban village of Nantou Old Town, an event that received more than 550,000 visitors. Both iterations of this 'frozen' design experiment opened up questions about resolution, changing desires and what adaptable architecture could bring to urban settings.

This chapter reflects on (w)Ego as a performative housing prototype that invites the public to reflect on the future of collective housing: Could the (w)Ego experiment point the way to a more sustainable and equitable way of living, and to more communicative, human-centred built environments?

The (w)Ego House

The (w)Ego House is an installation first built on the market square of the city of Eindhoven and then installed in Nantou urban village in Shenzhen. It measures 9 m wide by 9 m tall, and is 3 m deep. The tailor-made wooden structure stands on top of a raised platform, 15 m wide by 9 m deep, whic h provides stability. On the ground floor, nine colourful doors lead to nine unique living units defined by their inhabitant's desires: The Window, The Jungle, The Grotto, The Panopticon, The Skyroom, The Stairs, The Bookshelf, The Tribune and The Waterfall. Its two facades, different on each side, reveal the interior spatial diversity and give the public glimpses of the complex imbrication of this three-dimensional puzzle, where shapes and colours are so knotted together that it is hard to isolate individual units just by looking.

Each unit has a double bed, a toilet, a shower, a sink and a private access, accommodating the basic needs of its potential inhabitant; all have distinct light, exterior views and circulation. As in the (w)Ego Game, these rooms are the building blocks of the collective building.

How buildable is this (w)Egoistic slab, in which the structure, amenities, circulation and mechanical, electrical and plumbing installations are shaped by the desires of each inhabitant? Another level of negotiation then comes into play, beyond agreeing about boundaries with your neighbour: the negotiation between physics, cost, structural integrity, building regulations, safety, comfort, and the multitude of individual desires imbedded in the slab.

Elevation 1

Elevation 2

The (w)Ego Rooms – 1

Each room represents a personalized world with singular characteristics and a unique atmosphere. Together, they form a kind of ecosystem – a world made of several independent smaller worlds.

Stepping into The Jungle, visitors enter a lush wilderness, discovering a succession of spaces filled with plants. Like in a tropical forest, vegetation hangs from the top, grows from the walls and spreads all over the floors, creating different micro climatic zones around the room's amenities. Some plants enjoy the humidity of the bathroom while others participate in the acoustic isolation of the ceiling. When we zoom out, The Jungle acts as the green lung of the slab and its surroundings.

Next door, a guitar player is sitting on the edge of The Window, located in the bottom centre of the slab. This room offers a long horizontal plain window, connected in some parts with the street and acting as a stage for public performances.

On the ground level, a tiny beige entrance invites visitors to enter The Grotto. This hidden habitable volume is roomier than its entrance suggests. From the outside, visitors can only see one hole through which they could crawl down. Once inside, it feels like a vaulted grotto, and is painted in luxurious gold. The grotto acts as the foundation of the whole slab, on which all other rooms are stacked.

Dream version **Negotiation outcome**

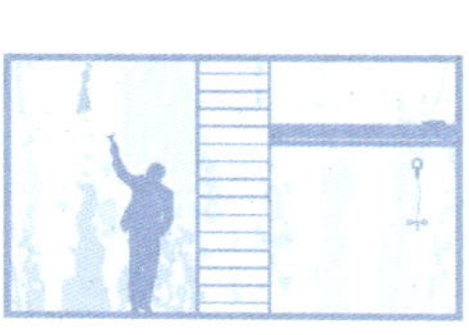

The Window

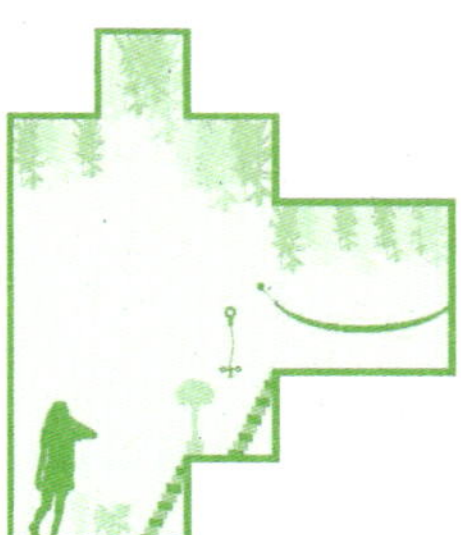

The Jungle

The Grotto

The (w)Ego Rooms – 2

Have you ever dreamt of looking in all directions simultaneously? In The Panopticon, the room is not a simple transversal unit. It offers multiple views of the city. Surrounded by mirrored walls, floors and ceilings, the space acts both as a periscope, reflecting other views into the space, and simultaneously as a kaleidoscope: breaking up and reframing multiple perspectives. This interior space also reflects the surrounding skyline back down to passers-by at street level, opening up this privileged view to the public.

Entering from the side, a yellow door leads visitors up a series of ladders and through a steep tunnel to The Skyroom. This route goes through five other neighbours' rooms before reaching the highest place in the slab. At the top, visitors can contemplate the sky, or city life, from a bed raised eight metres above the square.

An orange door is an invitation to climb up alternating stairs that revolve around other units. In this room one becomes active, by moving around – which is to say up or down. In The Stairs you literally live on a staircase: with a bed, shower, toilet and other facilities, as well as any possible activity, all found on the steps.

Dream version **Negotiation outcome**

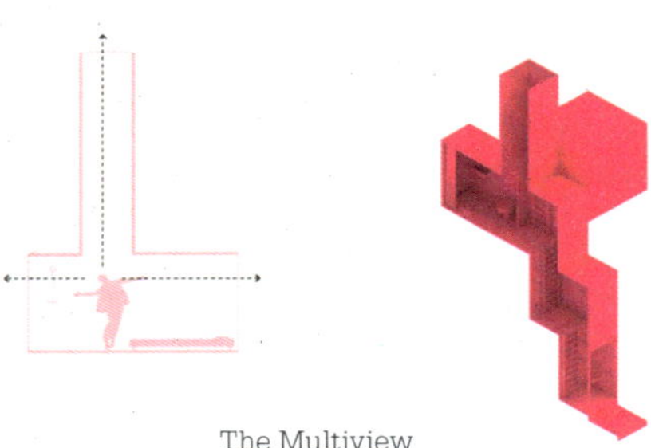

The Multiview

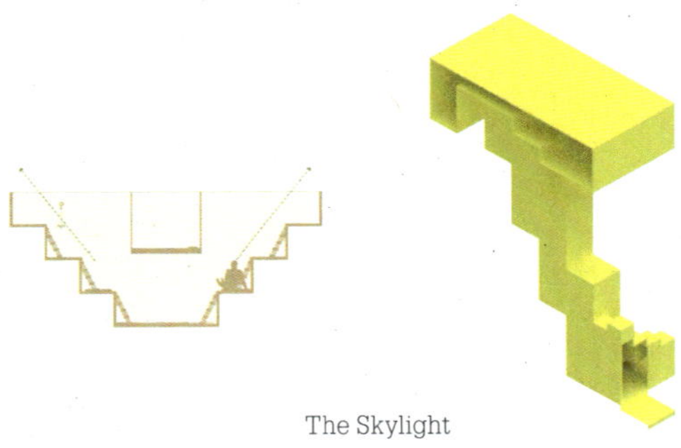

The Skylight

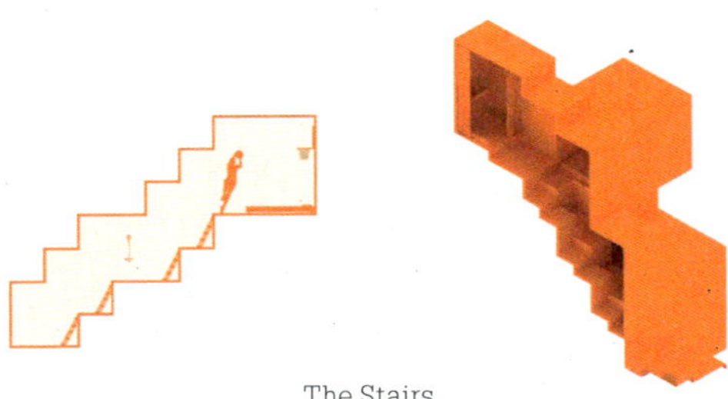

The Stairs

The (w)Ego Rooms – 3

In The Bookshelf, the surface of the walls is maximized, allowing for the display of a large collection of books. Like in a traditional library, some books can only be accessed by climbing up a tall ladder. Here one nine-metre high wall provides the room with the most space for storage. To reach the bed, one must walk up past book shelves, seeing at a glance and sequentially the whole library, which is also visible to passers-by.

Opening a red door, visitors enter a private theatre. Being in this room is like standing on a tribune, which can become a place to watch or a place to perform. As with The Stairs, amenities are organized on the steps. By opening up the facade, The Tribune can form part of the public realm, extending the city square into the slab and offering the public a space to gather, shelter or stage an event.

The Waterfall is a room where all the pipes of the eight other rooms converge, cascading down this room's levels to create a dreamy micro-climate. In The Waterfall, surrounded by blue, you can take a six-metre high shower, as if you were bathing in a cascade. At the right temperature, the splashing foam at the bottom can become a steam bath or a spa. The room acts like a climatic regulator for the whole slab and its surroundings.

Dream version | **Negotiation outcome**

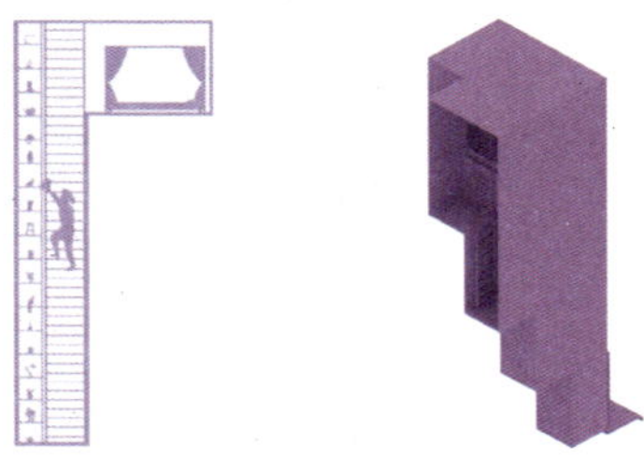

The Bookshelf

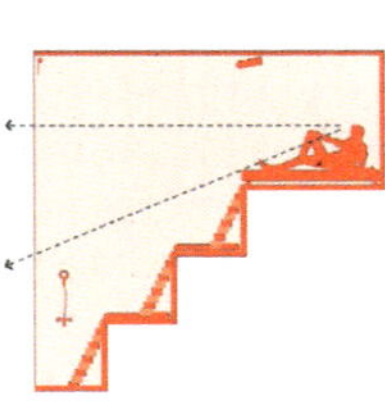

The Tribune

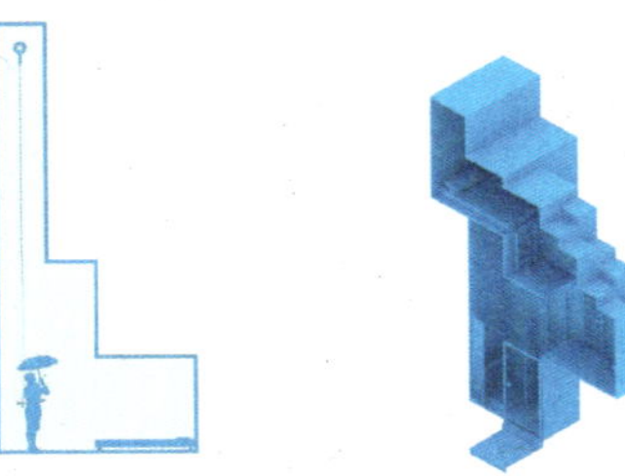

The Waterfall

The (w)Ego Block

The nine rooms support each other. Their overlaps become potentials rather than limitations. With this set of complex interrelations at play, the slab somehow becomes more sustainable and performative than if all the rooms existed alone. The Waterfall regulates climate, The Jungle mitigates temperature and cleans up the air, The Tribune engages with public space, The Cave supports the rest of the slab, and The Stairs promote an active lifestyle, while The Panopticon and The Bookshelf offer multiple perspectives, through new views of the city and access to an extensive library. Together they form an urban, structural, programmatic and environmental ecosystem for the city.

The (w)Ego installation showcased just one of the countless possible outcomes from the negotiation process between nine individuals. Just like when a video game is paused, the 1:1 model represents a frozen moment of this collective design process.

As we scaled up this moment into a 1:1 prototype, the digital voxels became standardized cubes of 1 × 1 × 1 m made from wooden panels – each tagged with a specific number indicating its position in the slab. The panels were assembled together on site in one day, stacked from the bottom to the top like a three-dimensional Tetris game.

When the way the rooms were stacked was not self-supporting, wooden columns were added to carry the load of other rooms. Could those extra columns have been avoided if a structural parameter had been pre-scripted in the digital version of the game? With the construction of the 1:1 model, some components and parameters that were abstracted or not visible in the digital version were exposed and questioned.

For example, the building process revealed the necessity to work and negotiate at a higher resolution. The 1 × 1 m panels were small enough to be carried by one person, and could be easily assembled, disassembled, transported and reassembled. However, the standardized dimension of those modules could not always accommodate specific and more refined solutions. Sometimes, we would have to break the logic of the 1 × 1 m panels and increase the detail of negotiation between neighbours. Some parts of the slab were therefore built with 50 cm panels for split levels, or 25 cm for the steps of a stair. The negotiation became more detailed and more ergonomic at these points. We realized that the resolution at which we negotiate our ideal space could vary, going up or down according to what each space or negotiation process requires. A negotiation held in centimetres could define furniture, fixings, and spaces that are directly based on the human body, opening up the potential to negotiate finer grain detail within dividing walls.

Axonometric view 1

Axonometric view 2

Floorplan - Level 01

Floorplan - Level 02

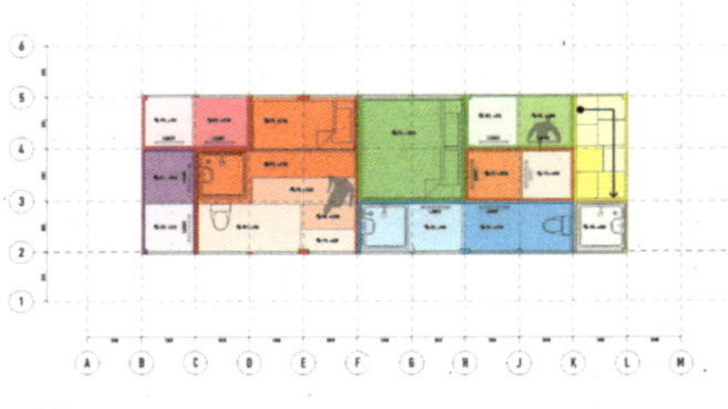

Floorplan - Level 03

Floorplan - Level 04

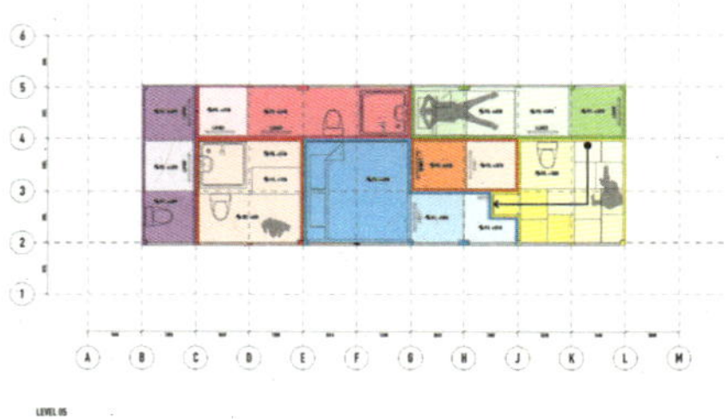

Floorplan - Level 05

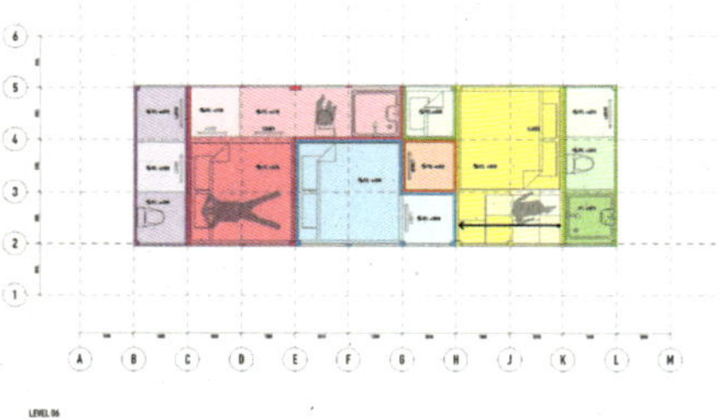

Floorplan - Level 06

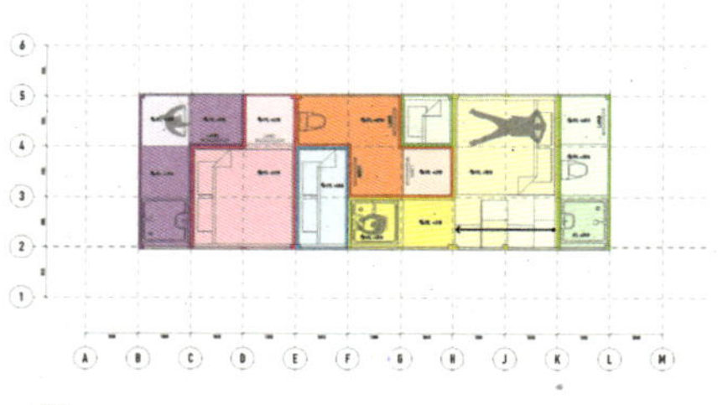

Floorplan - Level 07

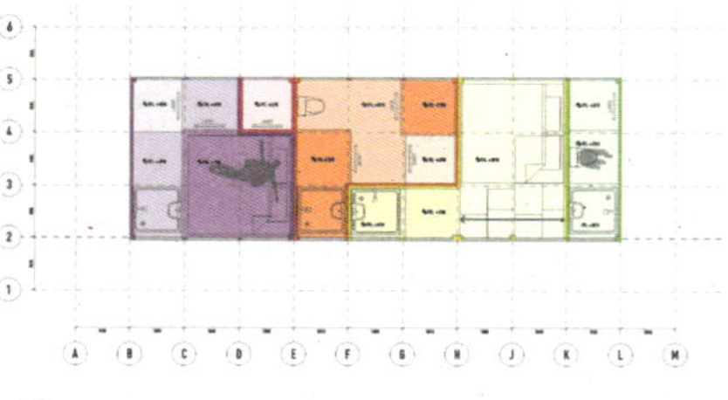

Floorplan - Level 08

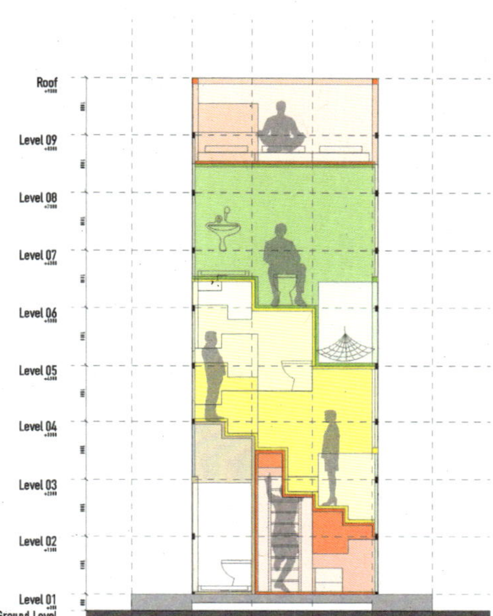

Lateral section

Longitudinal section

(w)Ego Eindhoven

It's late October, in 2017. On the market square of Eindhoven, visitors walk around the (w)Ego House. From the terraces and cafes surrounding the square, they look at the colourful facade, comparing the different rooms, mentally decomposing the building process, and imagining how it could evolve. Visitors try to map which door leads to which room before entering. How would it feel to spend a night in one of those rooms? Which one would you choose? Could those two merge, shift or move? What would your ideal room be, given all this choice? What might you negotiate hardest for, and what wouldn't you mind compromising on?

A hide and seek game is improvised, there's music in one room, someone is waving out from another and children have quickly worked out how to interact across and between the spaces. A collective choreography starts to emerge. As visitors act and react, they begin creating something bigger than themselves, collectively engaging with the question of how the building came to be and what it could become.

The slab is not completely finished. This deliberate design decision aims to reveal the slab's potential evolution. It invites visitors to see more, to explore its latent potential, to wonder about its future. (w)Ego could become something else. It could change over the nine days of the design week. It could move every 24 hours, reconfiguring the rooms in response to its visitors' dreams.

(w)Ego is a public invitation to dream of a future architecture where desires are not static, and neither are our environments. (w)Ego aims to show that a responsive, evolutionary and flexible architecture is possible. (w)Ego brings together a belief that buildings can, and should, meet our needs at every moment with an urgent call to optimize the use of our limited urban space.

View from the market square in Eindhoven, The Netherlands

The Skylight

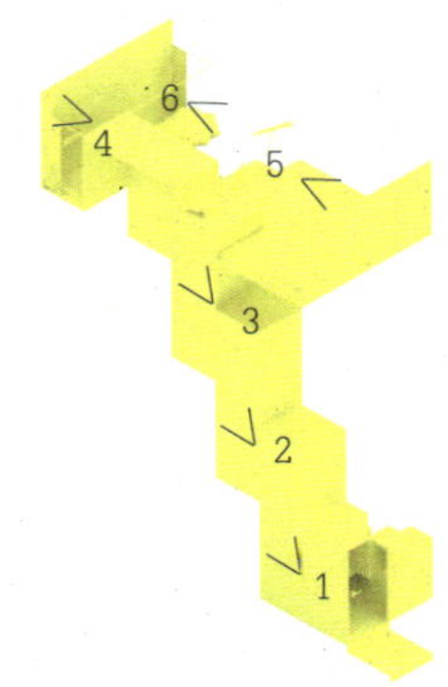

1

2

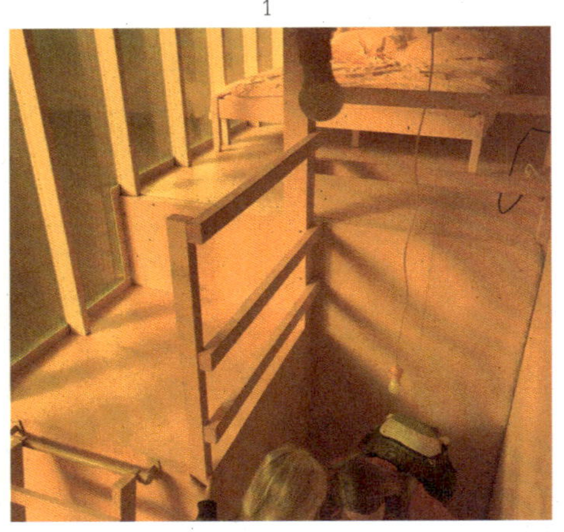

3

4

5

6

The Tribune

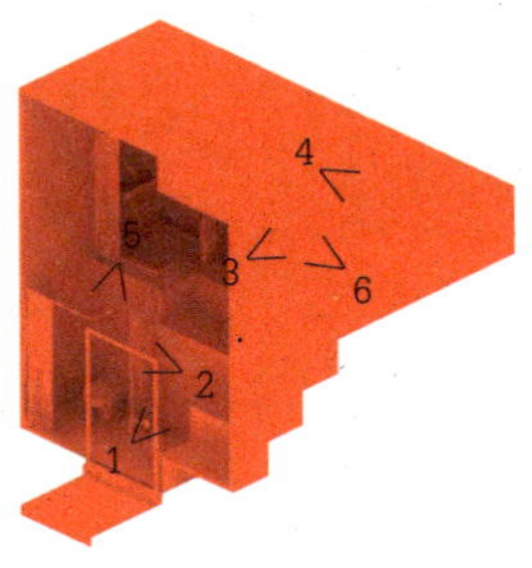

1

2

3

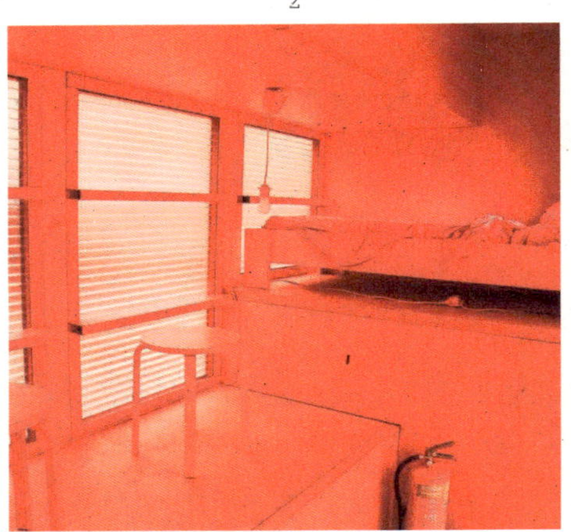
4

5

6

The Stairs

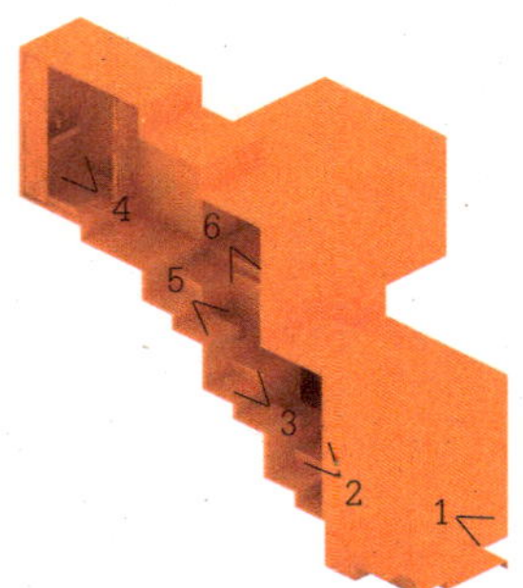

1

2

3

4

5

6

(w)Ego Eindhoven

Brought to life by thousands of visitors, the facade displays the negotiation of new possibilities and new sets of questions opened up by the building of the (w)Ego slab block at 1:1.

MINT
MINT
VOOR

(w)Ego Eindhoven

What impact would (w)Ego have in different contexts and densities?

For example, does (w)Ego tell the same story or push the same boundaries and preconceptions in the city centre of Eindhoven and in

an urban village in Shenzhen?

(w)Ego Shenzen

The Why Factory (TU Delft) and MVRDV were invited by curator and critic Hou Hanru, architects Liu Xiaodu and Meng Yan, founding partners of URBANUS, artist Yang Yong and urban researcher Zhu Ye, to participate in

the 7th Bi-City Biennale of Urbanism, hosted in Shenzhen, entitled 'Cities, Grow in Difference'.

(w)Ego Shenzen

On 15 December 2017, the (w)Ego House was opened again in the urban village of Nantou Old Town, in Shenzen. After welcoming more than 550,000 visitors, it received an Architectural Media Jury Award at

the 7th Bi-City Biennale of Urbanism
and Architecture

Part 3

Desires are not static. The 1:1 model built in Eindhoven and Shenzhen represented one frozen version of this dynamic puzzle. But as we grow up and get older, our housing needs and desires change. Over a lifespan, the size and make-up of homes and households evolve. Based on a recent US census, the average American moves home 11 times in their life [10]. Even in one day, the needs and desires that make up our ideal dwelling vary drastically. During the day, most homes are vacant. While we sleep, bedrooms are generally the only space in use. And when we are throwing a party with a large number of guests, we often dream of pushing out the walls to make more space.

What if we could? As what we need from our homes changes and evolves over time, could these grow, move, shrink, reconfigure and adapt to different situations? What materials and technology could allow for such flexibility? How can we design walls that move to suit us? How would it feel to live in a home in which the layout is being constantly reconfigured? Could buildings change as fast as we do? How might adaptability make our cities less vacant? Building on visions or experiments such as Cedric Price's Fun Palace or the Schröder House in Utrecht by Gerrit Rietveld, this chapter explores the expanded and real-world potential of housing adaptability.

OntheGo

The Sketch

The Why Factory (TU Delft) with RMIT Melbourne and Bezalel Academy, Jerusalem

Students: Temitope Adesina, Tom Asiskovich, Mordechai Bachar, Yuval Bar-Adon, Manor Brown, Philip Chang, William Christian, Bryan Chung, Dookee Chung, Hadassah Lehman Cohen, Tomer Deren Peretz, Stav Dror, Nadav Etkin, Rotem Gilboa, Michael Ifergan, Katherine Kai-Cin Jou, Neal Kaldor, Liran Messer, Bradley Mitchell, Tamar Over, Jarrod Palmier, Shelly Shmulewich Shalev, Omry Spasser, Laura Szymon, Jian Yang

Tutors: Winy Maas, Javier Arpa Fernández, Felix Madrazo, Adrien Ravon, Vivian Mitsogianni, Ben Milbourne, Ifat Finkelman, Deborah Pinto Fdeda

Text by Vivian Mitsogianni and Ben Milbourne

Until now we have focused on the construction of a permanent dwelling that can fulfil our sedentary dreams of home and settlement, even as our needs and desires change. In this chapter, we start exploring modes of temporary living for populations on the move. As humans continue to leave their homes in search of work, land, education, safety, opportunity or leisure, how could the design of our cities accommodate their dream homes on arrival?

As with the other experiments in this book, we start with a predefined envelope, and the principle that no space should be wasted: the (w)Ego Hotel will cater to all those that need it, without ever leaving vacancies. In this chapter, we explore the dynamic process of accommodating the variable needs of transient guests. What sort of organizing principle is needed in order to accomplish 100 per cent occupancy, 100 per cent of the time for a fluctuating set of users and needs? How might sets of needs take up varying amounts of space, according to competing demand? How much disappointment can a guest take, when expectations and space are compressed to a minimum? Can a guest's needs fill the space when vacancies are low? How can we use spatial resources to their maximum potential?

In the (w)Ego Hotel, only the envelope and a limited number of reconfigurable elements are fixed, with occupancy and configuration changing in real time. Students developed a number of architectural solutions for negotiating the wishes of a wide variety of guests dynamically, responding to the availability of space and how the rooms relate: maximum customization for maximum, constant, satisfaction.

The (w)Ego Hotel

This hotel maintains a strict 100 per cent occupancy policy. Because of this, the volume of your room may not stay constant during your stay. During high season, your room might shrink and change dramatically. Please stay calm. Here nothing is fixed, but we guarantee that your basic needs will be satisfied.

You will have entered your desires into our website at the time of booking. We kindly advise you to read the room manual prior to your stay, and to fill in the registration form attentively. When you arrive, don't go to reception – it does not exist. Please wait at the entrance for your personal moving circulation to arrive. In some cases, you may be asked to actively take part in reformatting your room and its fixtures. Your room space will be designed according to your personal booking preferences, and may continue to adapt to you throughout your stay; please note that all room spaces may be affected by other guests' desires at any time.

Things will change. Please don't panic. Enjoy your stay.

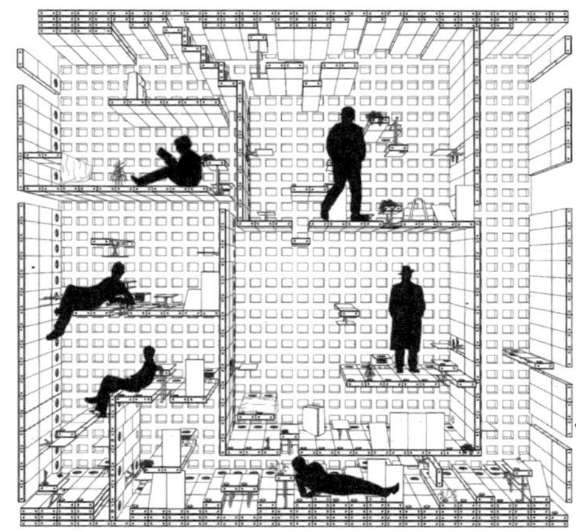

6 guests occupancy

12 guests occupancy

Introducing Time

This chapter takes as a point of departure questions around temporary housing for populations on the move and how our cities can meet the needs of mobile populations. The hotel as a type – a pit stop for those on the go, and a point of welcome to a new city – is, in this context, a productive area for speculation on an architecture that is adaptable and responsive to increasing transience.

The preceding iterations of (w)Ego research utilize multi-unit

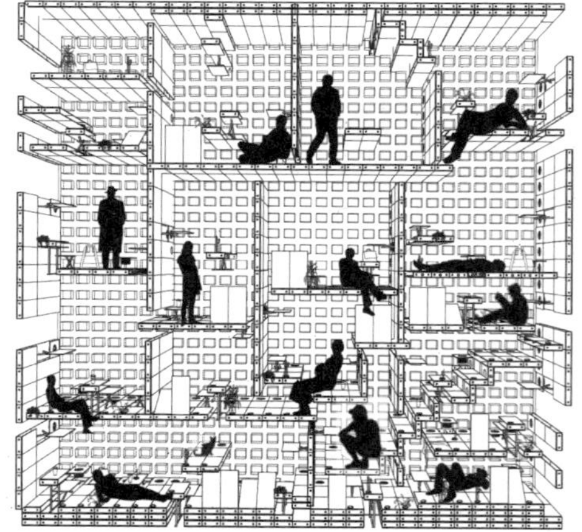

24 guests occupancy

housing as a lens to investigate the tension between the desires of individual occupants (egos) and the collective spatial outcome of the interplay of these desires: (w)Ego. These earlier investigations largely omitted the question of time, or more specifically what happens when our desires or our spatial requirements change. While what we need from our home changes as we age, or as our tastes or lifestyles change, these changes occur relatively slowly. In contrast, temporary housing, and in particular the hotel in its various forms, must accommodate a wide variety of desires and needs, and it must do so with a much greater turn-over of occupants than other forms of housing. This can create characterless spaces, resilient to the projections of any visitor, but satisfying few.

The (w)Ego Hotel speculates on the impact that constant and rapid changes can have on the relationship between personal desire and spatial configuration – and the tension that can build up between them over time. It is a first step in an exploration of the potential for flexible architecture to develop in new directions, stretching what flexibility in our built environment could mean.

Seeing Beyond the Stars

The conventional approach to catering for a variety of needs or desires is to differentiate hotels via a standardized rating or 'star' system, as a proxy for the type and quality of each hotel's offer. While this system can accommodate guests with different expectations (and budgets), it does so in a highly impersonal way. For example, HOTREC (Hotels, Restaurants & Cafes in Europe), the organization administering the European star system, requires all 5-star hotels to provide a personalized greeting for each guest along with fresh flowers or a present in the room on arrival. Some guests want to be left alone and some hate flowers. How can a hotel realistically please everyone?

Hotels must also negotiate fluctuating levels of occupancy. Resource optimization and financial return fluctuate wildly with low and high seasons: the cost of running a hotel at 10 per cent occupancy is nearly the same as running it at 100 per cent occupancy. Is this built-in variability sustainable today, as we grow increasingly aware of the need to use our limited spatial resources in as sustainable a way as possible?

Luxury for Everyone

The (w)Ego Hotel imagines that luxury is not standardized, as in the 'personalized' greeting of a 5-star hotel, but rather a genuinely tailored space furnished with the things and facilities that you need and want – and without those that you don't.

Could this hotel simultaneously offer all the star ratings – and would these even mean something, if you knew, 100 per cent guaranteed, that you'd find your ideal room when checking in? What if standardized expectations could be replaced with a room that would be responsive to your desires not just when you book and check in, but throughout your stay?

And could this responsive hotel function without empty rooms, while always being able to make room for new guests – so that every guest was always given as generous a space as possible? What would 100 per cent occupancy look and feel like with only one guest? How might this guest's needs still be met when sharing the space with another 39 guests? How might it be technically possible to have this much change within a set space?

Real-Time Customization

We tested these speculations within an envelope of 9 m × 2.1 m × 9 m, or 27,000 voxels (units of volume equivalent to a pixel). The task was to develop a continuously reconfigurable architecture that not only met the varied and changing needs of a fluctuating number of guests, but also had 100 per cent occupancy, 100 per cent of the time.

The first challenge is identifying the needs of each individual guest. Students collectively designed a hotel booking website interface that involved the completion of a questionnaire. Along with standard questions (number of beds, duration of stay), we asked questions aimed at evaluating other personal preferences, such as desired view and location, the amount and size of window openings, the size of bed, shower and toilet, preference for spatial configuration, and other personal preferences relating to the use of a room.

On arrival, the check-in procedure then translates the guest's desires into a spatial configuration expressed as an allocation of 'voxels' (volume), its composition and a set of specific facilities or services – all in relation to how many other occupants are already in the hotel, and in negotiation with their desires. This interface builds on the earlier iterations of the research, gamifying the relationships between occupiers to negotiate potentially conflicting interests to arrive at the optimal spatial arrangement.

In order to test different numbers and combinations of occupants and their desires over time, we developed a set of exaggeratedly different characters, giving all of them occupations, ages and other demographic and personal data, including fictional stories and needs.

Catalogue Of Systems

How can the hotel physically change to accommodate an ever-changing environment and ever-changing levels of occupation? We set out a range of structural and technical building systems that could be used to physically and formally make this possible.

This suite of strategies investigates the physical implementation of voxel arrangements, and more importantly how to transition from one voxel configuration to another as the hotel's internal configuration recalibrates in accordance with the departure and arrival of guests. These initial strategies included inflatable volumes whose expansion is limited by the pressure of adjacent rooms; Voronoi volumes that are based on a combination of retractable rods and tensile surfaces, optimising the subdivision of the hotel by defining the arrival/departure of guests as points within the Voronoi field; and tensile surfaces that roll and unroll from suspended rods, dividing rooms to accommodate new guests, or retracting to connect adjacent rooms as guests depart.

Each strategy was evaluated against a range of criteria, including the range of spaces that they made possible and whether they allowed for multiple room configurations; whether the scheme is buildable and achievable with current commercial technology; and whether guests could remain happy with different levels of occupancy, as the room sizes changed to facilitate greater

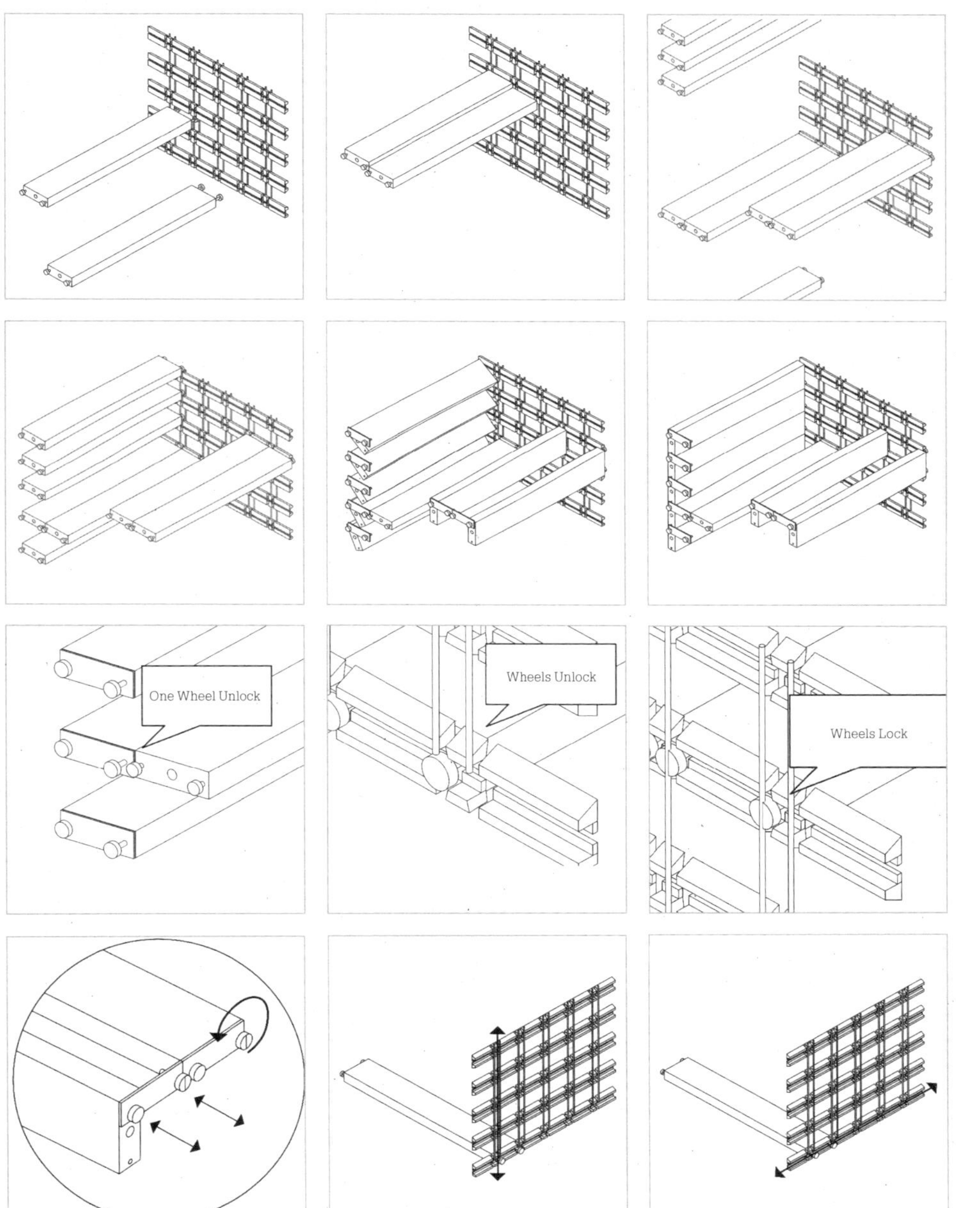

Planks and rails system

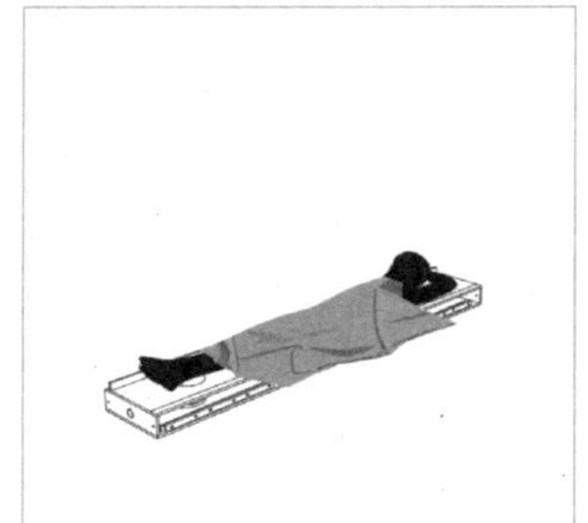

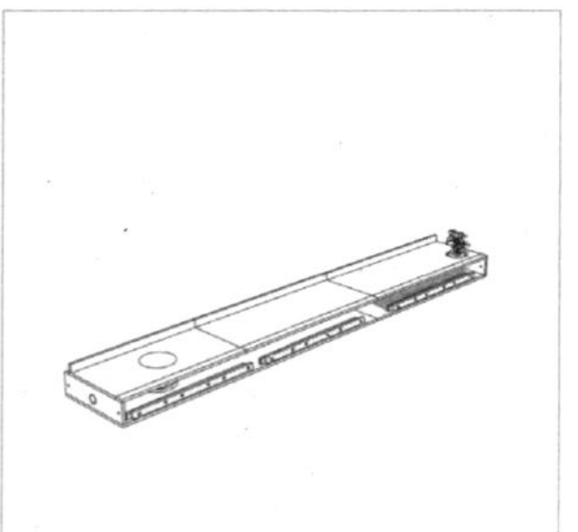

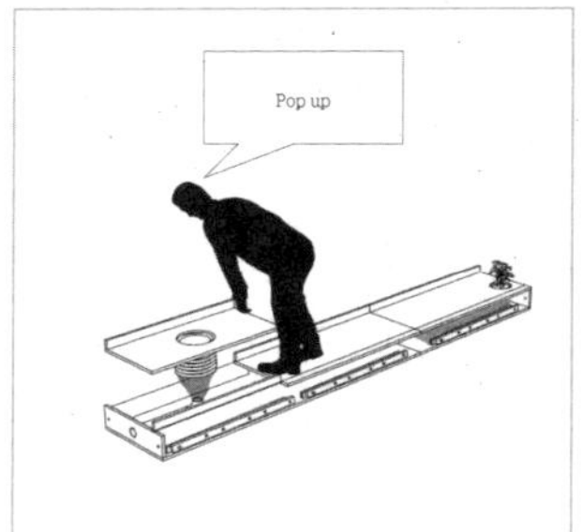

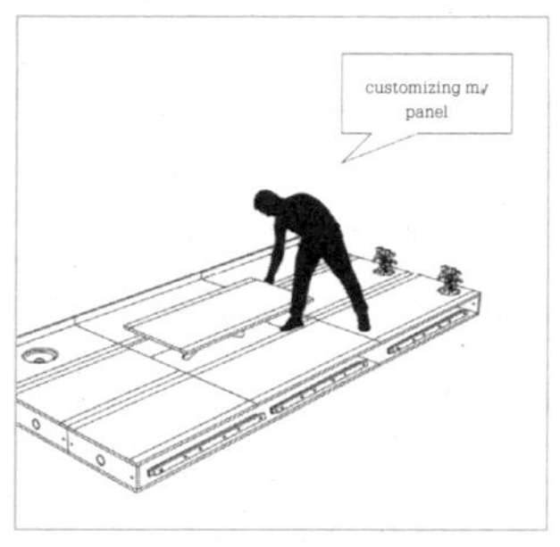

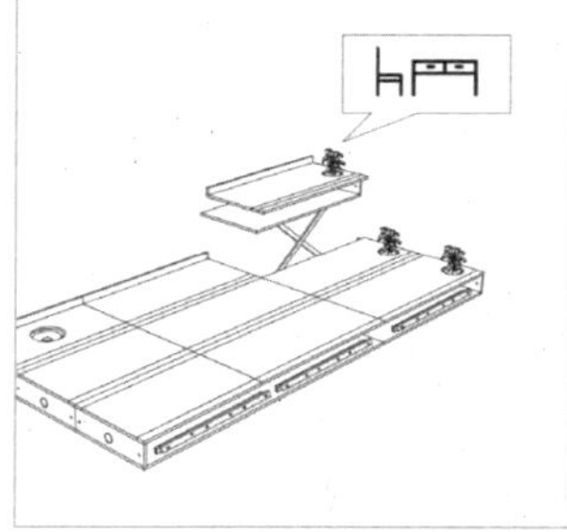
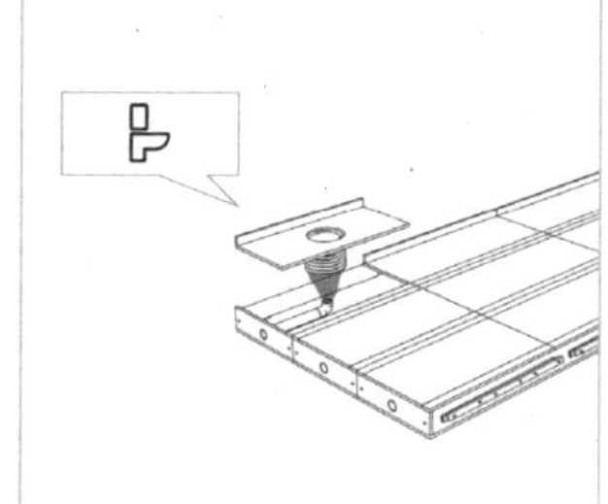

Planks – floor system

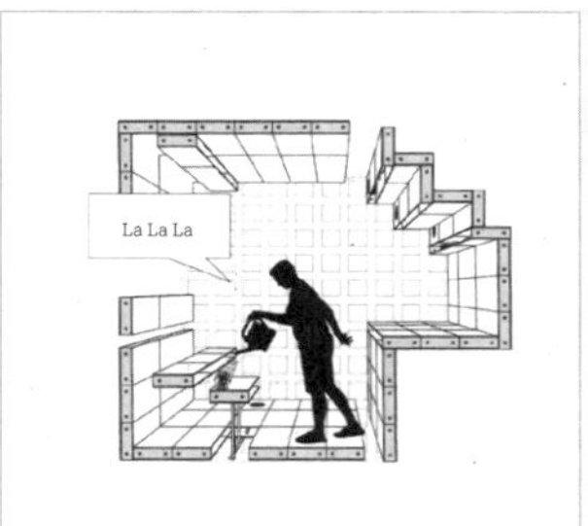

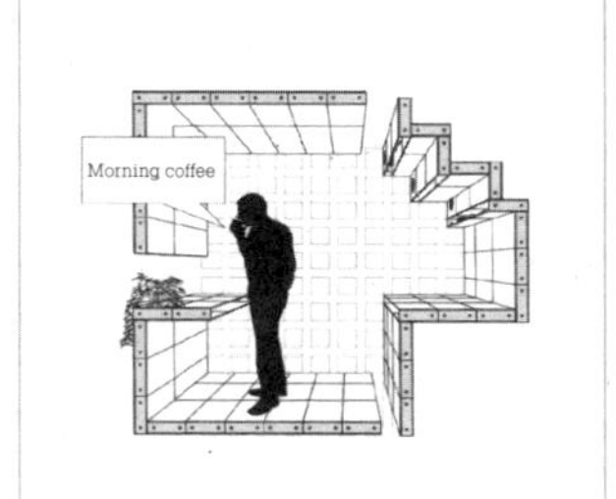

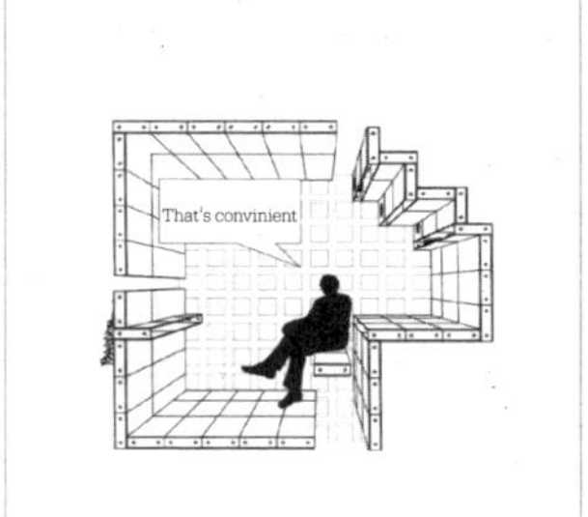

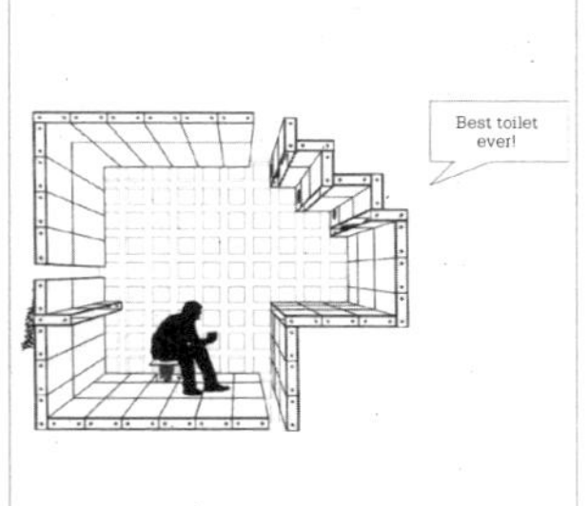

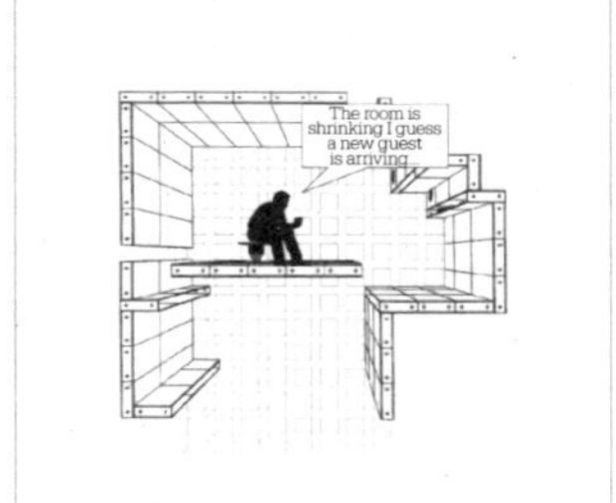

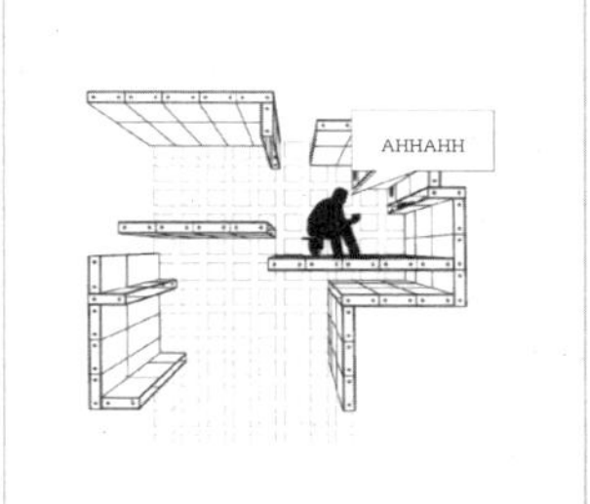

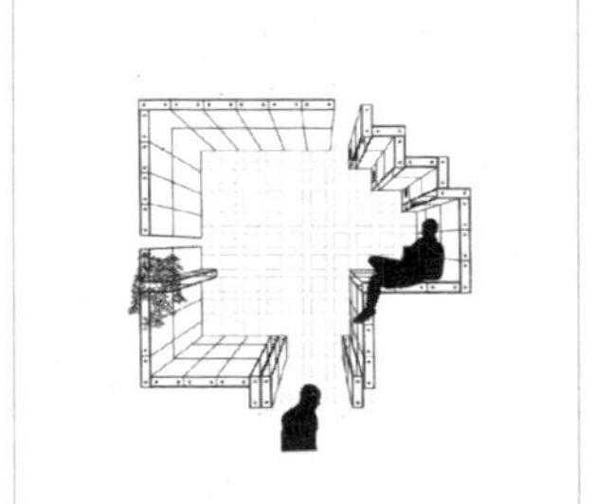

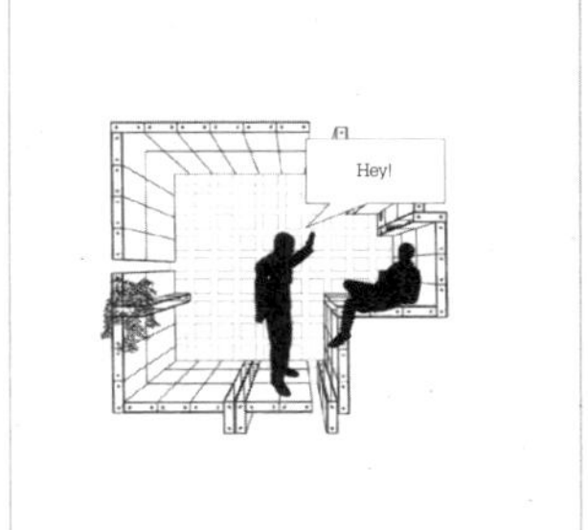

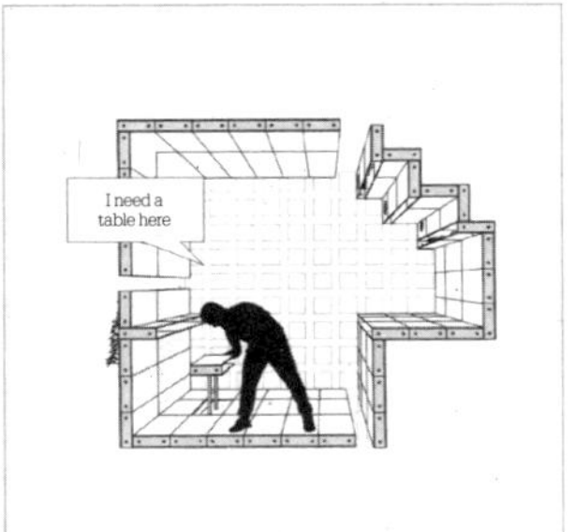

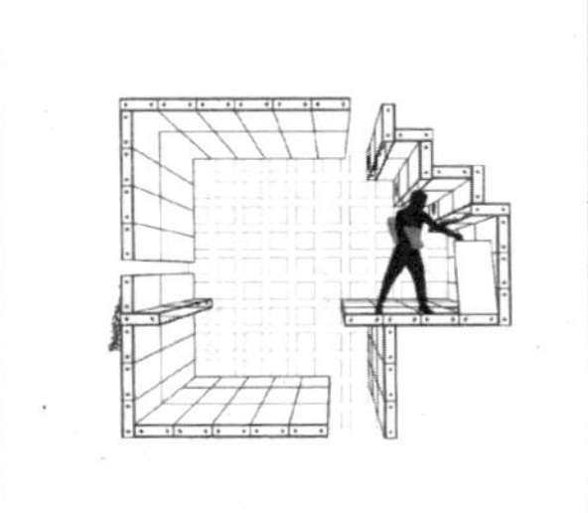

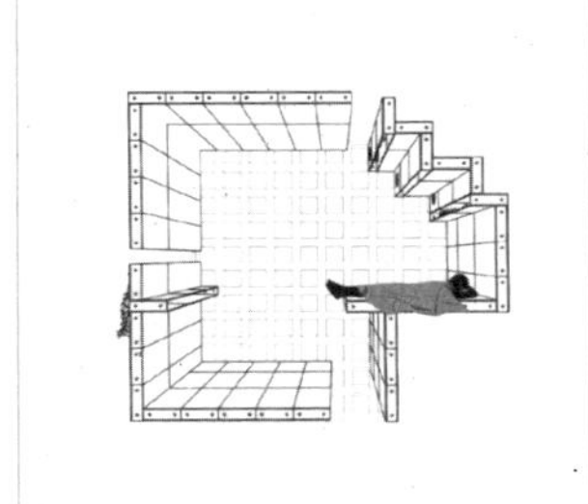

Floors and walls – room formation

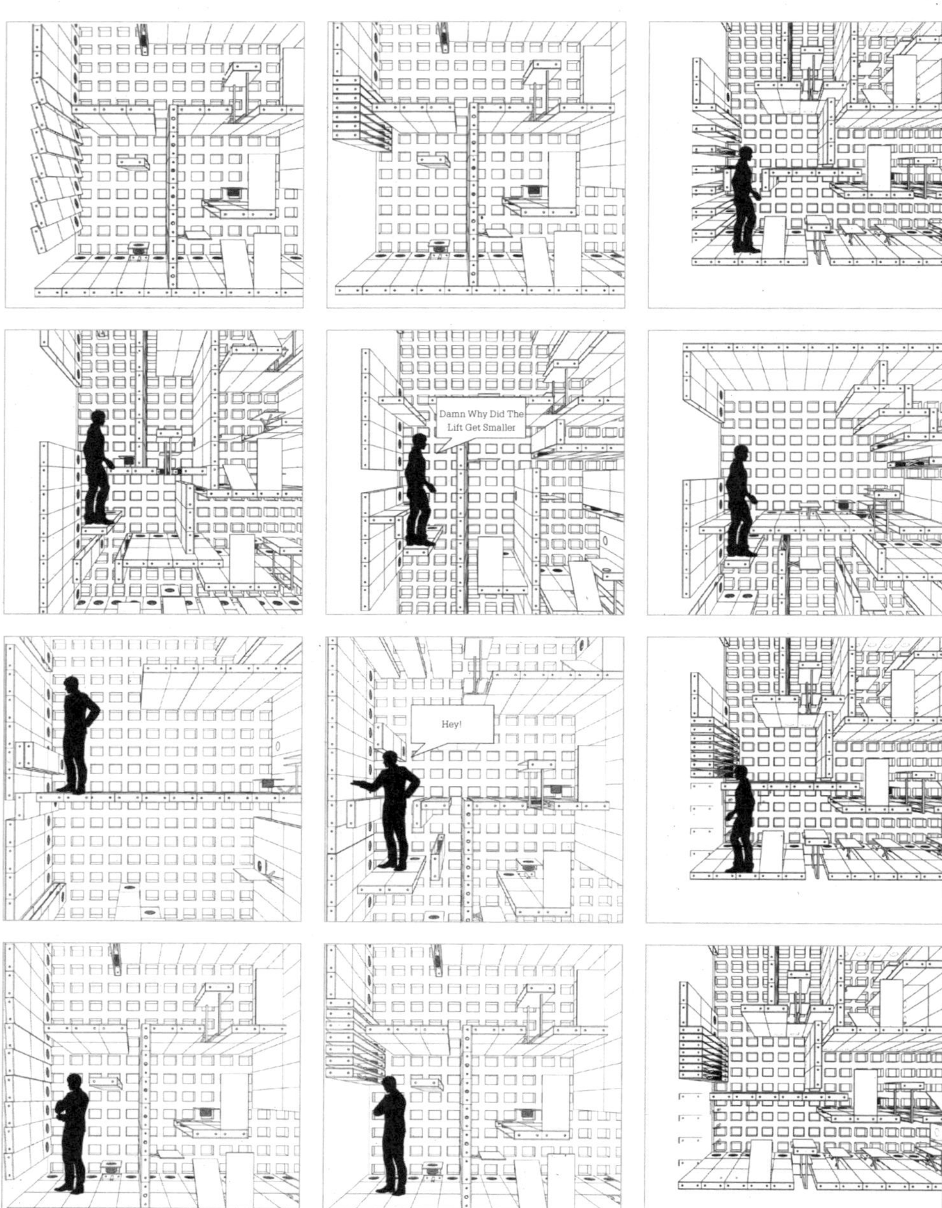

Planks and rail system – access

or less occupancy.

Three options were selected for development. Rooms in the 'Hang Inn' are created with hammock material hung between two rollers on each flank wall that can be rolled to expand and contract rooms on demand.

The 'AirPnP' project used stick systems on a load bearing track that allows it to slide on a horizontal plane, creating internal spaces within and containing interchangeable cartridges that house the window mechanisms, potable water, toilet, storage, minibar waste and batteries (for power).

The 'Flat O' tel' involved the deployment of 360 planks that can be moved between two parallel grids of tracks by a vertical pulley system. These tracks along which the planks move also provide connections to services (electricity, water etc.). Set out horizontally, a panel can serve as both floor and ceiling, and be flipped vertically to transform into a wall. When in motion, sets of planks can also act as transportation for guests.

The mobility of the planks also provides access to individual rooms and throughout the hotel, with some planks acting as a vertical and horizontal elevator, taking guests to their individual rooms along unique routes, while other planks simultaneously reconfigure to create the volume of the new guest room in the space expanded between adjacent rooms.

Structural systems, air, lighting and ventilation were readily solved by each of the strategies described above with varying levels of success. One of the most challenging aspects of this research was to try and resolve how to deal with the elements of a hotel – and in fact all buildings – that are by necessity fixed and also traditionally vertically stacked, such as plumbing and waste removal.

The distinguishing feature of the plank system is how it deals with waste water through a modular system. A number of the planks contain ablutions facilities (showers, toilets and basins) that fold out of the plank to provide services to occupants on demand. The track structures serve as a continuous interface with each of the planks, providing electricity, water supply and a pathway for waste water to be evacuated from the rooms.

Flexible Architecture

This chapter asks many more questions, especially technical and engineering ones, than it answers. It presents a speculative future in which our relationship to buildings (and a building's relationship to us) is fundamentally altered: no longer a static building-to-occupant relationship, it images a future in which an active or reciprocal relationship between building and occupant can make sharing space not just efficient but also luxurious, surprising and sustainable.

The explorations in this research can also be seen as a heuristic process or pedagogical experiment to introduce students to new ways of considering architectural configuration and composition, questioning what it is that our cities are composed of. Through the step-by-step process of exploration, students identified and challenged their underlying assumptions about architecture itself and discussed how we might explore its limits, and our ambitions for its future.

It is also an exercise in testing, spatially and in terms of reproducible systems, one of the key concerns of architectural thinking in the last century.

Flexibility, or the interplay of time and spatial occupation, was a key concern in Modernist architectural discourse, arising as a strategy for negotiating a dichotomy described by Walter Gropius: that the architect's concern is the human use and occupation of a building, but the architect's involvement in a building ceases at the very moment that occupation begins[1]. This understanding of one of the key roles of the architect is based on predicting not only the way in which occupants will use a design on the first day of occupation, but in all the ways they might use it in the days and decades after that.

Two principal threads developed in architectural approaches to flexibility. The first deploys neutral (or 'loose fit') containers that can accommodate a large variety of uses, but are arguably a good fit for none – take for example multi-sport courts, or generic 'white box' galleries. This approach is exemplified by Mies van der Rohe's New National Gallery in Berlin, in which a flexible field of spaces can accommodate an open-ended range of activities and installations. Mies argued that this type of emptiness, which he called 'universal space', provides a scaffold for the emergence of heterogeneous modes of occupation[11]. However, the extreme emptiness of Mies' universal space can be inversely viewed as totalitarian in requiring everything and everybody to conform to the grid.

A second approach is a reconfigurable architecture that actively responds to changes in user needs, often offering both occupational variety on a day-to-day basis and an ability to adapt to change over longer periods of time: think sliding walls, soundproof curtains, retractable canopies and even garden extensions. This dynamic approach to spatial configurations was demonstrated in Gerrit Rietveld's Schröder House, in which moveable screens replaced fixed dividing walls to allow the configuration of the rooms to be altered easily. A variation on this approach deploys the unfinished or modular building as a 'scaffold' for responding to uncertain needs, where the building can be readily adapted or reconfigured in response to new demands. The Pompidou Centre by Richard Rogers, Renzo Piano and Gianfranco Franchini is perhaps exemplary of this line of investigation, although claims made for its 'flexibility' have proven to be more emblematic than operational, borne out by the need for its recent lengthy closure for repairs[12].

Many of these historic examples and strategies for adaptable or dynamic architecture offer either relatively limited sets of spatial configurations (as in the Schröder House), require extensive (and often time consuming) remodelling to address new requirements (as in the Pompidou Centre), or require strict adherence to their particular brand of flexibility (as in the New National Gallery). As a result, a common feature of these built investigations into flexible, dynamic or responsive architecture is that the initial configuration of operable or reconfigurable systems is generally the last or most common one – that is, users do not 'operate' the buildings or engage with them in the way the designers imagined that they would.

But these limitations are being increasingly challenged as the range of technologies that architecture can draw on is expanding. Contemporary advances in robotics and user-interface design, combined with our willingness to provide massive amounts of real-time personal data, suggest that real-time, dynamically reconfigurable architecture is not only possible, but likely in some form in the near future.

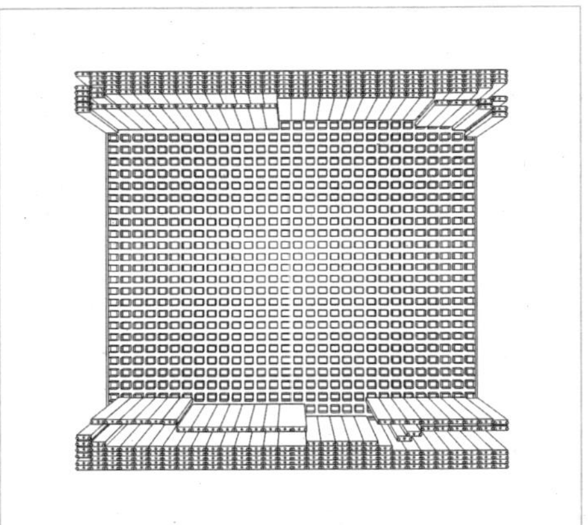
t1

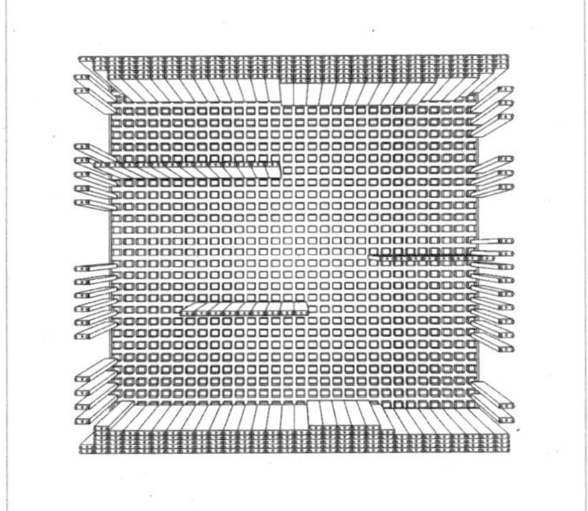
t2

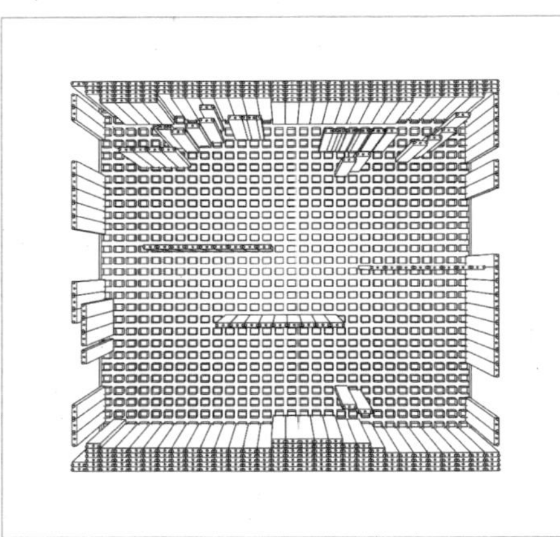
t3

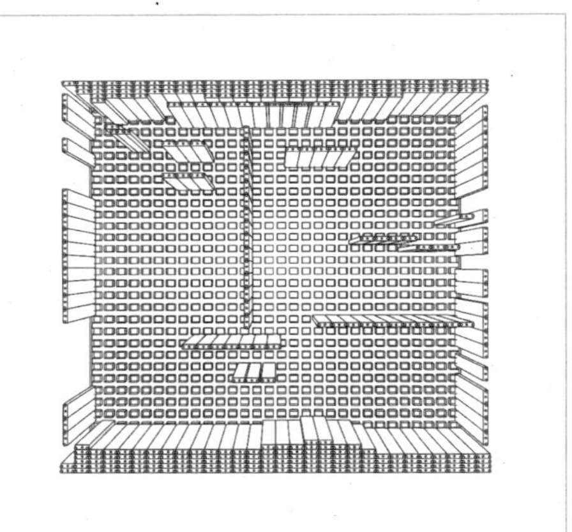
t4

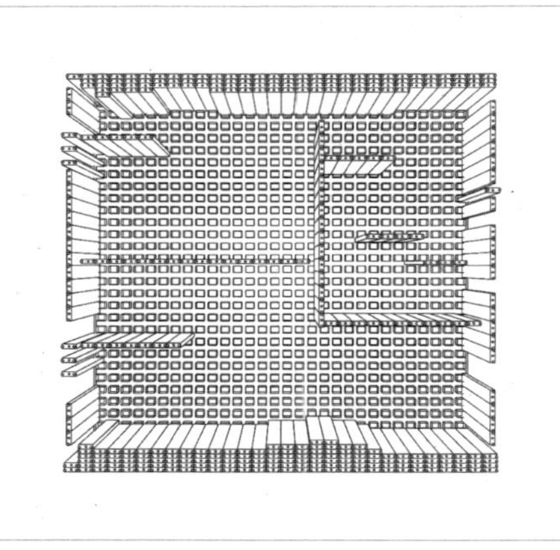
t5

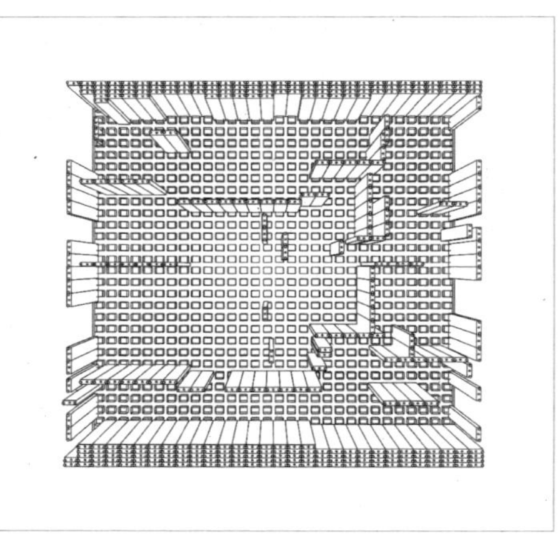
t6

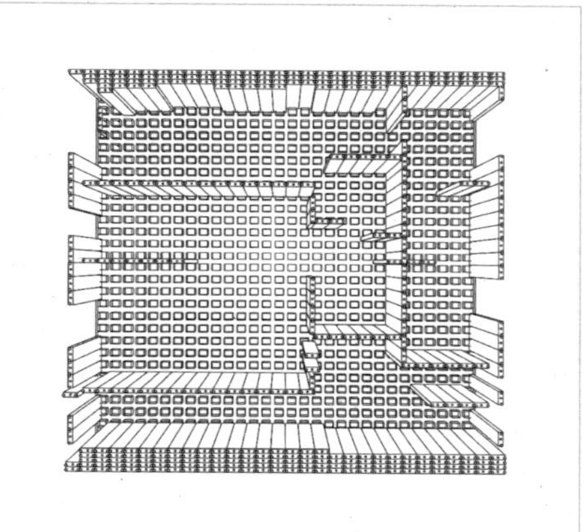

t7

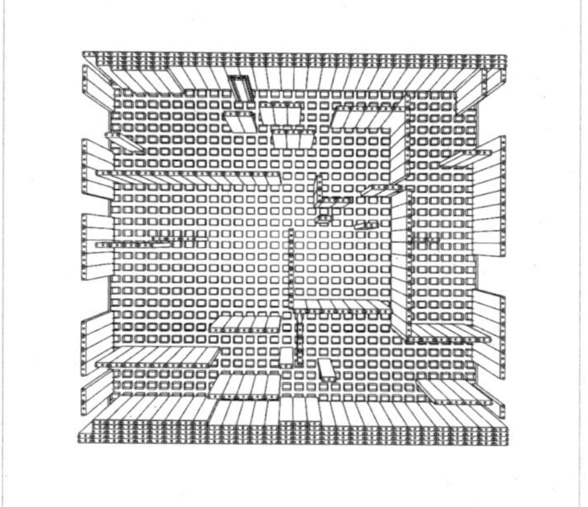

t8

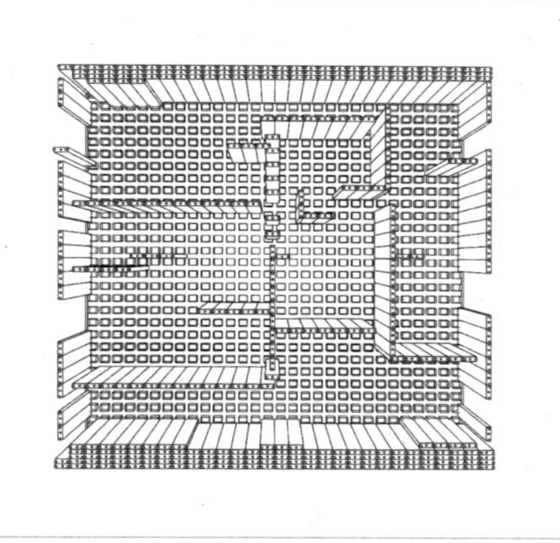

t9

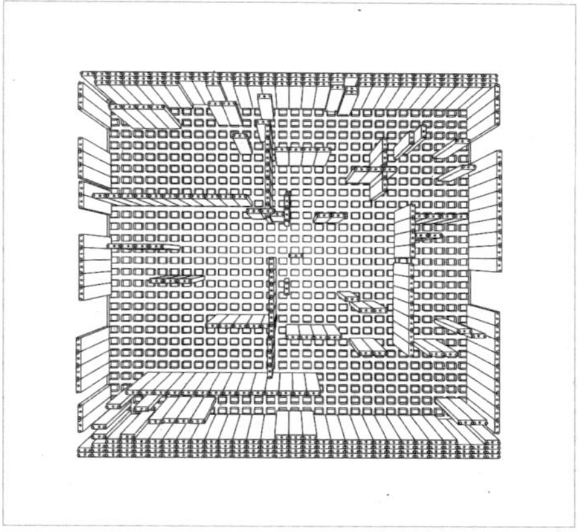

t10

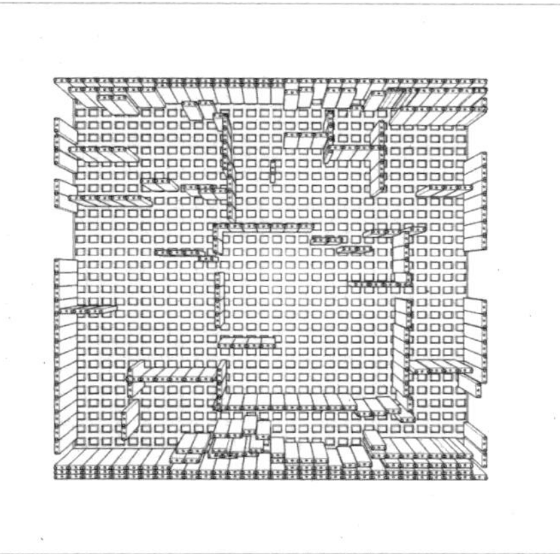

t11

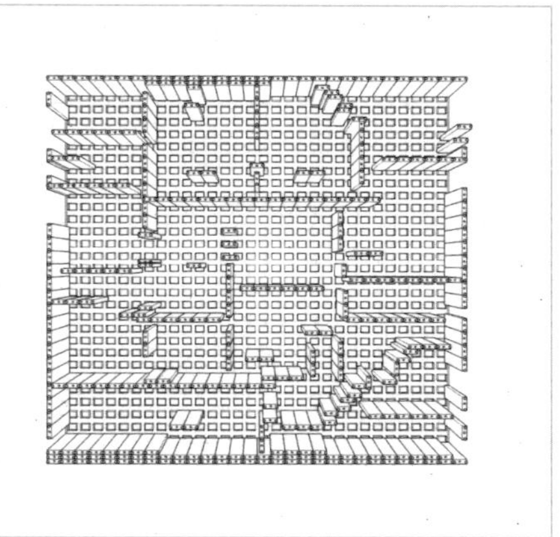

t12

The Script

The Why Factory (TU Delft) with IIT Chicago

Students: Karina Andree, Nour Abuzaid, Emily Aquilina, Shervin Azadi, Rick Blankestijn, Ruben Büno Heslinga, Alex Da Costa Gomez, Helena Daher Gomes, Karim Daw, Ana da Fonseca, Justin Frank, Twan Goossens, Yuan Guo, Shirin Hadi, Qiongjun Hu, Maria Kaik, Thomas Krall, Jimmy Lei, Zach Mellas, Danica Mijonic, August Persson, Jeanique Romeijnders, Berend Schenk, Ángela Shepherd Díaz, Eileen Stornebrink, Jitske Swagemakers, Mesut Ulkü, Emma van der Staaij, Amanda Verschuur, Philipp Wenzl, Zerrin Yüksel, Xiaomi Zhi

Tutors: Winy Maas, Felix Madrazo, John Manaves, Stavros Gargaretas, Leo Stuckardt, Lex te Loo, Pirouz Nourian, Hans Hoogenboom, Friso Gouwetor, Arend Jan Krooneman

Guest Critic: Wiel Arets

Text by Felix Madrazo

Imagine a housing block that could constantly reconfigure itself to best suit the habits and schedules of its residents. Continuing the investigation started by (w)Ego Hotel, OntheGo investigates the potential design of a building capable of compressing and expanding its component spaces to accommodate the changing needs of each of its users, while maximizing the space available to each at any one time.

OntheGo tests the capacity of architecture to evolve over time, instantly, as people come and go, coincidingly being at home for a few minutes, passing each other in a rush or suddenly all dawdling in one space all at once. In this chapter, we explore the potential translation of activities, planned and unplanned, into spatial requirements. What is the minimum envelope for a static user? How much extra comfort can be provided if residents start to share space and coordinate activities? How can a system negotiate and solve the inevitable conflicts caused by spaces in flux?

OntheGo explores a series of computational models that can facilitate the design and management of this four-dimensional puzzle. It asks: How can we engineer real-time adaptability and automation into mass housing?

OntheGo

Humans consume and demand more and more space. Since time immemorial, the solution for this has been to compress the living quarters of those at the bottom of society, to give to those at the top the sensation of power through spatial abundance. Density has come with great advantages; it has brought affordable dwelling to millions and with it access to transport, infrastructure, schools and so on. But the cost of this is that whole families have to live in fixed environments of 35 m2, even in rich Europe. Can we challenge this rigidity of a dense space?

Think of a city at a given moment. Traffic jams mean that most people are in transit, going to work or returning home, while work spaces and living spaces both remain unused. During the day, suburbs and residential neighbourhoods stand almost empty. If one made a heat map of activities in the city, it would not be surprising to find that a big chunk of it (even in a dense city) is unused or, more precisely, latent, waiting for the users to activate it. The inverse has been true during the Covid pandemic, with mass working-from-home leaving city centres and office blocks close to vacant for months at a time.

In homes or offices, the bathroom gets used for one to 15 minutes at a time, then remains empty until used again. The bedroom is mostly used once a day, not to mention storage spaces which, from one perspective, are hardly 'in use' at all. You can query the redundancy built into most functions of the housing block or the city in a similar way. This observation would be irrelevant if space was endless and the environment was in perfect shape. But it is not.

As new technology emerges, we are now able to locate our position in real time; and crucially for architecture, we can manipulate our space from a distance. Software and architecture seem to be merging into one. At last, it seems plausible to rethink what density means and introduce a key factor to the equation that has been largely ignored: time.

With time in the mix, another conception of architecture is possible: an architecture that can provide what users need in real time, and then compress and transform into other functions to achieve maximum use. In an ideal scenario, a city could shrink enormously if it offers only the space that real time demands. Or we could think of keeping our current footprint, but instead of accepting that households are limited to 35 m2 of living space, we could ditch this concept of austerity for one where current use and user needs are what matters, and space responds to these. Another generous scenario could see our cities hosting double or triple our current densities, without compromising on space, and without expanding beyond their current boundaries.

Would there be enough redundancy in this system? Or too much, overall? One could say that if everyone goes to work at the same time and returns at the same time, there would be little space for improvement. But the contemporary city, where everyone is on the move, is far more complex and diverse. This chapter tests the scenario with the daily schedules of a range of users.

OntheGo is a design studio that took place at both Delft University of Technology and the Illinois Institute of Technology in Chicago. It explores the design of a housing block capable of accommodating the different needs of each of its temporary residents and maximizing the space in use.

The model arrives at new levels of efficiency and comfort through both compression and expansion. To achieve a responsive density, one that prioritizes the specific requirements of all its users, OntheGo is not only tailor-made – it is housing on the move!

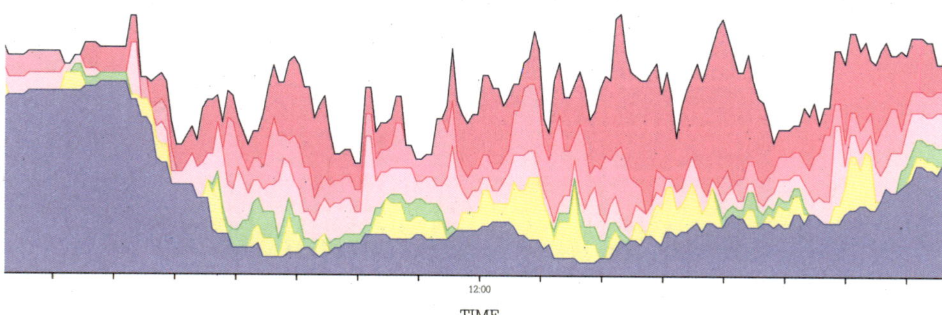

Users schedule generated timetables

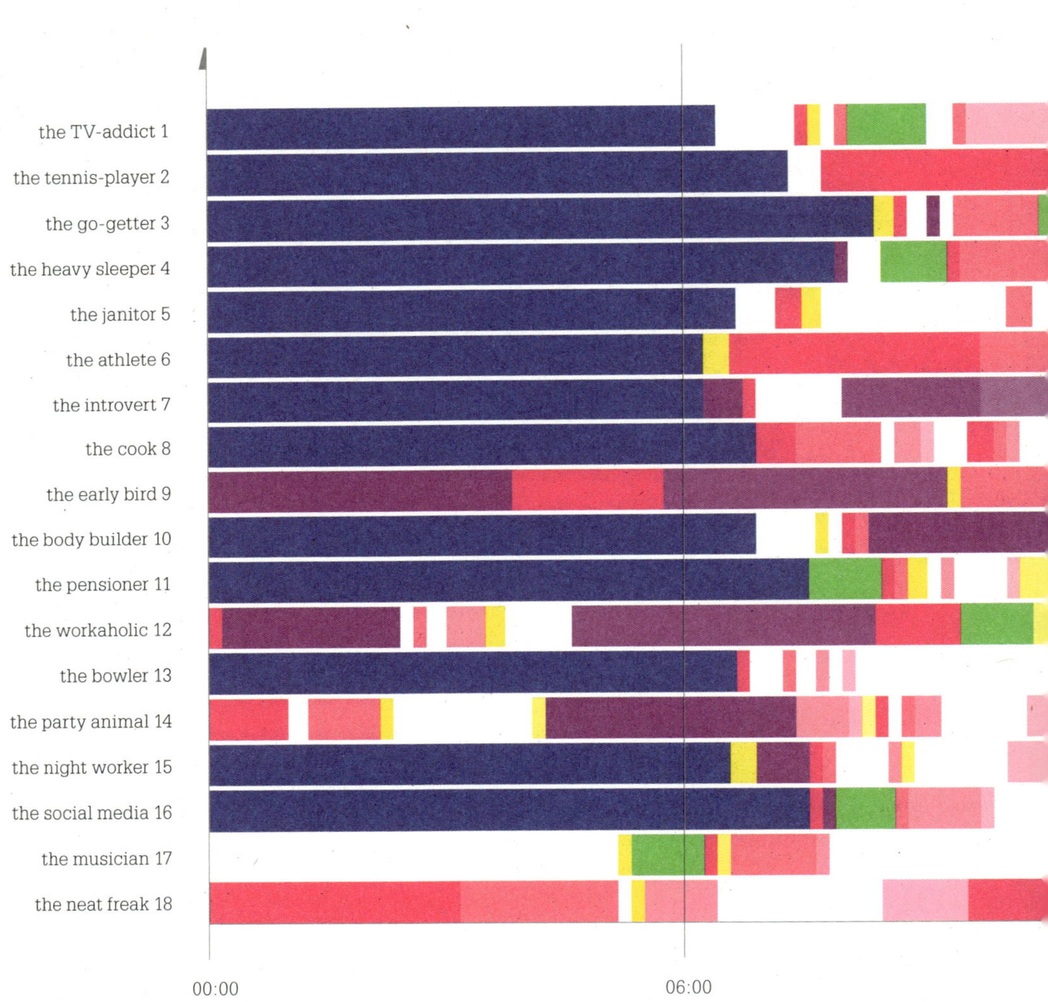

Users schedule generated timetables

12:00
18:00
24:00
sleeping
work/study
leisure
food
care
out

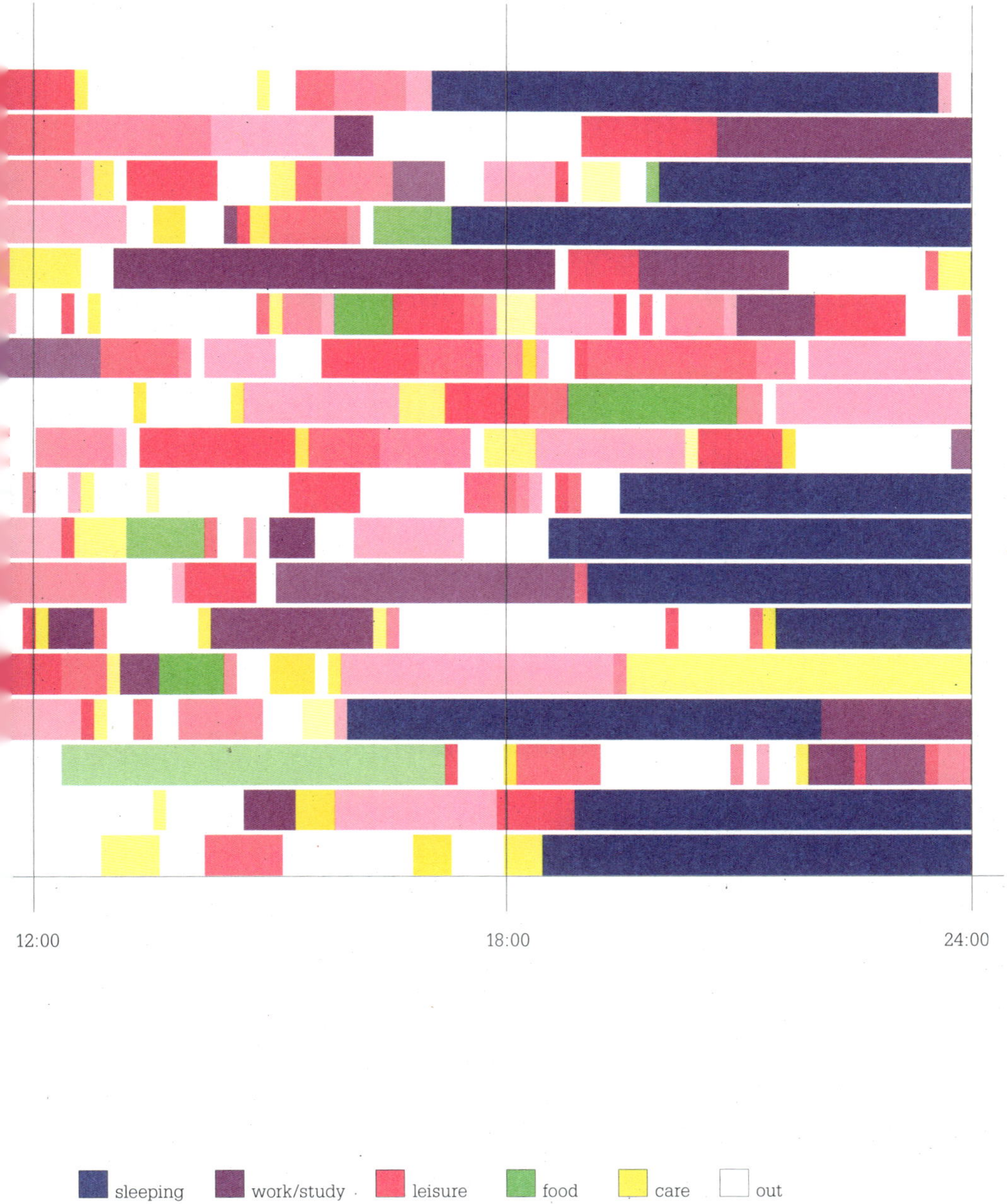

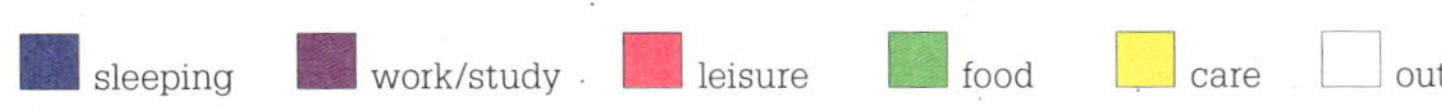

User Schedule

This phase aims to understand the type of users that inhabit the project, with a focus on their daily occupations. The User Generator is a dynamic model that processes data to create realistic users and timetables on demand. Each user is generated with a profile that includes data on their daily schedules, activities and habits. This experiment allows us to observe when particular functions of the home are unused and hence unnecessary. What kind of usage patterns can we derive for each user over the course of a 24 hour day?

The TV-addict

The Tennis Player

The Go-getter

The Heavy Sleeper

The Janitor

The Athlete

The Introvert

The Cook

The Early Bird

The Body Builder

The Pensioner

The Workaholic

The Bowler

The Party Animal

The Insomniac

The Social Media Addict

The Musician

The Neat Freak

Users timetable diagrams

Scheduled Volumes

Through this series of graphs, we aim to understand what the spatial requirements are when carrying out different activities related to the home. Having established the users of the building and the activities they undertake, we must translate this data in volumetric requirements. Based on motion tracking technology, this experiment attributes space to each activity. Rooms become dynamic. The graph above shows peaks of activity as well as the inactive moments in which space is unused, and so, somehow wasted.

The TV-addict

The Tennis Player

The Go-getter

The Heavy Sleeper

The Janitor

The Athlete

The Introvert

The Cook

The Early Bird

The Body Builder

The Pensioner

The Workaholic

The Bowler

The Party Animal

The Insomniac

The Social Media Addict

The Musician

The Neat Freak

Users volume activity diagrams

Voxel Size

Making a building that is constantly adaptable requires a minimum module that is small enough to react to a wide variety of situations, but large enough to not become inconvenient. While a very small module would provide the most flexibility, it requires much more computational power because it must constantly change with each movement. A larger module is spatially less efficient, but computationally more so. The module should also relate to building standards, both for ease of construction but also to incorporate standardized components, such as kitchen amenities. All of these factors require a balance, and this balance defines the building 'resolution'.
The conclusion of this experiment is that the ideal voxel size is 30 cm. This offers a balance of spatial and computational flexibility.

Unit 10 × 10 cm

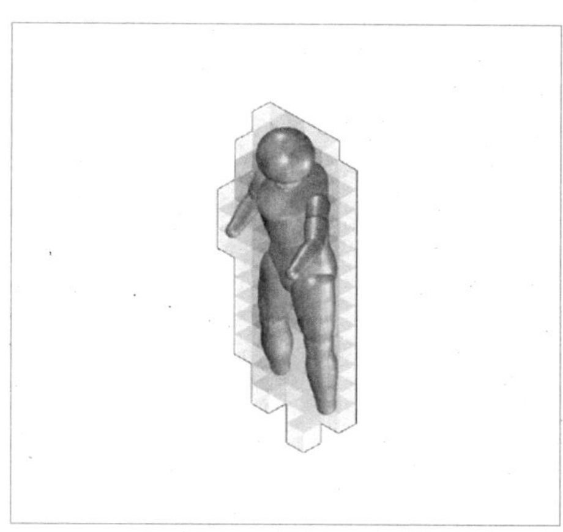

Unit 30 × 30 cm

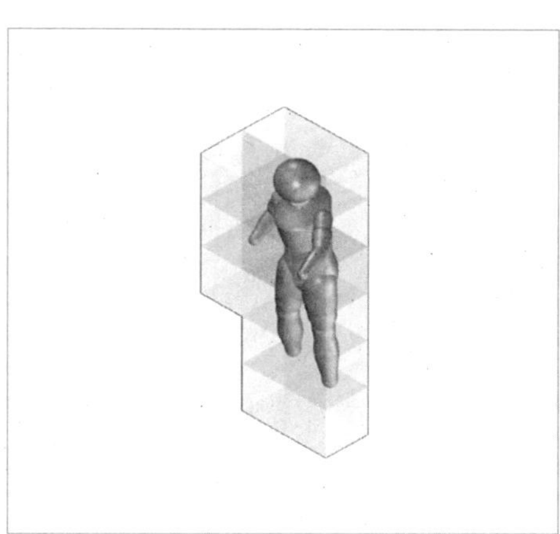

Unit 60 × 60 cm

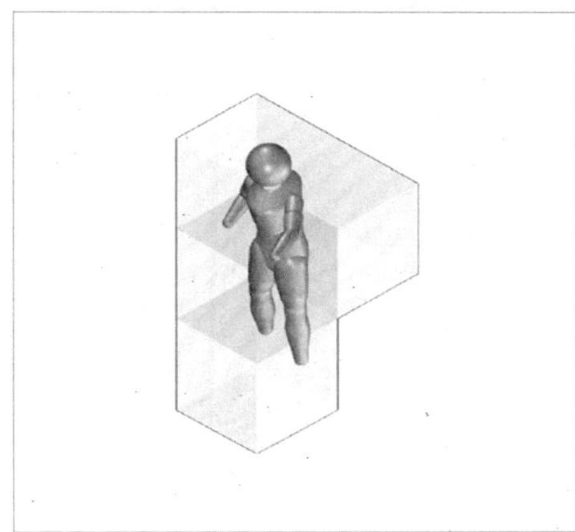

Voxel Suit

1 Minimum Volume
The voxel suit consists of only the voxels needed to envelop the user at any given moment. It adapts to the users' movements in an instant. This is the minimum and most spatially efficient suit, although the space resulting is uncomfortably tight.

2 Activity Volume
The activity volume is the space created by overlaying all the voxels needed through the entire activity. This results in a fixed space that can accommodate all required movements.

3 View Cone Volume
A view cone is a representation of the visual field within a geometry that cannot be restricted or compromised. This is added to the activity volume to ensure that the user always feels comfortable and can see all the required things during any activity.

4 Storage Volume
Nearly every activity requires storage, although the amount varies widely. Assigning voxels of storage to each activity, we ensure the user has all the required items to fulfil the activity.

5 Desired Volume
The desired volumes are spaces that are individual to every user, and every activity. Every user can set their own preferences. While some may prefer a large, wide space for a given activity, others may want a small, tall one.

6 Shared Volume
When multiple people are doing the same activities at the same times, they can share space. The space they use is therefore reduced at the scale of the building but enlarged experientially, because shared with others.

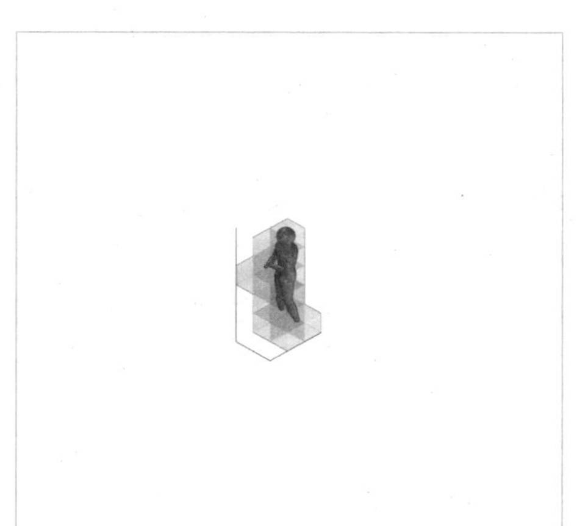

1. Minimum Volume

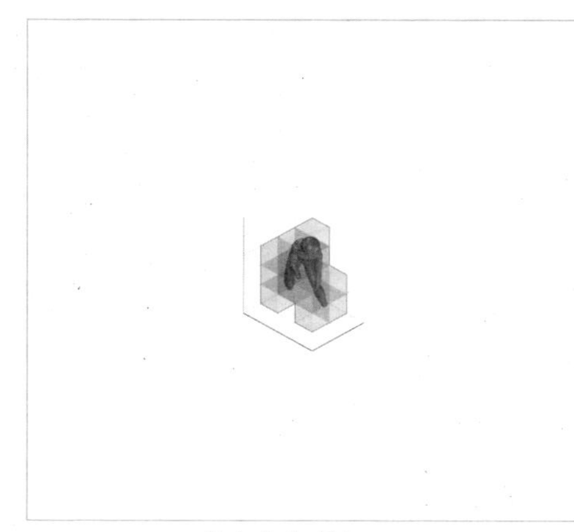

2. Activity Volume

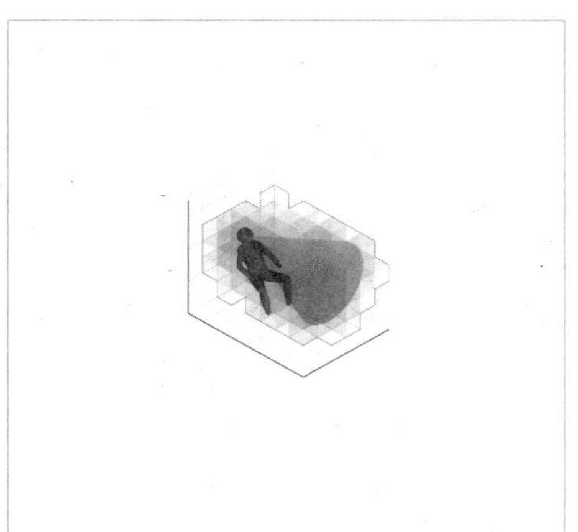

3. View Cone Volume

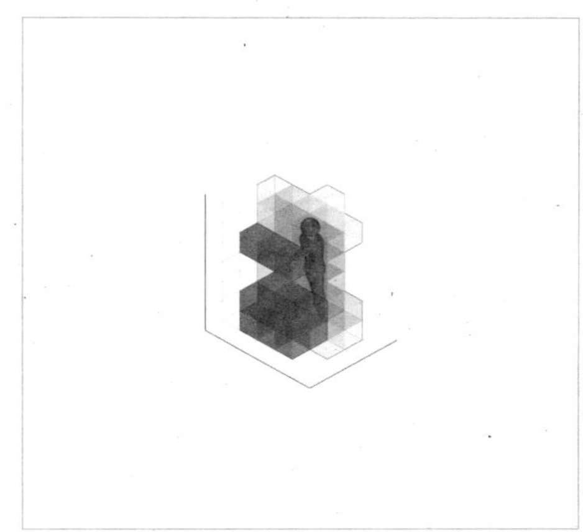

4. Storage Volume

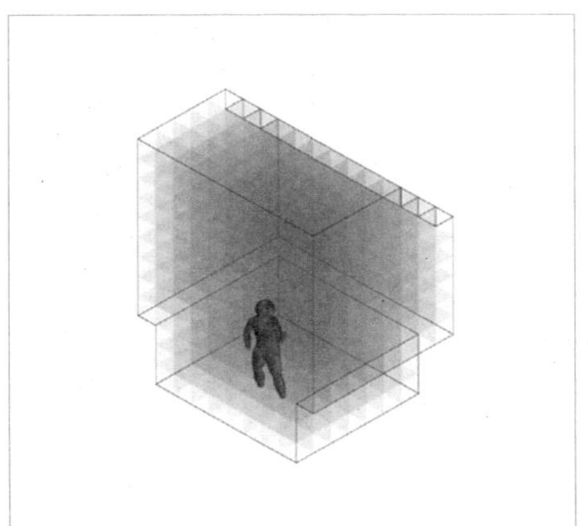

5. Desired Space

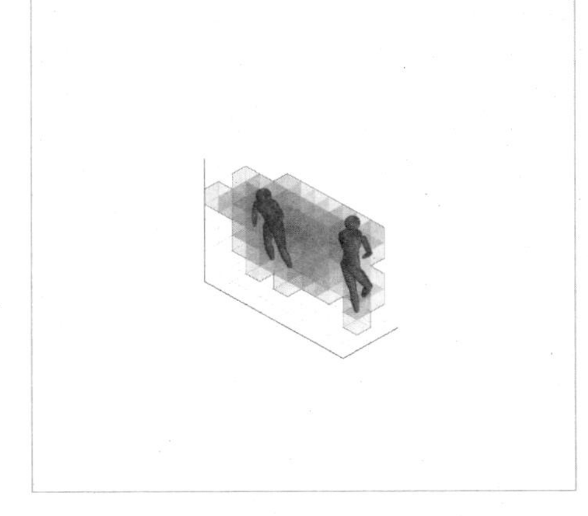

Voxel Cloud

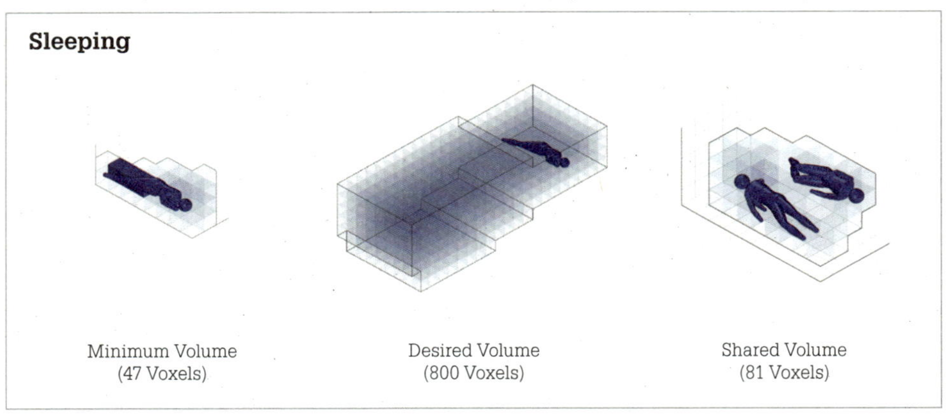

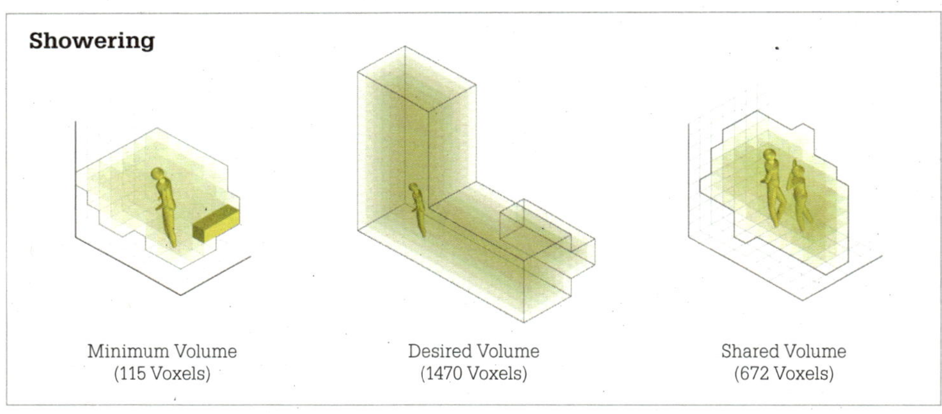

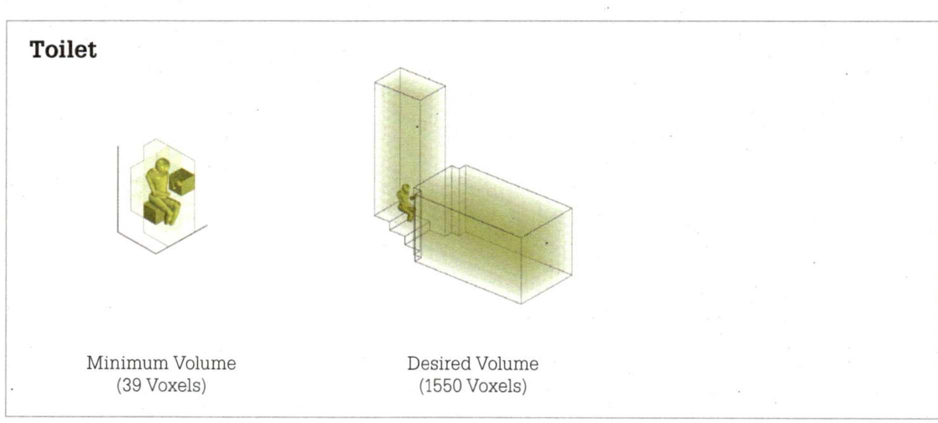

Volumetric catalogue of activities

Voxel Cloud

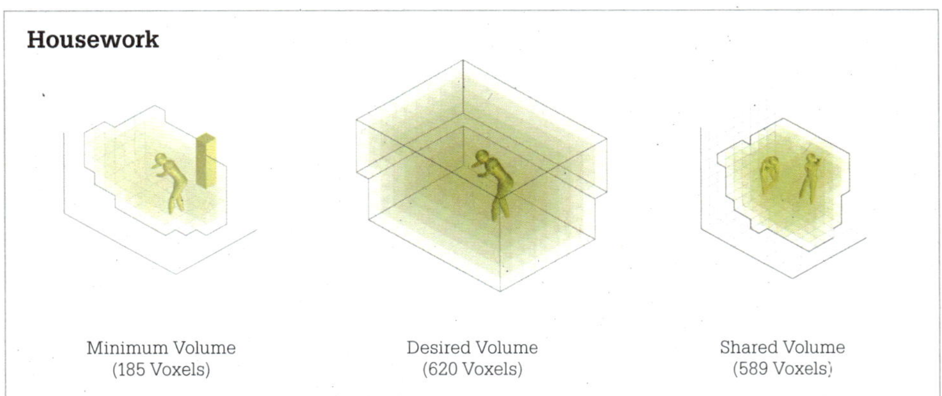

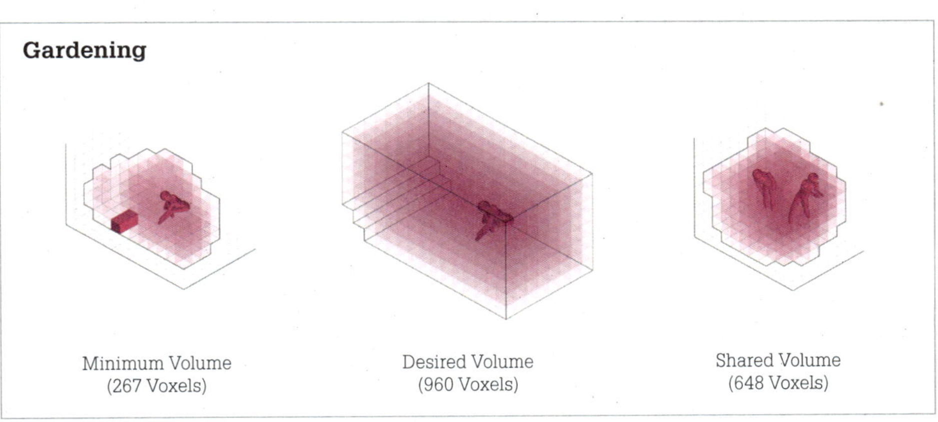

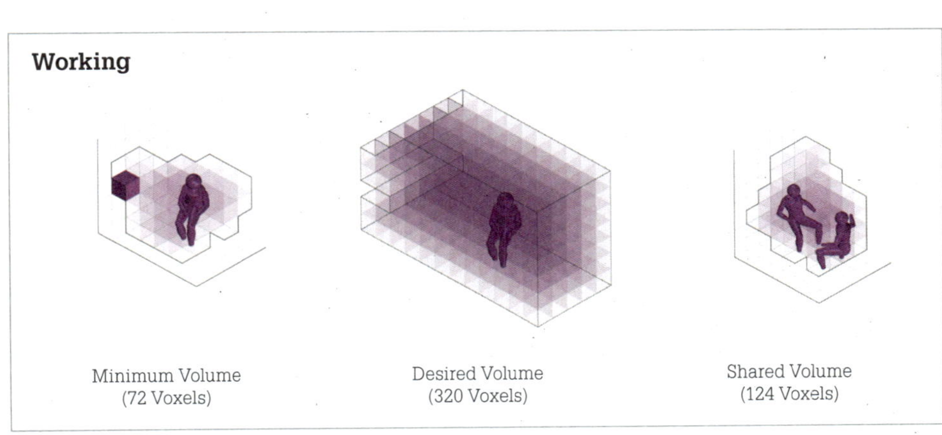

Volumetric catalogue of activities

Voxel Cloud

Education

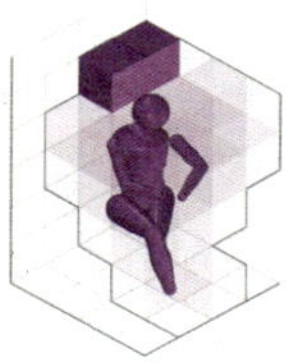

Minimum Volume
(51 Voxels)

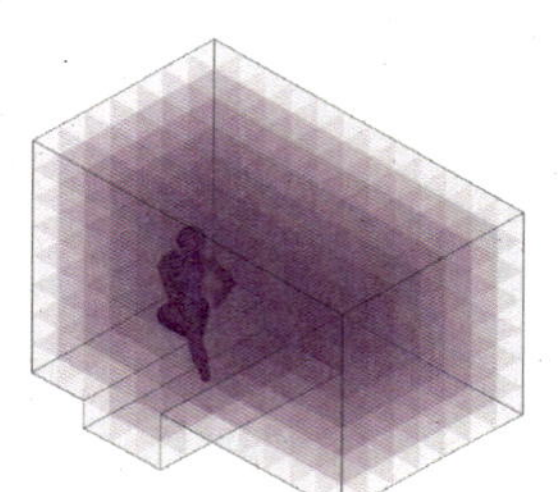

Desired Volume
(310 Voxels)

Shared Volume
(86 Voxels)

Dining

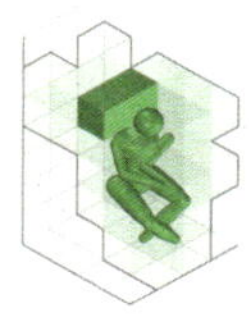

Minimum Volume
(58 Voxels)

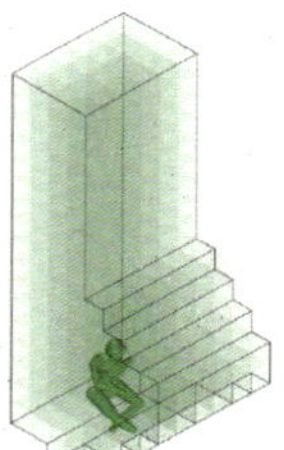

Desired Volume
(540 Voxels)

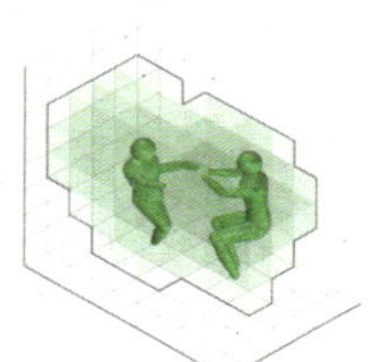

Shared Volume
(193 Voxels)

Circulation

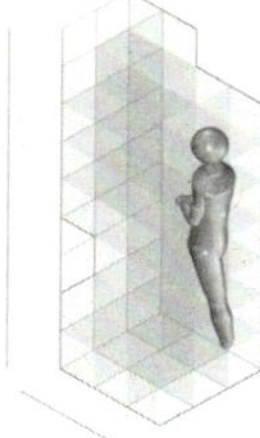

Minimum Volume
(81 Voxels)

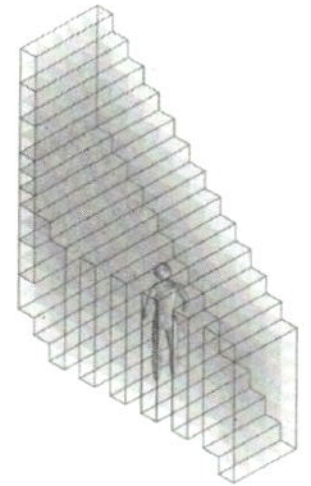

Desired Volume
(546 Voxels)

Volumetric catalogue of activities

Voxel Cloud

Doing Aerobics

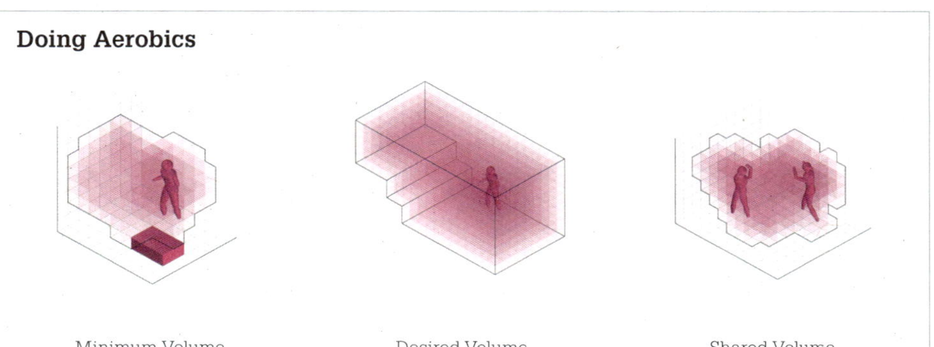

Minimum Volume
(202 Voxels)

Desired Volume
(1134 Voxels)

Shared Volume
(521 Voxels)

Doing Yoga

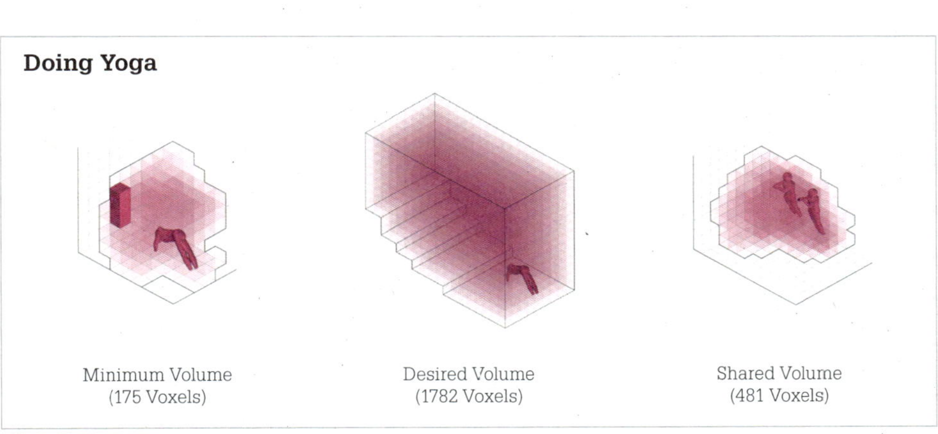

Minimum Volume
(175 Voxels)

Desired Volume
(1782 Voxels)

Shared Volume
(481 Voxels)

Dancing

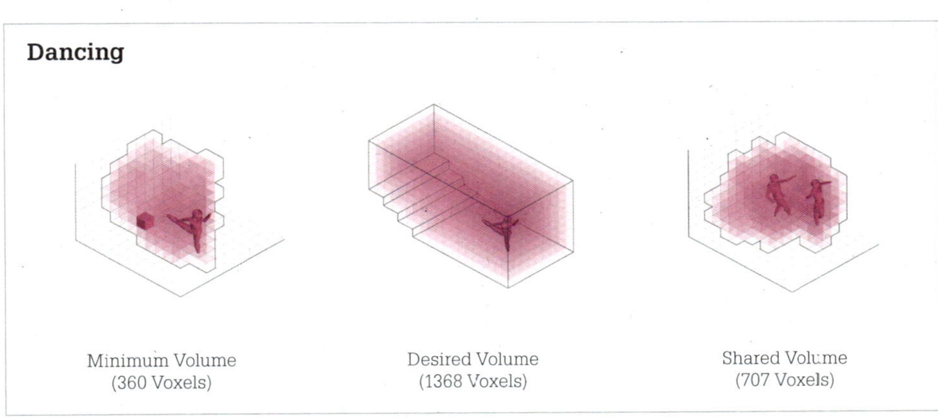

Minimum Volume
(360 Voxels)

Desired Volume
(1368 Voxels)

Shared Volume
(707 Voxels)

Volumetric catalogue of activities

Initial Position

Inside the envelope, voxel clouds are considered as points distributed in space. Each point represents a user in the building. It starts from a random distribution. Each point searches through all the other points and find the nearest one. Then they simultaneously move away from these nearest points. This allows for a fair organization method, through which an initial state for our simulation is determined. In order to determine the best starting position with the least number of conflicts, more than 1,000 iterations were generated.

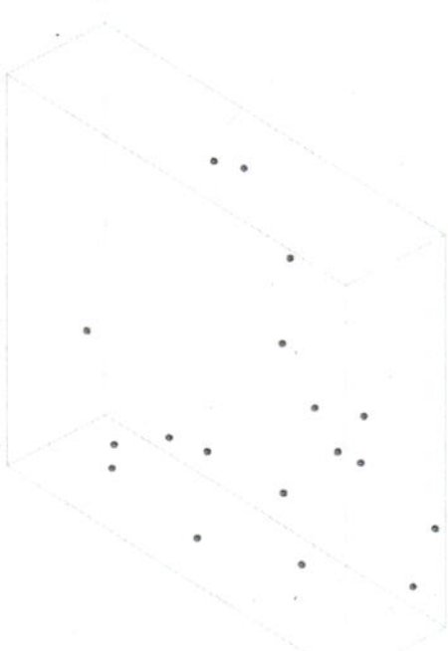

Seed 3, initial position

Seed 3, t=n+2w

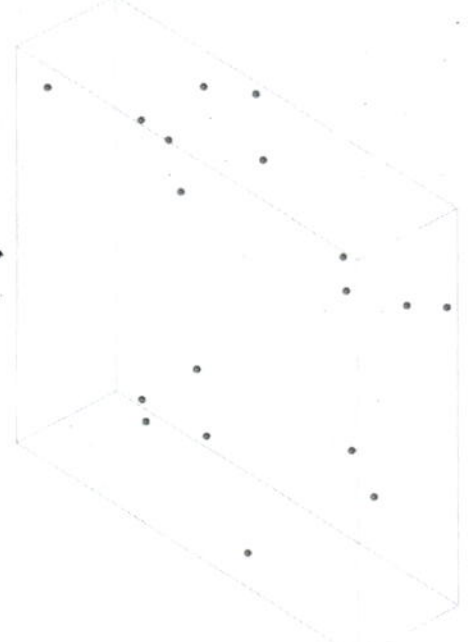

Seed 12, initial position

Seed 12, t=n+2

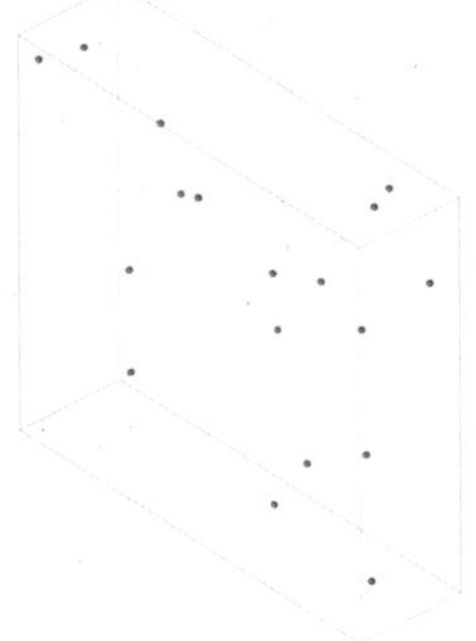

Seed 0, initial position

Seed 0, t=n+2

Enveloping

Several envelope sizes have been tested to fulfil the needs of every virtual inhabitant. The optimal size has been determined based on a zero-conflict detection. The following diagrams show several iterations that go from 28 × 28 × 9 voxels to 38 × 38 × 9 voxels.

Size 1 – 28x28
41 conflicts

Size 2 – 30x30
23 conflicts

Size 3 – 32x32
9 conflicts

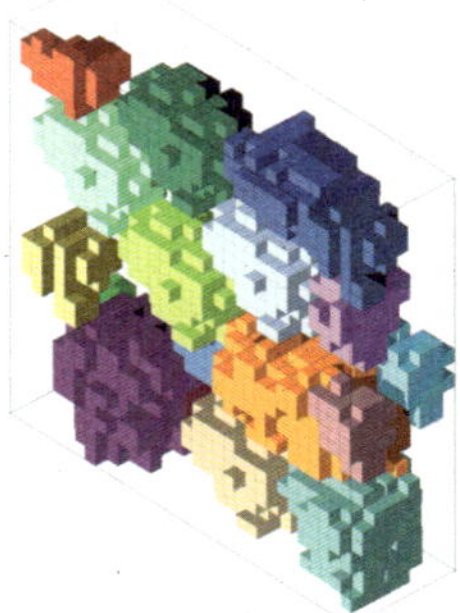

Size 4 – 34x34
0 conflicts

Size 5 – 36x36
0 conflicts

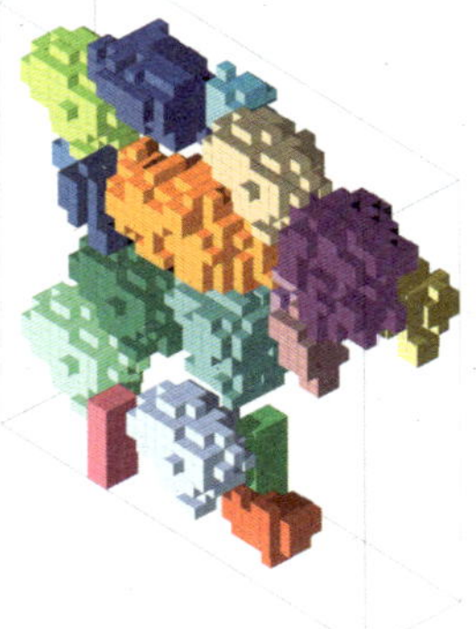

Size 6 – 38x38
0 conflicts

Negotiation Over Time

When users interact with and change their own spatial requirements, it directly affects their neighbours. This introduces elements of conflict and negotiation into the experiment. When different timeline and spatial requirements overlap, it creates conflicts. Those conflicts can be solved by the fact that other spaces are left vacant by other users.

An algorithm developed as part of this research is able to constantly identify and locate conflicts, and find a solution for them. For example, when a user is moving in or out, they send a notification to the envelop and their neighbours are moved away to accommodate an instant pathway.

1

2

3

4

5

6

Scripted Interactions

Conflicts in desire require negotiation. OntheGo operates based on an algorithm, able to accommodate any situation. It constantly evaluates every user's degree of satisfaction in order to adapt and iterate solutions to any tension in the fairest possible way.

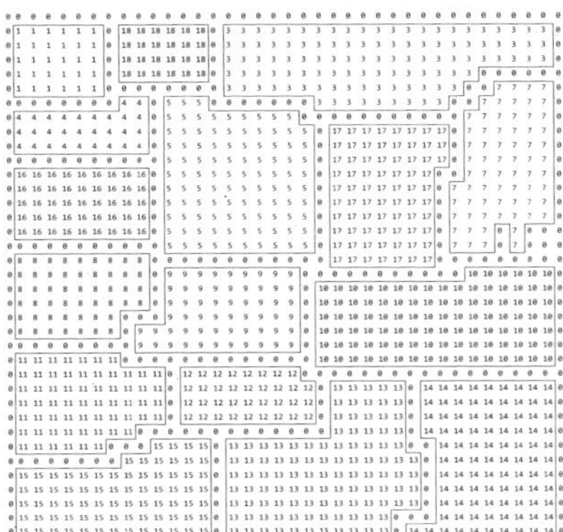
A matrix is generated using each person's ID and the coordinates they occupy

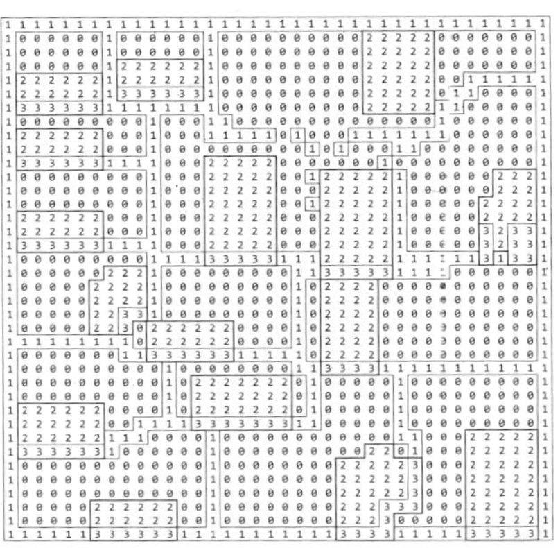
A matrix of boundaries (3) and spaces (2) is created from the organisation data

Each dynamic entry (beam or space that can move) is translated to a node

Neighbouring nodes are connected with edges, creating a graph representation

Visual representation of prioritisation with espect to time in the pathfinder

Visual representation of the path calculated for one set of start- and endpoint

From Voxel to Beams

Voxel clouds are reconditioned to fit the envelope of the building better. By extruding each voxel cloud towards the sides of the slab, it makes the overall arrangement more efficient. No space is left unused. In addition, it creates an opportunity to translate each beam, spanning over the depth of the slab, into a constructive element.

1

2

3

4

5

6

Using Sliding Beams

The initial intention of the structure and mechanism was to free up the front facade. This would allow for a light, transparent facade membrane to maximize daylight. In addition, it would make full observation of the inner movements of the planks possible: a window for the city to appreciate the inner workings of a new dynamic architecture.

The second alternative is a symmetrical assemblage where both facades support the beams' weight and their movement. It allows for a more stable configuration. Both facades are permeable, creating richly patterned lighting inside the spaces, which spills out at night. The inner movements of the building are not completely revealed to passers-by, but this permeability does offer some level of visual porosity.

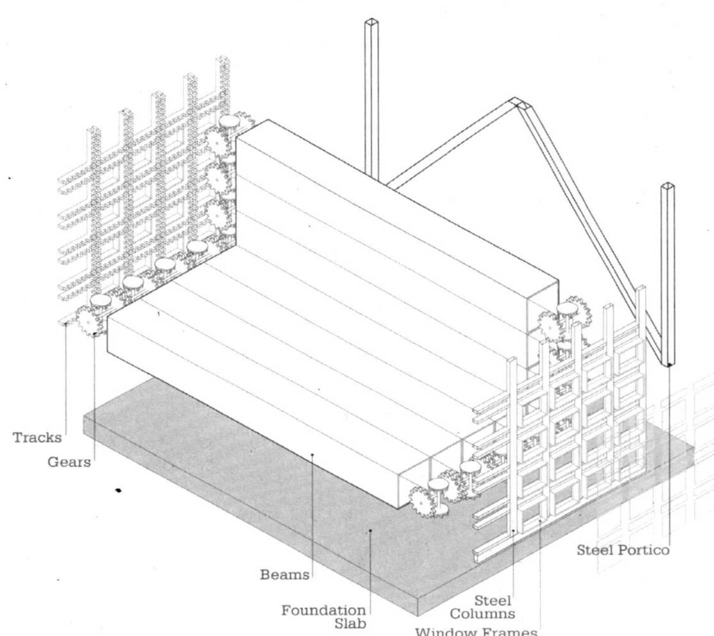
Tracks
Gears
Beams
Foundation Slab
Steel Columns
Window Frames
Steel Portico

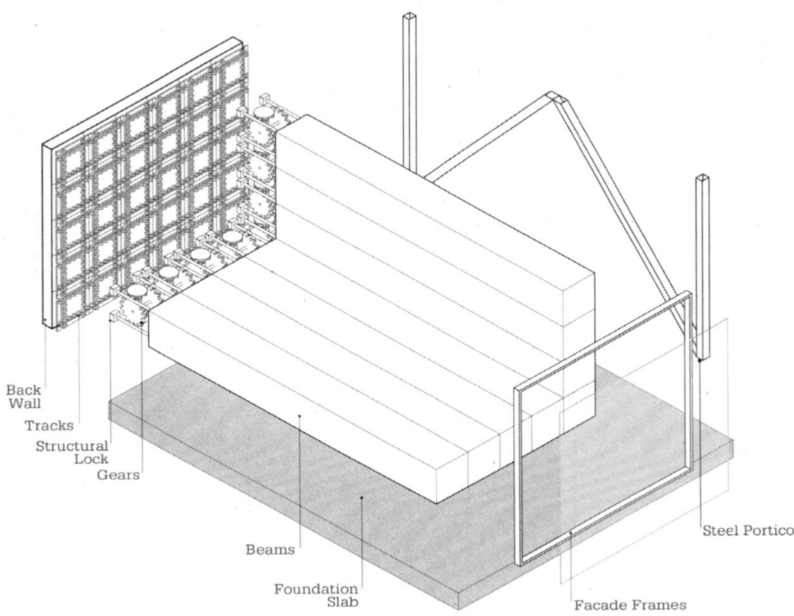
Back Wall
Tracks
Structural Lock
Gears
Beams
Foundation Slab
Facade Frames
Steel Portico

A Day OntheGo

These images are stills from a movie, produced to simulate how the housing block gets transformed over time. The movie shows in detail how each element (walls, ceiling, floor, lift, stairs, pipes) adapts to the changing demand for customization, and also how each of these elements gets compressed when not in use. The scenes follow a series of transformations based on user needs over a typical day.

1

2

3

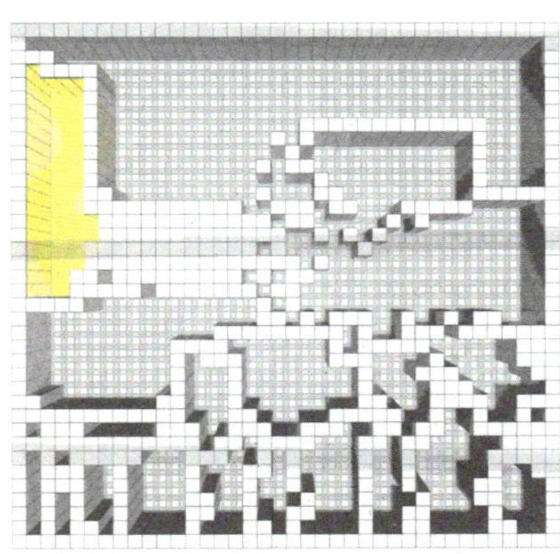

4

5

6

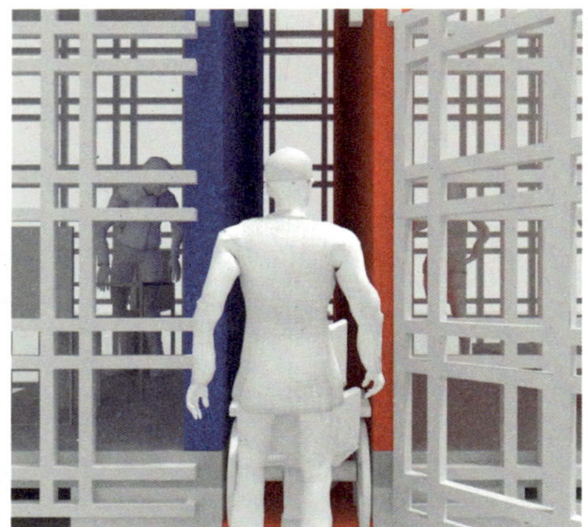
t1

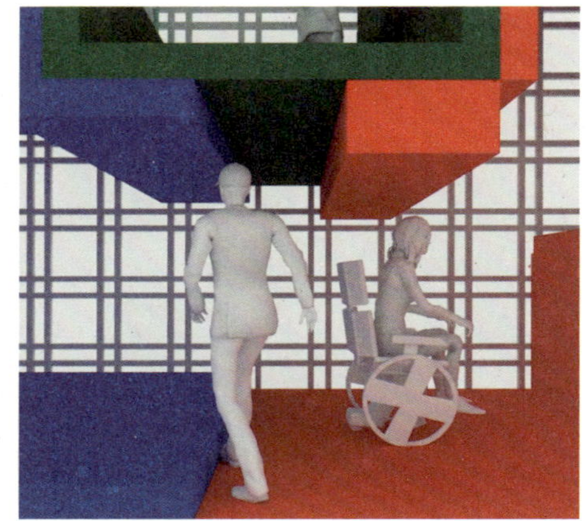
t2

t3

t4

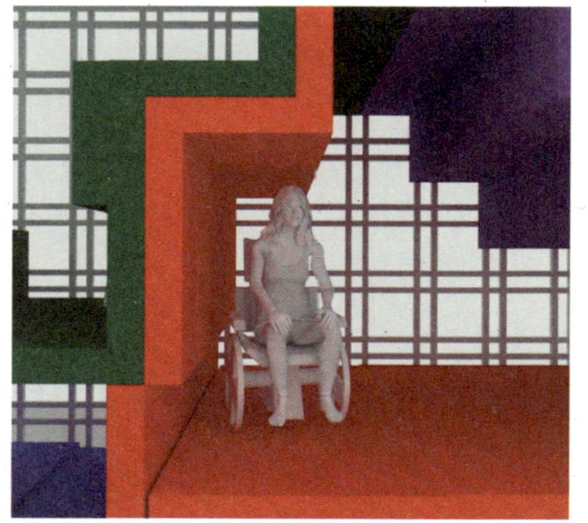
t5

t6

t7

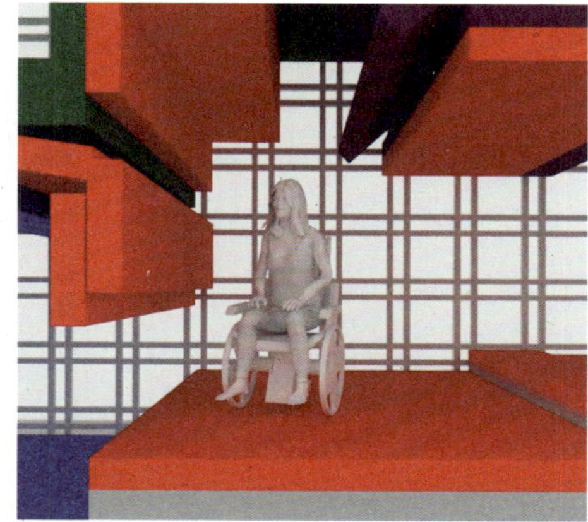

t8

t9

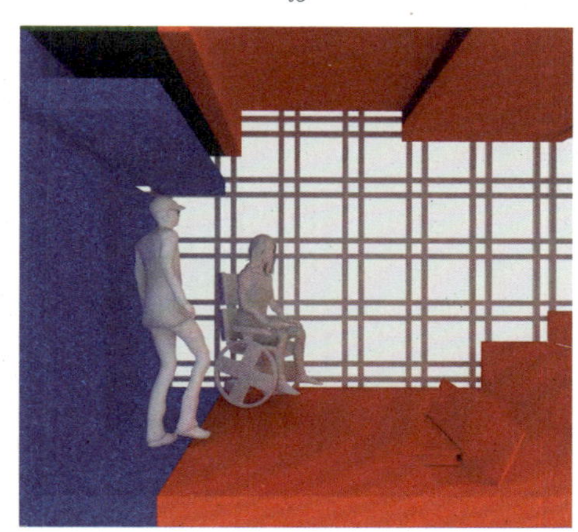

t10

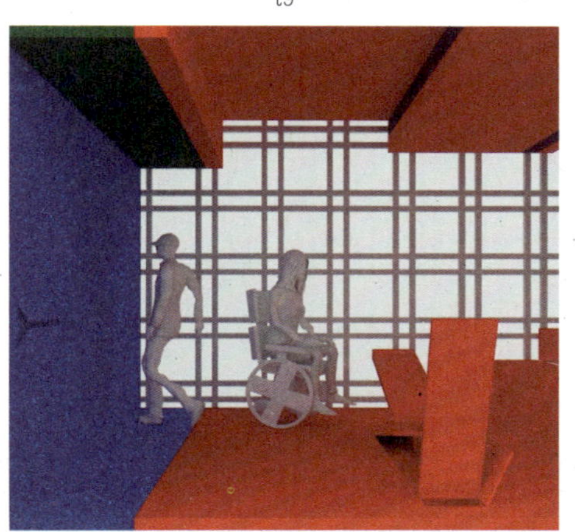

t11

t12

The Prototype

The Why Factory (TU Delft) with IIT Chicago

Students: Karina Andree, Nour Abuzaid, Emily Aquilina, Shervin Azadi, Rick Blankestijn, Ruben Büno Heslinga, Alex Da Costa Gomez, Helena Daher Gomes, Karim Daw, Ana da Fonseca, Justin Frank, Twan Goossens, Yuan Guo, Shirin Hadi, Qiongjun Hu, Maria Kaik, Thomas Krall, Jimmy Lei, Zach Mellas, Danica Mijonic, August Persson, Jeanique Romeijnders, Berend Schenk, Ángela Shepherd Díaz, Eileen Stornebrink, Jitske Swagemakers, Mesut Ulkü, Emma van der Staaij, Amanda Verschuur, Philipp Wenzl, Zerrin Yüksel, Xiaomi Zhi

Tutors: Winy Maas, Felix Madrazo, John Manaves, Stavros Gargaretas, Leo Stuckardt, Lex te Loo, Pirouz Nourian, Hans Hoogenboom, Friso Gouwetor, Arend Jan Krooneman

Guest Critic: Wiel Arets

Text by John Manaves

Having sketched and scripted OntheGo, there is now a need to understand what current and emerging technologies can offer in terms of material possibilities for accelerating transformation. The next step in this research aims to find solutions beyond architecture, incorporating high and low tech. How can we make OntheGo buildable in the near future? What common structure can host these transforming spaces? How do walls, ceilings, roofs, furniture and pipes take form, and how do they facilitate this adaptability?

The initial development occurred while The Why Factory studios from Delft University of Technology and ITT visited the Aedes Campus in Berlin at the end of 2017. The research and prototyping continued at The Why Factory in Delft and at ITT in 2018 and 2019.

A Turning Point

The extruded elevator core has been in use since 1853. Invented by Peter Copper for the Cooper Union Building, it has been virtually unchanged as the basis for vertical travel within a building. MULTI, ThyssenKrupp's multidirectional elevator, no longer conforms to a single extruded core, allowing new possibilities in mobility and structure, but is still limited by the cab. Just as the elevator freed the building height from human physical limitations, determining it instead by engineering limits, the OntheGo and (w)Ego prototypes seek to free the building section from rigidity and, in doing so, to shift the framing of this exploration from the impossible to the possible.

The aims of the prototype studies were twofold: to demonstrate that the design could be functional, through engineering and fabrication tests, and to free the ongoing research from technical criticism. As in many fields, conceptual design and future models are a critical driver of momentum for innovation in architecture and the built environment. Establishing a functional prototype may allow for the re-imagination of the way we build and utilize buildings; allowing spaces to expand and contract and be rearranged based on occupants' needs and desires. This chapter is about the first attempt at constructing OntheGo, a robotic system that can respond to inputs and reconfigured space accordingly. This system could turn buildings, currently limited in their functionality by rigidity, from simple edifices into adaptable infrastructure: a living framework capable of change.

How Does It Work?

As with Elisha Otis' demonstration of the modern elevator at the Crystal Palace in New York, we set out to challenge the preconceptions of mobility by presenting a working model and showing clearly how it could operate. Through scaled mock-ups, the work pursued a linear development to demystify the mechanical complexity of the OntheGo and (w)Ego research. The assumption was that the technology required, and the speed of development, is easily within reach – especially with the advancement of digital controls, rapid prototyping, and open-source coding. A rigorous plan was developed, outlining how to design, produce, and test the prototypes needed to manoeuvre a surface capable of transforming from wall to floor and back while moving the resident and his or her possessions within the space. From the start, the intention was to develop a working prototype demonstrating the actual conditions of the proposed design, OntheGo.

In OntheGo studio research, digital simulations examined the transformation, expansion, and compression in relation to the desired space and its use over time. OntheGo was presented as a scientifically accurate depiction of how a building could be activated, allowing it to adapt to our schedules and changing spatial requirements. A common denominator or unit was developed to facilitate the change of walls, floors, ceilings, and furniture to facilitate the compression and expansion of the spatial consequences of user desires. Within the unit level of the most successful system lay the 'Plank'. Designed for a diverse set of purposes, this basic module can be deployed as

Prototype 1

furniture or building utilities, and act as the floor, ceiling or the walls of rooms. Planks constantly rise, descend, and turn, creating a platform for transportation through and transformation of the building's interior.

The focus of this prototype was on manoeuvring the individual plank unit as proof of concept of the more extensive system. The main objective was to develop a controlled, low-voltage, motorized movement with the emphasis on the ability to change axis and floor-to-wall-to-ceiling interchangeability.

The process consists of iterative design through rapid prototyping. Off-the-shelf parts and custom-designed 3D components were assembled and iterated in successive generations of details to test and improve plank mobility. Open-source software was utilized to control the movement of the plank.

There is little (or no) precedent for this work. Further research into controls, systems and logistics is needed to test the prototype's potential and functionality at scale.

Tests

Developed during the studio visit to Aedes Network Campus Berlin, the initial attempt was to create plank movement in one axis. This first trial revealed the complexity needed for single action motion, both in terms of hardware and software. Knowledge borrowed from open-source 3D motion control technology was the starting point in developing the drivetrain and controller systems. Stepper motors and controllers were purchased at local electric stores and managed via a programmable microprocessor employing a custom digital interface. A low-tech approach was used for the track and plank, and a hand-cut foam core demonstrated the ability of controlled movement along a linear path. We made several observations. The software and electrical components were the more straightforward hurdles; the robustness, precision, and durability of the mechanical parts would be more challenging.

Prototype 1 aimed to develop a full working prototype in multiple phases, with each phase focusing on a particular problem and building upon its predecessor.

Prototype 2 focused on developing a more robust track as well as striving to create movements in two axes. As in the OntheGo studio research, this model included a superstructure for the tracking system along which the planks could move. The central structural system was divided into a repeating modular unit. The unit measured 1.0 metre wide by 1.0 metre high by 2.7 metres deep. The dimensions and offsets of the tracks were developed based on digital animated studies and simulated movements. Pivoting nodes were added at the intersection of the tracks to enable planks to switch directions, from moving forward and backward to moving up and down. The addition of the central nodes completed the mechanics needed to allow for the full range of movement required to manoeuvre the plank into all positions. This model was constructed out of more durable materials, consisting mainly of laser cut medium-density fibreboard (MDF).

The plank's design has two axes that engage the track and measure 1.0 metre wide by 1.0 metre high by 2.7 metres deep. The plank operates in a similar way to a 4 × 4 vehicle with four stepper motors, one at each corner. A stepper controller for each

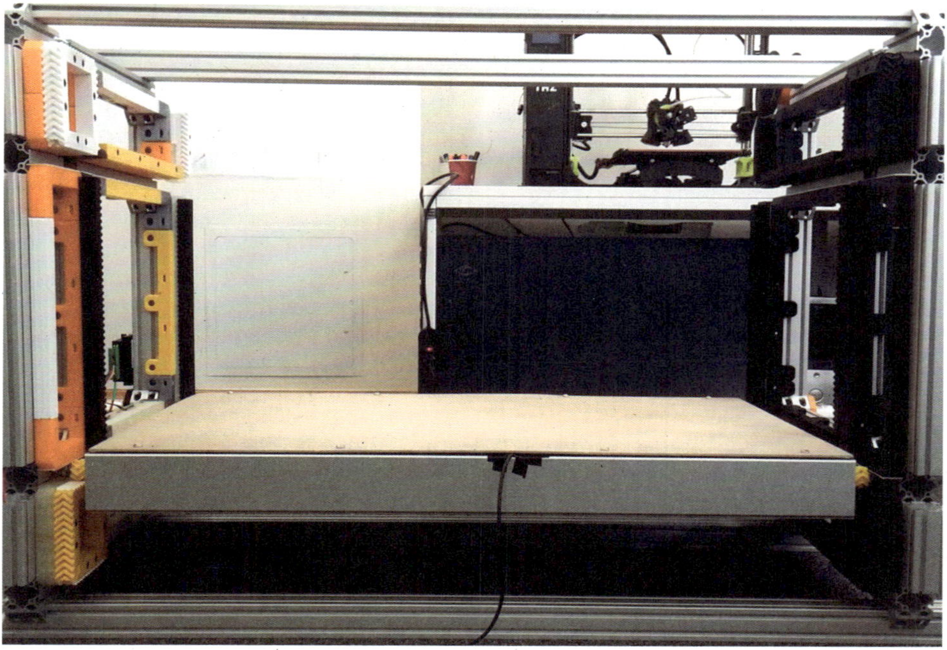

Prototype 2

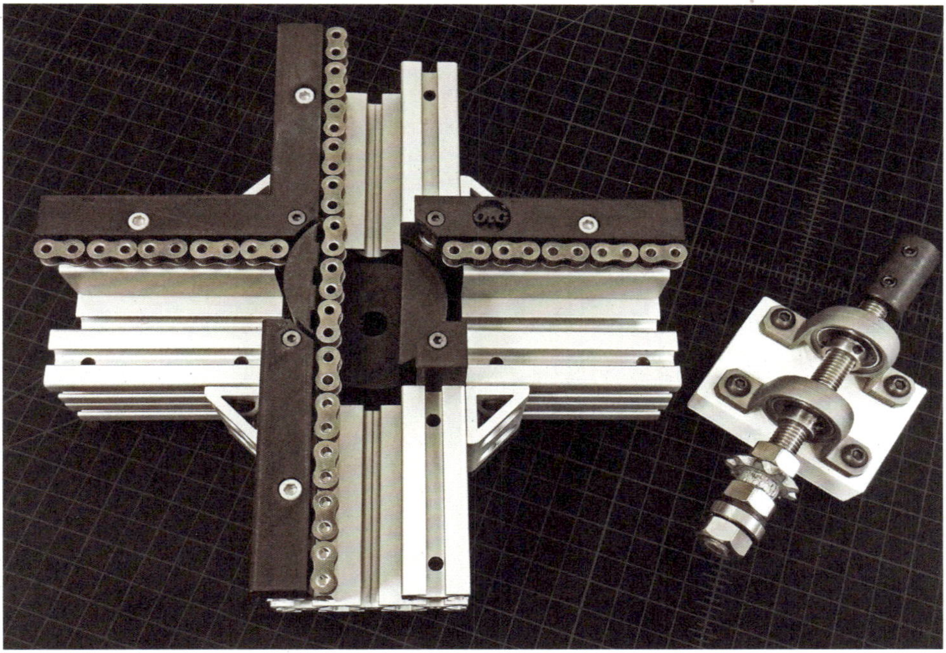

Prototype 2 – detail

axis synchronizes the movements allowing for the arrangement of the multiple manoeuvres needed to position a plank within the assemblage.

Prototype 2 was a scaled model at 1:2. During assembly, precision continued to be an obstacle, as the moving parts required an underestimated level of tight tolerances. A series of consecutive test movements were performed to assess the limitations the current design may have in terms of mechanics. Forward/backward and upward/downward movements were successfully performed and replicated – confirming that the programming required to achieve these controls was in place. The precision of the gearing system and the superstructure and track were confirmed to be the weak link, and is the next challenge moving ahead.

As in the evolution of the modern elevator and its shift from the use of rope to iron cable to wire rope to steel belt, the prototyping had to follow a linear system: the precision of the plank movement would require a gearing system that would need to be tested and tailored. For the next iteration, a superstructure capable of tuning and customization was sought. The development of the gearing would be facilitated by rapid prototyping.

In Prototype 3, the emphasis was on full, uninterrupted motion along all axes. A comprehensive redesign was executed to achieve this outcome. The superstructure, the track system for the plank, and how the plank engaged the track were updated first. 3D printed components were used in combination with custom aluminium profiles to realize a precise system. A printed herringbone gear was designed to prevent misalignment of the plank as it moved along the track.

Prototype 3 was built at a 1:1 scale, which presented a new set of challenges. The heavier weight of components required higher strength materials and considerably more powerful motors and gearing, which in turn created slower and high torque movement, requiring safety precautions. The perfect balance between speed and torque seemed elusive. The final assembly revealed a robust structure and tracked system along with an operational plank geared to carry over 1,000 kilos. The prototype started to show what a real-world configuration may look like. The statics were studied and validated. The modularity of the unit could be expanded on to create a bigger, more complex structure.

The pivoting nodes were further improved upon, as were the turning capabilities of the plank. Turning the plank required the geared steppers to rotate at different, varying speeds, which added complexity to the stepper motor controls and programming. The different components were further tested, iterated, and refined. The hardware and software were developed to assure dependable assembly and user safety. The result was continuous full motion, demonstrating a successful working prototype. Prototype 3 was proof of concept. The final iteration of Prototype 3 was presented at the IIT College of Architecture Open House in 2017 and presented as one of the winning entries for the Neveling Foundation Award.

After the successful testing and presentation of Prototype 3, Prototype 4, a multi-plank operational system, will integrate all the requirements for multiple plank manoeuvring, including mechanical systems and controls to allow the unit to expand and reconfigure. The beginning details of Prototype 4 have been developed. The geared systems for the track and plank have

1

2

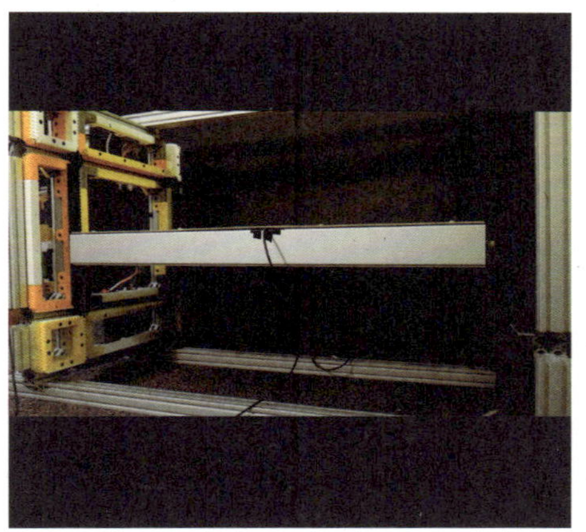

3

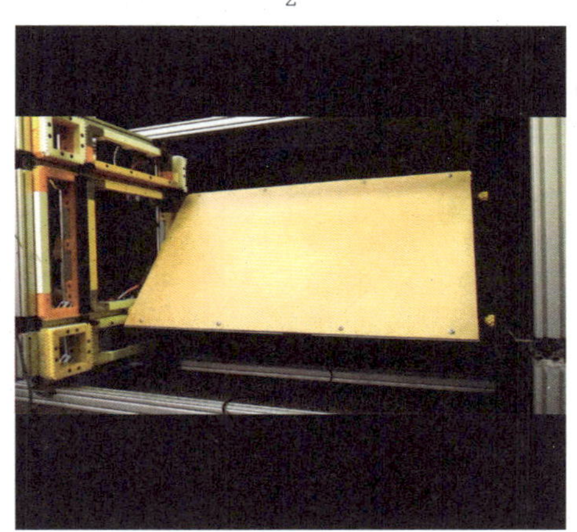

4

5

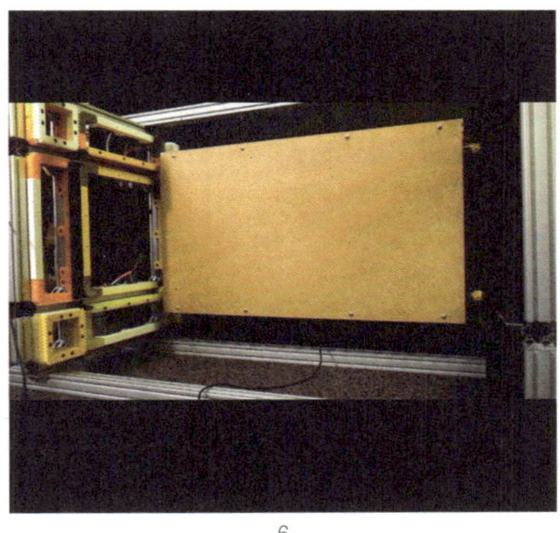

6

been redesigned, using high strength and mechanically precise roller chain to replace the double helical gear.

A wireless control system developed to send signals to the individual plank's microprocessor was a major improvement. All components are now powered by a low-voltage system with a power source at every module to energize both the stepper drive and internal electronic controllers. This distribution is accomplished by sending low-voltage power through a now insulated track, transferring electricity from the track into each plank. Similar to the initial phased development of the overall system in Prototype 1, individual components and subsystems are undergoing iterative development.

In conclusion, the findings during this ongoing research demonstrate that the 'impossible' can be, and has been, accomplished. The development of the prototype has shown how one can develop a physical working model of a never-before-realized concept within a short timeframe, utilizing existing knowledge and freely available tools. The development of the experimental and innovative OntheGo prototype, through a transnational collaboration between two institutions, is evidence that the architecture industry – and with it the future of our built environment – is on the verge of provocative change.

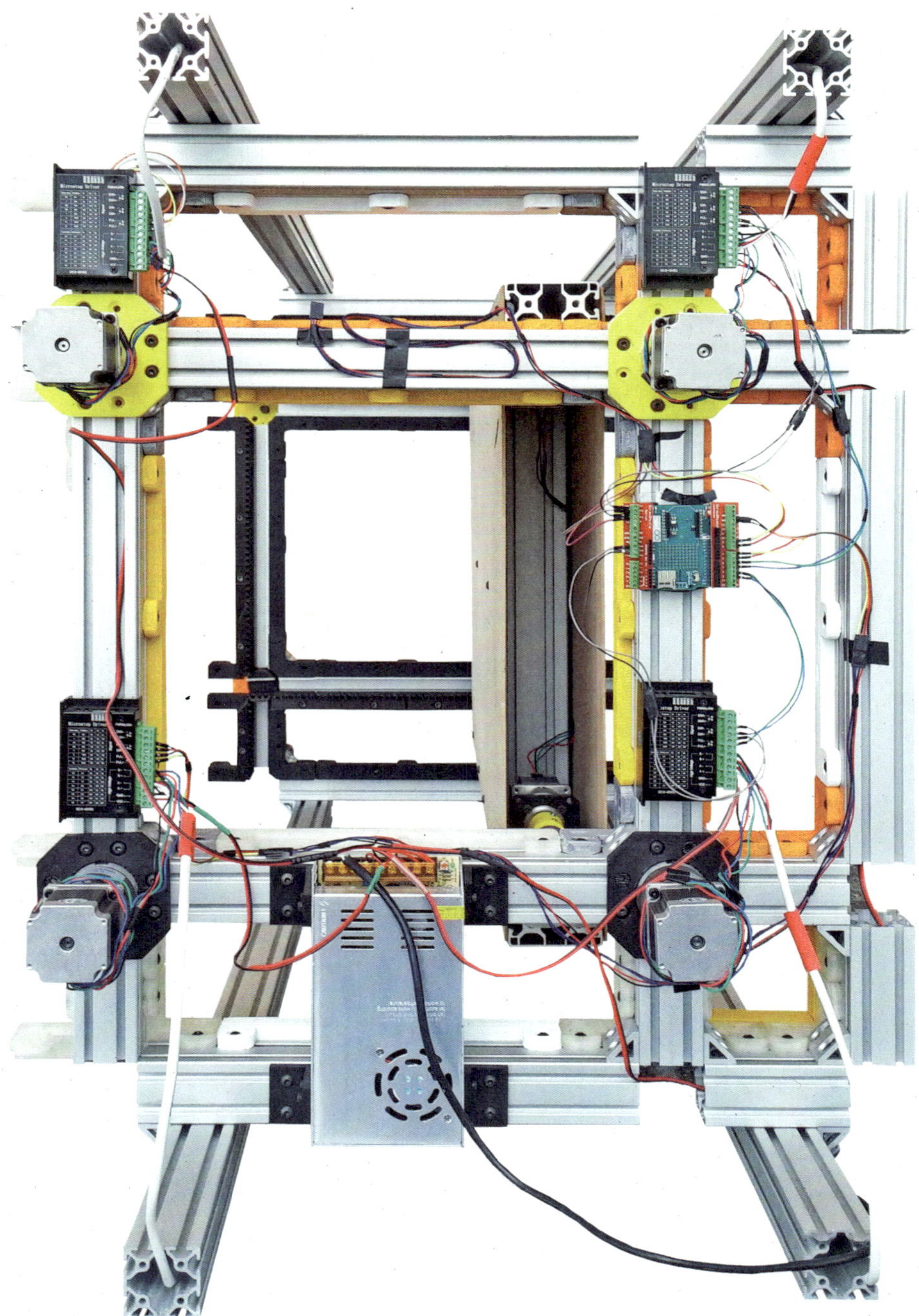

Prototype 3

Prototype 3, scale 1:1, Crown Hall, IIT, Chicago, USA

Where do (w)Ego Next?

Winy Maas

The Adaptable Building

How would it feel to live in a completely adaptable building? What would the impact on society be if our built environment could constantly be reshuffled by software, robots and sliding planks to better suit us? It's is a scenario that keeps on fascinating generations of architects, who create visions of a changing architecture suitable for a changing world, and explore materials and technologies that could allow buildings to constantly adapt to our bodies and desires.

The experiments in this book are part of that fascination. Like any research or prototype, they reveal both potentials and limitations. This chapter reflects on those experiments and on the interdependencies between innovation, the urban environment and society – questioning the future of buildings, materials and cities.

What's Next?

How can we build an urban environment that is constantly adapting to the desires of each inhabitant, within the space of a click? How would we live in this fully customizable city? How can we build an architecture that operates 24/7 and optimizes the use of cities to the fullest?

When we think of adaptability and housing, our architectural imagination is often constrained by contemporary case studies. In most of them, adaptability mainly

occurs in the interior of a building. A few doors can slide and a few walls rotate; the envelope and spatial organization of a building block remains rigid. How much have we moved forward from those examples through the experiments collected in this book?

Prefab

Prefab construction might be a next step, but it hasn't yet fulfilled its promise to be able to stack, change and customize units. The speed of cranes is still too slow to achieve an adaptability that can respond to our daily activities. Smaller elements might enlarge the potential and diversity of this option. Our upcoming research, Pixelworld, will address that.

The dream of fully automated housing remains in the realm of science fiction, where sensors, robots and artificial intelligence confound our lives with a series of technological hiccups rather than improving it. Still, curiosity about its promise is a driver to keep on investigating the potentials and limitations of automation. What could we learn from building blocks that behave like robots? What sort of organizing principle, materials and technologies are needed in order to accomplish 100 per cent adaptability to the ever-changing demands of temporary users in real time?

Nano

With The Why Factory's research and corresponding publication *Barba, Life in a Fully Adaptable Environment*[13], we explored a smaller (or maybe the smallest?) scale of elements that can congregate to form houses, buildings, cities: nanomaterials and molecular aggregation. The research depicts an environment made entirely of nanoparticles, able to solidify, to become malleable and transform responsively over and over. The research explores an environment which allows you to extend your space, shrink, merge, separate, and pull out a chair, a table, or shape or un-shape any objects when needed. We dreamt of a Barba-like material that would allow you to get the best space from your house at any moment. Buildings, acting as a second skin, give birth to a body-based urbanism.

Bio

That step might become even more inclusive when we transform the material from the inorganic to the organic. This might construct the adaptable city through biological components, adding 'life' to it – for 'programmable rooting', 'soil making', harvesting oxygen and CO2. For breeding, feeding and nurturing. For self-maintenance. For increasing plant life and habitats for animal life. Bio-construction with endless cyclic-ness.

Air

And where do (w)Ego next? Imagine that instead of moving walls and floors, those elements would accompany you wherever you are – just like a house made of drones. Like flying 'stuff'... With this new nomadism, each cubic metre that you currently occupy would move you around. This would completely redefine the way our cities are structured and the use and relevance of mobility infrastructure.

Through Sky City, we are exploring a model for such an environment. For centuries, the dream of a city floating in the sky has stimulated the imaginations of novelists, movie directors, futurists, architects and engineers. Animated by those visions, and by the development and democratization of technologies, we are exploring the state of the art of air urbanization. The last decade has seen many developments and implementations towards such futures: from Project Loon (a network of stratospheric balloons designed to bring internet connectivity to rural and remote communities worldwide), to Amazon Prime Air (a future delivery system from Amazon designed to safely get packages to customers in 30 minutes or less using aerial vehicles) and the implementation of flying cars as a solid solution for urban air mobility.

However, current visions of flying cities appear to be out of scale and proportion. In current sci-fi scenarios, entire chunks of the existing city fabric are lifted up into the sky. They oddly replicate actual cities. These massive, top-down urban spaceships seem to go against our desire for flexibility and freedom. Why should our cities look the same if we are able to fly?

How can we devise a flying city that would be completely bottom-up? Where everyone would be able to fly around, meet, connect, detach, and move freely? Can we envision a flying urbanism that would be silent, energy friendly and affordable? A frictionless urbanism[14]?

What are the devices and materials which would make that possible? We could think of air balloons, made of recycled materials. We could think of billions of drones autonomously flying like bees.

If we extrapolate those scenarios, what kind of city and planet would emerge? The built environment would take the shape of clouds. Every single cell, every single cubic metre that we inhabit would be floating in the air. Buildings would densify and dissolve depending on the needs and desires of each resident. There would be no more streets, no more infrastructure, no more commuting, and no more footprint on the planet. How long would it take for nature to recover? How long would it take for endangered species to regenerate? The urbanization of the world would be one self-sufficient, floating cloud drifting around and above the earth.

Everyone could define a preferred diameter of personal space. This three-dimensional halo would react to those of your neighbours, depending on activities and preferred degrees of privacy. This multitude of halos would allow our cities to be more porous. We could maximize views, daylight, sun exposure and natural ventilation depending on environmental conditions, individual desires and collective aspirations. This eleven-million-people flying settlement would respond and adapt to weather conditions. It could even participate to improve air quality, filtering particles and mitigating rainfall, taking an active role in cloud formation.

What would the future of our food production be in such aerial environment? Could we grow all our food with aeroponics? What kind of gardens could we dream of? What about birds? And then, what kind of collective events could self-organize? How would a stadium look if we could all fly? A truly ‘eventful’ city could emerge.

Would we need traffic laws or just simple basic rules

of proximity in order to ensure sustainable, equal and safe interactions? Just like a flock of birds, constantly reshuffling positions, keeping a distance while flying, allowing for speed and deceleration, and preventing collisions… Would we need 3D zoning of the sky to regulate velocity? Or would Sky City be able to disperse to let someone go through and then regroup? How could the cells cluster and aggregate? How would they form a collective structure? A constantly reorganizing 3D Tetris challenging laws of density, a cumulonimbus when we need to densify and regroup, a cumulus evolving into a stratocumulus to maximize sun exposure, an altocumulus becoming more porous, a cirrocumulus when everybody is on their own, a nimbostratus when we need rain… Would such cities form a new planet? Made of gas and particles? A molecular urbanism? Does real estate become surreal estate?

Sharing

From science to fiction and back, this vision is an invitation to keep exploring such scenarios. There is so much to learn from the convergence of technology, art, science and biology, so as to model and understand such behaviours. The future city needs more disciplines to come together, from computation to chemical and biochemical engineering, sociology, real estate, architecture and botany. We need more cross-disciplinary approaches to the future, just as we need to learn to share space, resources and dreams.

There (w)Ego

And there we go. Towards a world where every part of the built environment would be able to fly around freely, and where each part composes a constantly changing city and landscape. That collaborates, that transforms, that adapts. Individually and collectively. It prepares our planet (countering our drive to colonize and to escape) to act as an enormous biomorphic 'sponge' or 'cloud', acting responsively and responsibly.

SkyCity, Msc1 Studio Fall 2020, The Why Factory (TU Delft)

OFFICE
OFFICE
OFFICE

The Why Factory is a global think tank and research institute, based at the Faculty of Architecture and the Built Environment (Delft University of Technology) and led by professor Winy Maas, co-founder of the architecture and urbanism practice MVRDV. The Why Factory's Future Cities Research Programme explores possibilities for the development of future cities by focusing on the production of models and visualizations. The results of this research programme are being presented in a series of books —the Future Cities series— published in association with nai010 Publishers in Rotterdam. *(w)Ego* is the thirteenth publication in this series, following *The Why Factor(y), Visionary Cities, Green Dream, Vertical Village, Hong Kong Fantasies, City Shocks, We Want World Wonders, Barba, Absolute Leisure* and *Copy Paste, PoroCity* and *Towers of Choice*. For more information see: www.thewhyfactory.com

Credits

Authors

Winy Maas

The 'M' of MVRDV, Founding Partner and Principal Architect Winy Maas has received international acclaim for his broad range of urban planning and building projects, across all typologies and scales. These are often self-generated, innovative, experimental, and theoretical. Maas challenges colleagues, clients, students and collaborators at TU Delft's The Why Factory – an internationally engaged think tank Maas established in 2008 – to challenge the boundaries of established standards in order to produce solutions that reimagine how we live, work, and play. Aside from his dedicated leadership role at MVRDV and professorship at TU Delft and elsewhere, Maas is widely published, actively engaged in the advancement of the design profession, and sits on numerous boards and juries, including the Spatial Quality Boards of Rotterdam, Eindhoven, and Barcelona.

> *'I advocate denser, greener, more attractive and liveable cities, with an approach to design that centres around user-defined, innovative and sustainable ideas for the built environment, regardless of typology or scale.'*
> - Maas

Javier Arpa Fernández

Javier Arpa Fernández is an architecture and urbanism teacher, researcher, author and curator. Having completed a Master of Science in Architecture at the Delft University of Technology, Javier specializes in the dissemination of architectural and urbanism practice. Javier is the Research and Education Coordinator of The Why Factory. He is the Curator of Public Programs at the Faculty of Architecture of TU Delft and Editor-In-Chief at the architecture firm MVRDV. Javier gives public lectures and participates in colloquia worldwide. Javier has been lecturer at the University of Pennsylvania, Design Critic at Harvard GSD, Adjunct Professor at Columbia GSAPP, Visiting Professor at ENSA-Belleville and ENSA-Versailles, and lecturer at IE University. He was Deputy Editor of *Domus Magazine* and Senior Editor for a+t research group. He is the co-author of a+t's *Density, Hybrids, Civilities, In Common* and the *Strategy* series, and *The Public Chance* volume. He was the curator of the exhibition Paris Habitat, about a century of social housing in Paris, held in 2015 at the Pavillon de l'Arsenal in Paris, and the author of the monograph *Paris Habitat: One Hundred Years of City, One Hundred Years of Life.*

Adrien Ravon

Adrien Ravon is an architect and academic. In September 2011, he joined The Why Factory at the Faculty of Architecture and the Built Environment, TU Delft. He has participated in research and education projects, been responsible for the production of digital design tools and actively collaborated in the public dissemination of ideas about the city of the future. He co-authored The Why Factory's Future Cities Series publications *Barba, Life in a Fully Adaptable Environment* (2015), *Copy Paste, the Badass Copy Guide* (2017), *PoroCity, Opening up Solidity* (2018), *Le Grand Puzzle, Manifesta 13 Marseille* (2020). He has collaborated with numerous international institutions, including ETH (Zurich), KTH (Stockholm), GSAPP (New York), IAAC (Barcelona), Design Indaba (Cape Town), Centre Pompidou (Paris), Dutch Design Week (Eindhoven), Manifesta 13 (Marseille) and Mori Art Museum (Tokyo). Adrien has worked as an architect and consultant for firms in Argentina, France and the Netherlands. He is currently a scientific council member for the Franco-Dutch network for higher education and research.

Felix Madrazo

Felix Madrazo is an architect, urbanist, researcher and lecturer. He is a founding partner of the architecture studio IND [Inter.National.Design], co-founder of the research collective Supersudaca and lecturer in various universities including TU Delft/The Why Factory. He studied architecture in La Salle University in Mexico City and has a master of architecture from the Berlage Institute. He is co-author with Prof. Winy Maas of the books *City Shocks* and *Copy Paste* published by Nai010 Press.

Content Credits

(w)Ego by The Why Factory (TU Delft)
with IIT Chicago, RMIT Melbourne, Bezalel Academy, Jerusalem

Authors: Winy Maas, Javier Arpa Fernández, Adrien Ravon, Felix Madrazo

Contributors: Marja Elsinga, Deborah Pinto Fdeda, Ifat Finkelman, Dick van Gameren, Birgit Hausleiner, Paul Kuitenbrouwer, Lex te Loo, Felix Madrazo, John Manaves, Ben Milbourne, Vivian Mitsogianni, Nelson Mota, and Mo Shegadi

Text Editor: Diana Ibáñez López

From Me to We
The Why Factory (TU Delft)
Text by Winy Maas

Part 1
Ego

Landscapes of Egoism
The Why Factory (TU Delft)
Winy Maas, Javier Arpa Fernández, Adrien Ravon, Lex te Loo and Léandre Sassi
Text by The Why Factory

Dream Homes?
The Why Factory (TU Delft)
Developed and illustrated by Jayson Johnstone during The Why Factory's 'Adaptive City' Msc3/4 graduation studio at the Faculty of Architecture and the Built Environment (TU Delft) during the Fall of 2013.
Tutors: Winy Maas, Ulf Hackauf, Adrien Ravon
Student: Jayson Johnstone
Text by Adrien Ravon

I-City
The Why Factory (TU Delft), MVRDV
The Why Factory: Winy Maas, Bas Kalmeyer, Tihamer Salij, Leo Stuckardt, Sander MuldersJeroen Zuidgeest
Based on the study developed and illustrated by Dalia Zakaite during The Why Factory's 'Anarchy' Msc1 Design Studio at the Faculty of Architecture and the Built Environment (TU Delft) during the Fall of 2011.
Tutors: Winy Maas, Felix Madrazo, Sander Mulders, Ania Molenda
Student: Dalia Zakaite
Text by The Why Factory / MVRDV

Part 2
(w)Ego

Housing Dialogues
The Why Factory (TU Delft)
Interviews conducted by Javier Arpa Fernández and Adrien Ravon during the Fall of 2019.
Interviews with Dick van Gameren, Marja Elsinga, Nelson Mota, Paul Kuitenbrouwer, Mo Sedighi, Birgit Hausleiner
Text by Javier Arpa Fernández and Adrien Ravon

Better Together!
The Why Factory (TU Delft)
Developed and illustrated by the students of The Why Factory's 'Egocity' Msc1 Design Studio at the Faculty of Architecture and the Built Environment (TU Delft) during the Fall of 2011.
Tutors: Winy Maas, Felix Madrazo, Adrien Ravon, Arend van Waart
Students: Niels Baljet, Francesco Barone, Félix Borel, Charles Ducerisier, Lucile Dugal, Chun Hoi Hui, Tarryn Leeferink, Zichen Liu, Javier López-Menchero Ortiz de Salazar, Prokop Matej, Marek Nosek, Matteo Pavanello, Woo Soojung, Iason Stathatos, Wen Jun Tan, Olina Terzi, Loes Thijssen
Text by Adrien Ravon

The (w)Ego Game
The Why Factory (TU Delft)
Developed and illustrated by the students of The Why Factory's 'Egocity' Msc1 Design Studio at the Faculty of Architecture and the Built Environment (TU Delft) during the Fall of 2011.
Tutors: Winy Maas, Felix Madrazo, Adrien Ravon, Arend van Waart
Students: Niels Baljet, Francesco Barone, Félix Borel, Charles Ducerisier, Lucile Dugal, Chun Hoi Hui, Tarryn Leeferink, Zichen Liu, Javier López-Menchero Ortiz de Salazar, Prokop Matej, Marek Nosek, Matteo Pavanello, Woo Soojung, Iason Stathatos, Wen Jun Tan, Olina Terzi, Loes Thijssen
Guest Critics: Jeroen Zuidgeest, Ekim Tan, Huib Plomb
Text by Adrien Ravon

Building (w)Ego
The Why Factory (TU Delft), MVRDV
for Dutch Design Week 2017 and Shenzhen Architecture Biennale 2017
Research and concept design: The Why Factory (TU Delft)
Definitive design and construction drawings: MVRDV
The installations have been made possible with help from sponsors including De Meeuw, Dutch Design Week, City of Eindhoven, Van Beek Art Supplies, TU Delft, TU Eindhoven and Keeper Development
Text by Adrien Ravon

Part 3
OntheGo

The Sketch
The Why Factory (TU Delft) with Bezalel University and RMIT Melbourne
Developed and illustrated by the students of The Why Factory with Bezalel Academy Jerusalem and RMIT Melbourne during The Why Factory's '(w)Ego Hotel' Workshop at the Faculty of Architecture and

the Built Environment (TU Delft) during the Spring of 2017.
Students: Temitope Adesina, Tom Asiskovich, Mordechai Bachar, Yuval Bar-Adon, Manor Brown, Philip Chang, William Christian, Bryan Chung, Dookee Chung, Hadassah Lehman Cohen, Tomer Deren Peretz, Stav Dror, Nadav Etkin, Rotem Gilboa, Michael Ifergan, Katherine Kai-Cin Jou, Neal Kaldor, Liran Messer, Bradley Mitchell, Tamar Over, Jarrod Palmier, Shelly Shmulewich Shalev, Omry Spasser, Laura Szymon, Jian Yang
Tutors: Winy Maas, Javier Arpa Fernández, Felix Madrazo, Adrien Ravon, Vivian Mitsogianni, Ben Milbourne, Ifat Finkelman, Deborah Pinto Fdeda
Text by Vivian Mitsogianni and Ben Milbourne

The Script
The Why Factory (TU Delft) with IIT Chicago
Developed and illustrated by the students of The Why Factory's 'OntheGo' Msc1 Design Studio, with IIT Chicago at the Faculty of Architecture and the Built Environment (TU Delft), during the Fall 2017.
Students: Karina Andree, Nour Abuzaid, Emily Aquilina, Shervin Azadi, Rick Blankestijn, Ruben Büno Heslinga, Alex Da Costa Gomez, Helena Daher Gomes, Karim Daw, Ana da Fonseca, Justin Frank, Twan Goossens, Yuan Guo, Shirin Hadi, Qiongjun Hu, Maria Kaik, Thomas Krall, Jimmy Lei, Zach Mellas, Danica Mijonic, August Persson, Jeanique Romeijnders, Berend Schenk, Ángela Shepherd Díaz, Eileen Stornebrink, Jitske Swagemakers, Mesut Ulkü, Emma van der Staaij, Amanda Verschuur, Philipp Wenzl, Zerrin Yüksel, Xiaomi Zhi
Tutors: Winy Maas, Felix Madrazo, John Manaves, Stavros Gargaretas, Leo Stuckardt, Lex te Loo, Pirouz Nourian, Hans Hoogenboom, Friso Gouwetor, Arend Jan Krooneman
Guest Critic: Wiel Arets
Text by Felix Madrazo

The Prototype
The Why Factory (TU Delft) with IIT Chicago
Developed and illustrated by the students of The Why Factory's 'OntheGo' Msc1 Design Studio, with IIT Chicago at the Faculty of Architecture and the Built Environment (TU Delft), during the Fall of 2017.
Students: Karina Andree, Nour Abuzaid, Emily Aquilina, Shervin Azadi, Rick Blankestijn, Ruben Büno Heslinga, Alex Da Costa Gomez, Helena Daher Gomes, Karim Daw, Ana da Fonseca, Justin Frank, Twan Goossens, Yuan Guo, Shirin Hadi, Qiongjun Hu, Maria Kaik, Thomas Krall, Jimmy Lei, Zach Mellas, Danica Mijonic, August Persson, Jeanique Romeijnders, Berend Schenk, Ángela Shepherd Díaz, Eileen Stornebrink, Jitske Swagemakers, Mesut Ulkü, Emma van der Staaij, Amanda Verschuur, Philipp Wenzl, Zerrin Yüksel, Xiaomi Zhi
Tutors: Winy Maas, Felix Madrazo, John Manaves, Stavros Gargaretas, Leo Stuckardt, Lex te Loo, Pirouz Nourian, Hans Hoogenboom, Friso Gouwetor, Arend Jan Krooneman
Guest Critic: Wiel Arets
Text by John Manaves

Where do (w)Ego Next?
The Why Factory (TU Delft)
Text by Winy Maas

Image Credits

All images in this publication were produced by The Why Factory, which holds their copyright, with the exception of the following images:

p.1 Photo: Ossip
p.16 Berlin Voids, Berlin, Germany – MVRDV, 1991
p.16 Double House, Utrecht, Netherlands – MVRDV, 1997
p.17 Silodam, Amsterdam, Netherlands – MVRDV, 2003
p.17 Ypenburg, The Hague, Netherlands – MVRDV, 2005
p.18 Oosterwold, Almere, Netherlands – MVRDV, 2011
p.18 Vertical Village, Individual, Informal, Intense – The Why Factory (TU Delft) and MVRDV, 2011
p.19 PoroCity, Opening up Solidity – The Why Factory (TU Delft), 2018
p.19 Barba, Life in the Fully Adaptable Environment – The Why Factory (TU Delft), 2015
p.25-61 Photo: Google Earth Pro
p.121 Incremental housing Aranya, Indore, India. Designed by Balkrishna Doshi (Photo: Dick van Gameren)
p.123 Thalmatt 1, Bern, Switzerland. Designed by Atelier 5 (Photo: Dick van Gameren)
p.123 Thalmatt 1, Bern, Switzerland. Designed by Atelier 5 (Photo: Dick van Gameren)
p.124-125 Incremental housing Belapur, Navy Mumbai, India. Designed by Charles Correa (Photo: Dick van Gameren)
p.128 WikiHouse, De Stripmaker, Almere, The Netherlands (Source: WikiHouse.cc)
p.129 WikiHouse building parts (Source: WikiHouse.cc)
p.130-131 BouwEXPO Tiny Housing, Woningbouw Atelier, Almere, The Netherlands (Source: woningbouwatelier.nl)
p.133 Bouça Housing in Porto, Portugal. Designed by Alvaro Siza (Photo: Nelson Mota)
p.135 La Borda, Cooperative Housing, Barcelona, Spain. Designed by LACOL (Image: Lacol i Lluc Miralles)
p.136 Axonometry of a cluster in the Charkop sites and services scheme in Mumbai, India (Drawing: Freya Crijns)
p.137 View of a cluster in the Charkop sites and services scheme in Mumbai, India (Photo: Nelson Mota)
p.138-139 View of a street in Aranya township, Indore, India. Designed by Balkrishna Doshi (Photo: Rohan Varma)
p.141 Intense Low-Rise, Groningen, The Netherlands. Green Dice, a proposal for intense small-scale housing (Jarmund/Vigsnæs AS Arkitekter MNAL, Norway)
p.142 Een Zee van Huizen | A Sea of Houses by Brigitte de Maar
p.142 Intense Low-Rise, Groningen, The Netherlands. Green Dice, a proposal for intense small-scale housing (Jarmund/Vigsnæs AS Arkitekter MNAL, Norway)
p.144-145 Borneo-Sporenburg, The Netherlands. Urban plan designed by West 8
p.152-153 Shushtar-Nou in Iran. Designed by Kamran Diba in 1976 (Source: Iran's Cartographic Centre)
p.147 An example of experimental housing in the Netherlands: COUPERUSDUIN in The Hague, 1974. Designed by Sjoerd Schamhart (Source: The analytical drawings of students)
p.150 - 288 Housing Complex, Tehran, Iran. Designed by Mo Sedighi (Photo: Mo Sedighi)
p.150 An example of in-between realms as undefined spaces to stimulate self-expression, self-determination, and self-organization (Photo: Mo Sedighi)
p.152-153 Shushtar-Nou in Iran. Designed by Kamran Diba in 1976 (Photo: Mo Sedighi)
p.155 PREVI - Proyecto Experimental de Vivienda, Lima, Peru
p.156 PREVI - Proyecto Experimental de Vivienda, Lima, Peru
p.157 Rietveld-Schroeder House, Utrecht, The Netherlands
p.157 Puchenau Housing, Austria. Designed by Roland Rainer (Photo: Wolfgang Haderer)
p.159 Kowloon Walled City in the 1990s prior to demolition, Hong Kong
p.160-161 Kowloon Walled City in the 1990s prior to demolition, Hong Kong
p.172 Double House, 1997, MVRDV
p.248-259 Images: MVRDV
p.261 Photo: Ossip
p.263 Photo: Ossip
p.265 Photo: Ossip
p.277 Photo: Ossip
p.268-269 Photo: Ossip
p.270-271 Photo: Ossip
p.272-273 Photo: Zhang Chao
p.274-275 Photo: Zhang Chao

References

Landscape of Egoism

p.26–27
Sources: business-standard.com, caravandaily.com

p.28–29
Sources: timesofindia.idatimes.com, techblog.com, wikipedia.com

p.30–31
Source: jumbolair.com

p.32–33
Sources: wikipedia.com, foodnavigator-asia.com, bbc.com, williamscattleconpany.com

p.34–35
Source: steyncity.com

p.36–37
Sources: 432parkavenue.com, theguardian.com, wikipedia.org

p.38–39
Sources: theguardian.com, bloomberg.com

p.40–41
Sources: theguardian.com, wikipedia.org

p.42–43
Sources: wikipedia.org

p.44–45
Sources: wikipedia.org, mcmansionhell.com

p.46–47
Sources: archdaily.com, actualite.seloger-construire.com

p.48–49
Sources: wikipedia.org, idealista.com, elpais.com, lafincarealestate.com

p.50–51
Sources: wikipedia.org, bloomberg.com, theguardian.com, domusweb.com

p.52–53
Sources: chrisnorstorm.com, citylab.com, exclusive.multibriefs.com

p.54–55
Sources: wikipedia.org, archdaily.com, nationalgeographic.com

p.56–57
Sources: wikipedia.org, madinaty.com, theguardian.com

p.58–59
Source: theguardian.com

p.60–61
Sources: fortune.com, wsj.com, bbc.com

Dream Homes?

[1] pinterest.com
[2] statista.com
[3] Forbes.com

Housing Dialogues

[4] 1M Homes: tudelft.nl
[5] Vinex (Vierde Nota Ruimtelijke Ordening Extra) wikipedia.org
[6] Dutch Constitution, Art. 22.2
[7] worldbank.org

The (w)Ego Game

[8] playthecity.eu; Ekim Tan, 'Negotiation and Design for the Self-Organizing City: Gaming as a method for Urban Design' (2014), PhD publication, Delft University of Technology, Faculty of Architecture and the Built Environment.

OntheGo

[9] United States Census Bureau, American Community Survey (ACS), 2007; census.gov

The Script

[10] A. Forty, Words and Building (2000), 143.
[11] D. Mertins, et al, Mies (New York: Phaidon, 2014), 445.
[12] A. Forty (2000) 147.

Where Do (w)Ego Next?

[13] Maas W., Hackauf U., Ravon A., Healy P., Barba, life in a fully adaptable environment, nai010
[14] Madrazo F., Lana A., Cotrufo A., Frictionless urbanism, Five visions for urban aerial mobility, in Domus 1036

Acknowledgments

We would like to thank all the students of The Why Factory for their contributions to this book. We especially wish to thank Lex te Loo, for his valuable support in the production and editorial process. We are grateful to the Dutch Design Week, the Shenzen Biennale, the TU Delft, the HNI in Rotterdam, for exhibiting the results of this research.

We would like to thank TU Delft, RMIT Melbourne, IIT Chicago, and Bezalel Universities.

Finally, we thank MVRDV's staff, especially Jan Knikker, Irene Start, Isabel Pagel, Miruna Dunu and Nicolette Pot, for their continuous support for this project.

Book Credits

Authors: Winy Maas, Javier Arpa Fernández, Adrien Ravon, Felix Madrazo
Copy editing: Diana Ibáñez López
Proof reading: Jane Bemont
Graphic design execution: Selina Landis and Anna Moschioni at The Exercises
Design of The Why Factory logo + format: Thonik in collaboration with BENG
Printing and lithography: die Keure, Bruges
Paper: Circle Offset, 90 grs
Publisher: Marcel Witvoet, nai010 publishers, Rotterdam

nai010 publishers is an internationally orientated publisher specialized in developing, producing and distributing books in the fields of architecture, urbanism, art and design. www.nai010.com

nai010 books are available internationally at selected bookstores and from the following distribution partners:

North, Central and South America - Artbook | D.A.P., New York, USA, dap@dapinc.com

Rest of the world - Idea Books, Amsterdam, the Netherlands, idea@ideabooks.nl

For general questions, please contact nai010 publishers directly at sales@nai010.com or visit our website www.nai010.com for further information.

Printed and bound in Belgium

ISBN 978-94-6208-530-5
NUR 648
BISAC ARC00300